# BEYOND
# ROMANCE

# BEYOND

# ROMANCE

M. C. DILLON

STATE UNIVERSITY OF NEW YORK PRESS

Published by
STATE UNIVERSITY OF NEW YORK PRESS
ALBANY

For information, address
State University of New York Press
90 State Street, Suite 700, Albany, NY 12207

Production by Laurie Searl
Marketing by Fran Keneston

Library of Congress Cataloging-in-Publication Data

Dillon, M. C. (Martin C.). 1938–
  Beyond romance / M.C. Dillon.
    p. cm.
  Includes bibliographical references and index.
  ISBN 0–7914–5097–X (alk. paper)—ISBN 0–7914–5098–8 (pbk. : alk paper)
    1. Love. I. Title.

BF575.L8 D57 2001
128'.46—dc21                                          2001042919

        10    9    8    7    6    5    4    3    2    1

FOR

J. B. D.

Answere me this You Gods above:

What's lecherie withouten Love? —

A thinge less maym'd (They answer'd mee)

Than maym'd were Love sans lecherie.

—E. R. Eddison, *A Fish Dinner in Memison*

# CONTENTS

# PREFACE

This is a book about sexlove. It starts with a series of questions and continues with a series of attempts to give honest answers to them. Honesty is a paramount concern: it is the value that distinguishes the kind of love I argue is best, authentic love, from those, notably romantic love, that I find wanting and in need of correction. I have tried to write authentically about the kind of love I think is authentic. Authenticity is a kind of truthfulness; it requires facing up to unpleasantness from time to time, although I believe and try to show that in the long run it fosters happiness.

Our culture is suffering from erotic malaise. We do not seem to know how to love well, and that is manifest in the problems we seem unable to handle, the problems of bodily health apparent in the rise of sexually transmitted diseases, the problems of social health apparent in the proliferation of babies born to parents who are still children, and the problems of moral health apparent in our inability to make coherent policy decisions about abortion, commercial sex, homosexuality, extramarital sex, sexual harassment, and the like. Few will contest my claim that these ills are interrelated and betray confusion at the root level of our culture's values. Some will contest the solutions I propose, and many more will be offended by the critical stance I take with regard to intellectual and metaphysical turf they deem sacred.

I am, nonetheless, optimistic: I think that the ideas presented here are robust enough to gather strength under critical analysis, that they will eventually dissipate rather than compound the confusion. Something like the constellation of values presented here will prevail in the long run because the values, themselves, are genuine and true, and because truth has a way of becoming obtrusive. The mistakes I have inevitably made will be corrected by others who see the truth more clearly than I. Visions of truth are always perspectival, limited as well as guided by the capacities of those attempting to see, but truth also collects a diversity of perspectives and points to a place where they might intersect. The fact is that we need truth, that truth is itself a value, an object of human desire, because falsity generates human misery.

You will find no absolutes in this book just because it attempts to face authentically the truth that every claim to truth is limited, that in saying one thing it obscures another. You will find a sustained attempt to treat matters dialectically, that is, to seek balance by considering opposing views and granting to them the force that makes their opposition considerable. Every attempt to express truth betrays falsity in its limits, but the converse is also true: every falsity can be mined for the truth it obscures.

I respect the ideas I oppose. At the moment, they prevail, and they have gained this prevalence because they have strong and enduring appeal, because they show something that needs to be seen. I have tried to preserve the enduring value to be found in the traditions I criticize: the romantic tradition, its Platonic and Christian underpinnings, and its postmodern sequel. Critical analysis is, itself, a form of respect—respect in the sense of the Latin term (respicere)* from which the English word is derived, to look at something closely and admire it—an attempt to take a set of ideas apart, save what is valuable, and incorporate it into a stronger vision.

From the romantic tradition, we get the idea of love as a force that transforms us. From the Platonic tradition, we get the basis of that idea, that Eros is the demigod that draws us toward our highest potential. And from the Christian tradition, we get the idea that God is both truth and love, that the merging of these two ideas points to the transcendent global horizon of human existence. These ideas demand our respect and retain their validity. But they are surrounded by untruth; they are obscured by mystification, wishful thinking, and refusal to disabuse ourselves of infantile fantasy.

Freud shows us that Mother is a crucial figure in the development of our capacity to love, but the story of the Oedipus complex needs to be told again, and freed of its genital focus. Postmodernism demonstrates the validity of Nietzsche's claim that, although we are shrugging off the symbolism of bankrupt religion, we retain the bankrupt thinking—the division of everything into binary oppositions of good and evil, true and false—that those symbols

---

*To turn around to look at, hence to feel a regard or admiration for. Eric Partridge, *Origins: A Short Etymological Dictionary of Modern English* (New York: Greenwich House, 1983), 648.

represented. The bright side of human existence, life, love, goodness, and truth, is inextricably intertwined with the dark: life and death cannot be separated from each other, and neither can love and hate. But postmodernism has its own excesses and enthusiasms, which stand in need of correction: it replaces sacred symbols with secular symbols without realizing that the problem is with symbolism in general. And in its dismissal of absolute Truth, it neglects to retain the finite truths upon which life and love depend.

No absolutes, but no abject relativism, either. If you are a SCUBA diver, go down to 150 feet, take a deep breath, hold it in, and swim to the surface, the air in your lungs will expand with the decreasing pressure, and you will hurt yourself very badly. Boyle's law is true. If someone molests, rapes, and murders a child, that person has done a bad thing, regardless of motives or circumstances. Both examples can be recast in different contexts to introduce compounding variables requiring further thought and judgment, but the underlying facts and values are sound. What we need to love better than we now do are ideas that are truer than the ideas that now prevail. This book looks for those ideas and purports to find some important ones, ones that promise to work better, to work better for more people under more times and circumstances.

Truth, itself, is a problem. What is truth? A relation of propositions? Correspondence of proposition to fact? Coherence of adumbrations? This is a book about sexlove which purports to say things that are true. It is a theoretical work that claims to vindicate itself through pragmatic consequences, through the trial and error process of corroboration and falsification. Thus, it takes pragmatic consequence to be one measure of truth, perhaps the most important measure for a work of this kind, although not the most important measure for works of other kinds, for example, works in biology or physics. Nonetheless, it also purports to meet other legitimate measures of truth that might be applied: simplicity and cohesion with the body of knowledge gleaned through the arts and sciences; it even strives to attain a modicum of elegance. That is the nature of philosophy as I understand it: to synthesize material from all relevant domains into a coherent understanding that both fits the world of experience and illumines it.

To sustain this claim to truth, I have felt it necessary to address theoretical issues and to defend the views presented before the jury of experts. I want the respect of my colleagues in the academic world; I want these ideas to be taken seriously by them, to be tested and evaluated. The ideas are much bigger than I am, and they need to be taken up by the best minds they can attract. That means that I have had to employ the tools of my trade, the vocabulary that allows me to condense ideas to fit a manageable format and to do so with some precision. From time to time, it has been necessary to refer to the thinkers I draw upon in a manner that presupposes some familiarity with their work, thinkers that few outside the academic world have studied.

To sustain my claim to relevance, I want this book to reach beyond the academic sphere to the larger world of critical minds who bring other sorts of criteria and other funds of experience to bear, people who live their lives thoughtfully and want to dig a bit deeper than popular media sometimes allow. Ultimately, it will be these readers whose judgment will decide the fate of this work. And, for those readers, the technical terminology required for condensation and precision, and the references to the relevant works of other scholars may be regarded as merely jargonizing and name dropping, a posturing rhetoric of presumption, arrogance, and deliberate obfuscation. It is not that; it is a kind of academic shorthand that allows scholars to allude to complex thoughts without taking up limited time and space that can be turned to better use.

I think it is arrogant, a kind of arrogance I want to eschew, for academics to think we have a privileged claim on intelligence and judgment. We usually have intensive training in one field or another and can speak with some authority within those limits. As far as I can tell, however, our love lives are not demonstrably superior to those who keep the world going. I have asked some of these people to read portions of this book, and I have listened carefully to their feedback. They got it. They understood. And they managed to get through the tedious parts without missing much.

This is a hybrid work in the sense just explained. When I asked myself who I wanted to read my book, whom I wanted to address in my book, the answer was loud and clear—everybody I could reach. So, I have tried to reach everybody. Nietzsche wrote *Zarathustra* "for all and none." Nietzsche is one of my heroes, one of the thinkers from whom I take my measure. I had to try. So much for the all, what about the none? Well, I was writing for me, too. This book is not a personal statement in the autobiographical sense; I think I managed to identify and delete the anecdotal material. But it is an attempt to work out a lifetime of experience and thought, to find the patterns of meaning, and to develop their implications. I wanted to find out what I really thought. And I am a hybrid creature, one foot implanted in the groves of academe and the other, I hope, on the ground.

My intellectual background and most of my advanced training is in the phenomenological tradition. The credo that I take from that tradition is that all knowledge originates in the world of everyday experience, that the life-world is the source of knowledge, and also its measure of truth and validity. The world taught us that an object cannot move from point A to point B without traversing the intervening space. Then the world corrected that thought when we found electrons leaving one orbit and arriving at another without occupying the space in between. This credo needs to be acknowl-edged up front because it has two significant implications for the work in your hands.

The first is that this text is full of examples. I want you to know what my theories are *about*, where they came from, and where they will succeed or fail to articulate some aspect of your experience. This is a part of phenomenolog-ical methodology, and a fortuitous one for a hybrid work: the concrete de-scriptions will illumine the theory as well as be illumined by it. It may also complicate things in a healthy way. Life is richer and more complex than the-ory—that is why we construct theories, to try to understand the world of human existence. The theory never catches it all, cannot catch it all and still be theory; it sheds light where it does by leaving other parts dark. I hope to have shed light on important aspects of sexlove, but others will necessarily be left in the dark. This writing has thematically endeavored to keep itself aware of the fact that your judgment as to whether, where, and how it applies to your experience is an indispensable component of the overall project.

The second implication of the credo is that it has imposed limits on what I tried to say. In the domain of sexlove, my experience is that of a heterosex-ual male. I defend the rights of other genders and sexual preferences to live and love with dignity, but I do not dare to speak for or about them, except in-sofar as we are all human, except insofar as their lives are intertwined with mine in a shared world. With regard to women, I am both a realist and a nom-inalist. I think that biology and genetics do a pretty good job of saying what it is to be a female; beyond that I think that statements about females in gen-eral tend to be as trivial and vacuous—or just plain wrong—as statements about art in general, or about men. I think it is true to say that only women can bear children, although not all can or want to or should, and that this truth has bearing on women's lives. I also think it is true that we do not un-derstand as much as we could about the nature of this bearing. And I am con-vinced that, as a man, there are things about this and other aspects of female existence I could never fully appreciate. Prudence calls for silence in the face of ignorance.

Still, I am writing for everybody. Every body. Women's bodies differ among themselves, from men's bodies, and the bodies of other animals. All these bodies are born in some fashion or other, reproduce, and die. They all dwell in world space and time; although they may live the world in divergent modalities, some of us can sometimes successfully arrange to meet at a given place and time. My point here is that the range of application of what I have to say is variable: my truth claims quite deliberately do not apply universally to all times and places—after all, I am trying to *change* prevailing erotic praxis, to make tomorrow different from today—but neither are they limited to the solitary case of myself here and now. I will argue that carnal knowledge is crucial to sexlove, and that claim is couched in the timeless language of universalist discourse. I fully expect a celibate person to respond to it differently from a sexually active person, but I am also fully convinced that Augustine was as mistaken in his own time and place as he is now when he asserts that it would be better if we could avoid sex altogether and manage to reproduce another way. That time may come in a distant future I cannot conceive, much less care about, but it has not been, and is not now. In short, judgment is required to translate these ideas into their relevance for individuals. In long, one of the aims of this work is to prepare the way for its own surpassing.

The paths of truth and love have come together in many ways in human history; they have also diverged. The path I have tried to mark is the best I can see from the vantage of my position on it, but it is in the nature of paths to open new vistas as one proceeds along them.

Ambremerine
August 2000

# ACKNOWLEDGMENTS

Joanne Dillon's mark is on this manuscript: she inspired it, helped me write it, and smiled throughout.

My students and teaching assistants in the course I have been teaching on the philosophy of love and sexuality since 1976 have also touched this book. Two thousand two hundred forty-two minds, double that number of eyes and ears, helped me sort out the confusion and made rude noises when appropriate. They were impatient for me to stop stalling and finish the book. To them I say: now the book is out. Finally. So, buy it. There will be a test on the material. A test harder than the ones I gave.

Ethel S. Person, author of *Dreams of Love and Fateful Encounters: The Power of Romantic Passion,* persuaded me through her spoken and written words to take a closer look at romantic love, to treat it the way I would have romantic lovers treat each other. She helped me see beyond romance.

My colleagues in the Philosophy Department of Binghamton University, notably John Arthur, Leon J. Goldsten, Anthony Preus, Stephen David Ross, Donald D. Weiss, and especially my departed friend, Emilio Roma, were kind enough to read early drafts of much of this material and offer their insights, criticism, and encouragement. Jeanne Constable and Melanie Yaworski, secretaries and guardian angels, are the necessary conditions for the possibility of my professional life and exemplars of generosity and grace.

The members of the Merleau-Ponty Circle listened as this book took shape and responded with grace and acuity. Special thanks are due to Patrick Burke, Thomas Busch, John Carvalho, Chauncey Colwell, Edward Casey, Duane Davis, Fred Evans, Wayne Froman, Shaun Gallagher, Lawrence Hass, James Hatley, Sara Heinamaa, Marja-Liisa Honkasalo, Galen Johnson, Leonard Lawlor, Gary Madison, Glen Mazis, James Morley, Deborah Mullen,

Dorothea Olkowski, Isaac Ruedin, Hugh J. Silverman, Michael Smith, Jan Van der Veken, Stephen Watson, Gail Weiss, Carolin Woolson, Philips Young, and you, the person whose name is missing, who was too close for me to see in this memorial mode.

I am grateful to the International Association for Philosophy and Literature for providing a congenial forum in which to present many of the ideas developed here.

Amadeo Giorgi, Karsten Harries, Sungchul Ji, Alphonso Lingis, John McCarty, Harrison J. Pemberton, Elbridge Rand, Rosemary Rizo-Patrón, Calvin O. Schrag, Alan Soble, Frederick Wertz, Bruce and Donna Wilshire directly or indirectly nudged the thoughts trying to find expression here.

Elizabeth Dillon designed the graphic illustration. R. Kathleen Dillon caught mistakes I missed in the galleys.

Jane Bunker, editor extraordinaire, made the book happen.

Alan V. Hewat did what copy editors do, and did it very well, indeed.

Laurie Searl guided the manuscript and its author through the travails of production.

David Michael Strand compiled the index.

David Michael Levin read the completed manuscript and pointed it in the right direction.

Binghamton University and the Binghamton University Foundation provided funding and other forms of support.

The chapters listed below and reprinted here in varying degrees of revision were originally presented or published in other places; I am grateful to these sources for permission to reprint.

Chapter 1, "Names of Love," was presented at the Eighteenth Annual International Conference of the Merleau-Ponty Circle, Muhlenberg College, Allentown, Pennsylvania, 23–25 September 1993, and will be published in *Rereading Merleau-Ponty: Essays Beyond the Continental-Analytic Divide,* ed. Lawrence Hass and Dorothea Olkowski (Amherst, N.Y.: Humanity Books, 2001).

Chapter 2, "Aletheia, Poiesis, and Eros," was presented at the Eighteenth Annual Meeting of the International Association for Philosophy and Literature held at the University of Alberta, 4–7 May 1994, and published in *Philosophy and Desire* (Continental Philosophy VII), ed. Hugh J. Silverman (New York: Routledge, 2000).

Chapter 3, "Natural Law and Sexual Morality," was presented at the Nineteenth Annual Meeting of the Merleau-Ponty Circle held at Berry College, Rome, Georgia, 21–24 September 1994, and published in *The Ethics of*

*Postmodernity: Current Trends in Continental Thought,* ed. Gary B. Madison and Marty Fairbairn (Evanston, Ill.: Northwestern University Press, 1999).

Chapter 4, "Sexlove," was presented at the Twenty-first Annual Conference of The International Association for Philosophy and Literature, University of South Alabama, Mobile, Alabama, 6–10 May 1997.

Chapter 6, "Virtual Bodies / Bodies of Flesh," was presented at the Nineteenth Annual Meeting of the International Association for Philosophy and Literature held at Villanova University, 10–13 May 1995.

Chapter 7, "Motherlove and Sexlove," was initially presented at the Twentieth Anniversary Conference of The International Association for Philosophy and Literature held at George Mason University, 8–11 May 1996. It was subsequently revised and presented at The Association for the Advancement of Philosophy and Psychiatry, New England Regional Meeting, Saint Joseph College, 17–19 January 1997.

Sections I–III of Chapter 8, "Sex Objects and Sexual Objectification," was presented at the Thirty-second Annual Meeting of the Society for Phenomenology and Existential Philosophy, Clarion Hotel, New Orleans, 21–23 October 1993. Parts IV–VI were added in June 1997; the resulting manuscript was published in the *Journal of Phenomenological Psychology* 29, No. 1 (1998).

Chapter 9, "The Flesh of Love," was presented at The Twenty-First Annual International Conference of the Merleau-Ponty Circle at The University of Memphis, 19–21 September 1996, and published in *Areté: revista de filosofía* 9, No. 2 (1997) under the title "La carnalidad del amor: percepción e historia," trans. María Balarin and Rosemary Rizo-Patrón.

ONE

# NAMES OF LOVE

<hr/>

I long to talk with some old lover's ghost,
Who died before the god of love was born.

—John Donne, *Love's Deity*

## PHILOSOPHY AND LOVE

IF IT IS PHILOSOPHY that gives us ways of thinking of things, then there is more philosophy than bears the name. The names we have been given to summon love call forth a host of demons whose sting we have all felt. How many philosophers have loved wisely or well? How shall we listen to their words?

Words give us thoughts and thoughts give us deeds. The effect of deeds may be more or less satisfying. Has philosophy produced happiness? What good is it?

## CREDOS AND QUESTIONS

I believe that love, more than anything else, determines the quality of our lives. Fame, fortune, power, and the like do not guarantee happiness (whatever that might be), nor does the failure to attain all or any of these condemn us to a life unfulfilled. But failure in love *does* guarantee misery. We all love: we all care about ourselves and others, although that care may manifest itself in negative modes such as hate or indifference. But these negative modes are, nonetheless, forms of caring.[1] Everybody loves somebody in some mode or other, be it positive or negative, and the quality of the loving, more than anything else, determines the quality of our lives. That is the credo upon which this book is built. No good love, no good life.

What is love? What is the difference between good love, bad love, and the shades of love in between? That is a philosophical question, maybe *the* philosophical question, because it calls into question who we are, where we are in the midst of all that is, how to think and feel about all that is, and what it means for something to be good or bad. Philosophers have addressed this question, and their answers are as divergent here as they are on every other topic. There is no consensus, although some lovestyles prevail in certain times and places.

The Marquis de Sade gave his name to a way of thinking about love that regarded cruelty, incest, bestiality, coprophagy, homosexuality, and excess of all sorts as proper and natural forms of love. He lived a life qualitatively determined by his philosophy. Saint Thomas Aquinas also believed that nature grants propriety to certain kinds of love, specifically exclusive heterosexual monogamy designed to promote the propagation and nurture of offspring, and denies it to others, including just about everything that de Sade affirmed. He, too, lived a life qualitatively determined by his philosophy.

Fierce debate between these two positions goes on today. Is homosexuality natural? What about monogamy? Are love relations essentially power relations? What is natural, what is not, and does nature (whatever that might be) have anything to do with what is proper in love relations? Is it proper to evaluate the life of the person in the process of assessing a thinker's thoughts? Would it be possible to do that? Could we make an informed guess as to whether de Sade was happier in the eighteenth century than Aquinas was in the thirteenth? If Aquinas is in heaven, then de Sade is surely in hell, but do these places exist? We know that de Sade went to prison and that Aquinas did not, but how much does that matter? Nelson Mandela, like de Sade, spent much of his life in prison. And, following his own vision of what Aquinas wrote, the Grand Inquisitor tried infidels and set some of them aflame.

If we all love in some form or other, and if the quality of our lives depends in large measure on the quality of our loving—if how we think and feel about love affects our behavior, and if our actions produce consequences that produce happiness and misery—then the question concerning love is a momentous and forced question, one that we must face one way or another.

To ignore the question of love, to live uncritically assimilating the lovestyles of our times, is to relegate to others choices that affect who and how we *be*. How would you assess the happiness-producing quotient of the lovestyles manifest in contemporary life and the media that envelop us?

What is love? Do we know? If we don't know, if we can't discriminate between authentic love and fantasy, then what do we mean when we declare love—either in intimate moments or before an altar? And how are we to understand those declarations when we hear them from others? If we do know or think we do, then are we open to things as yet unseen? This is a portentous question.

## MENO'S PARADOX

If we knew what love is, we would not have to inquire about it.

But,

If we do not know what love is, we would not be able to recognize it if we were to encounter it.[2]

This is a famous dilemma, first posed by Plato in a dialogue called the *Meno*. Plato's response to this dilemma is also famous. He contests the unstated major premise: that is, that for any topic of inquiry, either we know what it is or we do not. Plato says that is wrong. He claims that, for any subject matter, it is the case *both* that we do and that we do not already know what it is.

On the surface, that looks like a contradiction, but it is not. Plato resolves the apparent contradiction in mythic terms with his doctrine of rebirth and recollection: we are exposed, between lives, to cosmic knowledge of what truly *is*. At birth, we forget. The knowledge is there, but inaccessible. Learning in this life is a matter of recognition. When we encounter the truth, we are able to recognize it because there is a kind of satori, a click of recollection, an awakening of the dormant knowledge we obtained between lives. Socrates is depicted as a midwife: someone who is capable of leading people who are seeking truth to the experience of recollection; he is adept at assisting at the birth of knowledge they already had.

Myths are frequently the source of profound truths, and Plato's myth is no exception. Plato's myth says that there is a kind of foreknowledge, a knowing ahead of time, that we somehow have, but which also eludes us in some way. What kind of knowing is this? Where does it come from? How reliable is it?

Consider the knowledge a child of ten or twelve, someone just about to enter puberty, has of sexuality. He or she knows enough about sexuality to be embarrassed about it. This person knows when to snicker, when to be ashamed, what parts of the body to hide, but does not know what sex is all about. For one thing, his or her body is not yet capable of experiencing orgasm. And yet, when, in adolescence, this person does encounter sexuality and does experience orgasm, he or she knows—already knew—what is happening. In non-mythological terms, one might say that the prepubescent child's foreknowledge of sexuality is horizonal, in the background of the child's experience. It simply has not yet become a conscious theme for the child. There is awareness of sexuality, but not a thematic, focused, or determinate awareness.

Where does this knowledge come from? In the case at hand, there are two obvious sources: the child's body, and the cultural environment.

The child has a bodily awareness of gender and sexuality which is not yet a fully conscious knowledge. Just as the prelinguistic infant's body is prefigured to become linguistic—and anticipates the conscious experience of language use—so the prepubescent body is already anticipating (or foreknowing) the sexual quality of experience that is about to dawn in conscious life. Generalizing, we may say that part of the inquiry about love is the task of becoming explicitly or thematically aware of what our bodies know implicitly or horizonally.

Moving now to the other source, we may point out that the prepubescent child has acquired a latent knowledge of sexuality from the cultural horizon. The child has been subject to a myriad of influences that affect his or her horizonal sexuality. Toilet training, enforcement of sex roles, imposition of taboos, etc. engender a kind of pre-thematic sexuality that will become explicit or thematic only when the child enters adolescence and begins that traumatic phase of sexual maturation. Here the role of language as a vehicle of culture is especially strong.

There is also increasing evidence supporting the view that adults tend to recapitulate in later life the quality of love they experienced as infants. Unloved children generally evolve into adults relatively incapable of loving their mates and their own children.

In sum, then, both nature (body) and nurture (environment) interact to generate the foreknowledge that guides inquiry.

How reliable are these pre-thematic or horizonal forms of foreknowledge? In the case of bodily foreknowledge, does the masculine or feminine body know how it will or should live out that biological gender in its sexual behavior? Is there an intrinsic relation between lingam and yoni, or are homosexual and other forms of sexual behavior equally valid? On another front, is there an intrinsic sex relation of dominance and submission, is sexuality pervaded by power relations? Freud boldly asserted that "anatomy is destiny," but then described the vicissitudes of instincts in which role reversals and dialectical shifts from dominance to submission are commonplace. The old nature versus nurture debate is still going strong: is one's erotic lifestyle prefigured by biology and physiology or by culture and language . . . or both?

In the case of cultural preconceptions, are the toilet rituals, mating rituals, societal sanctions on sexuality, etc. helpful or harmful to erotic maturation? They prepare us to live in accordance with the institutions of our times, but are these institutions, themselves, conducive to human fulfillment or frustration? Do we feel the satori, the click of recognition, because we have tapped into some fundamental truth? Or because some cultural influence has conditioned us to feel right about one kind of decision rather than another? Do we feel right about marrying a love object rather than extra-maritally loving that person because that is the way it really ought to be (i.e., because *homo sapiens* is intrinsically monogamous) or because a corrupt and antiquated social institution has been perpetuated through a bankrupt form of religion?

We already know what love is. We have the foreknowledge just described. Insofar as we play it by ear or do what feels right in regard to love, we are operating at the pre-thematic level. Letting our intuitions guide us.

The problems with this are manifest and pressing.

(a) Our intuitions frequently send conflicting signals. Our horizons contain confused and incoherent senses of what feels right.

(b) We are properly suspicious of our customs, institutions, and traditions. If they were entirely viable, the divorce statistics and other measures of erotic health in our culture would be different from what they are.

(c) Freud argued that our erotic impulses are grounded in our instincts, but also argued that instincts sometimes conflict with each other. Ego instincts are directed toward survival. Sex instincts are aimed at pleasure and reproduction. But sex acts are intrinsically dangerous (disease, unwanted pregnancy, violent competition for mates and with mates), hence a threat to the survival goal of ego instincts.

(d) Finally, and not so obvious, to play it by ear is to let oneself be controlled by external influences as opposed to taking responsibility for one's own life. The difference lies in reflective, critical scrutiny of preconceptions and foreknowledge.

It is necessary, then, to bring our implicit, pre-thematic, foreknowledge of love to thematic expression in order to make it available for scrutiny and criticism, thus for rejection, modification, or responsible acceptance.

Beyond that critical endeavor lies another that may be more important. This is the creative task of making conceptual room capable of opening ourselves to new qualities of experience. If our concepts of gender and power restrict how we think and act in the arena of sexlove, then we need better ways of thinking about them, new names that will allow us to discern ourselves and our possibilities more clearly.

For example, the commonly accepted (false) belief that it is impossible for me to feel your pain and pleasure implies that the sensations involved in acts of sexlove are private, that the only orgasm I can experience is my own. If I tacitly accept that belief, it keeps me from opening myself to my experience of your pleasure, numbs my attunement to your living flesh, reduces me to an instrument capable only of assisting in the production of your pleasure instead of participating in it, and tends to circumscribe sexlove relations within power relations. Suppose we had a new name—reversibility of flesh[3]—for the intertwining of pleasure and pain among bodies. Suppose that naming led us to look for something we had taken for granted, and thus overlooked and neglected to see. Suppose it allowed us to recognize that something explicitly, explore it, develop our capacities to enhance it. Would that not change our lives for the better?

## THE QUESTION OF TRUTH

Suppose life is like an upstream path with branches and forks and no way of going back. How do we know which way to go at the forks? This way fidelity, that way adventure. This way Roger now, that way someone else later. Having chosen Roger a while back and made a family with him, what to do at the branch that flows into an enchanted dark forest with some beckoning figure one knows well enough to know that he is not humdrum and boring, that on this Monday night he is more interested in you than in football and waist-thickening beer? When the years behind have taken their toll and the opportunities ahead are rapidly diminishing, is there an oracle where the waters part that tells you which path leads to happiness and which to misery? Or are there different figures on the banks with fingers pointing in different directions prophesying with terrible admonition? Is it possible to tell which voice tells the truth and which deceives?

The lovestyle that prevails in our time and place, romantic love, affirms the thrill of new love above all else. When Guinevere chose to break her vows to the aging King Arthur in order to consummate her love for the young Lancelot, she was true to a guiding precept of romance.[4] Romantic love affirms the intensity of the passion of youth, and seeks the forbidden as a way to fan that fire. The oracle of romance points toward the dark unknown, and warns us that not to seize the moment is to slip farther into old age and regret for lost chances.

The shadow of romantic love, and its constant companion, is enduring companionate love.[5] This lovestyle measures the truth of love by its longevity and seeks to ensure endurance through eternal vows and the ethical strictures demanding flawless adherence to them. The passions of youth are notoriously fleeting: it is immoral to desecrate the vow, to endanger the stability of the family institution, and, beyond that, foolhardy to jeopardize one's own chances for lifelong companionship with a familiar. Sometimes diversions flirt from the wings, but wisdom decrees that their appeal is illusory and that truth drains them of allure. The promise of love must be kept to be fulfilled.

Romantic love and its shadow are two fingers on the hand that grips our time, and they point in opposite directions. Each has its own truth, but, as they play out in our lives, these truths are irreconcilable. What is a philosopher to say?

Here is what one philosopher said.

> If you marry, you will regret it;
> if you do not marry, you will also regret it;
> if you marry or do not marry, you will regret both;
> whether you marry or do not marry, you will regret both.
> . . . . . . . . . . . . . . . . . . . . . . . . . . . . . . . . . . . .
> This, gentlemen, is the sum and substance of all philosophy.[6]

How are we to be guided by philosophy that speaks this way?

## ANOTHER CREDO

I believe that we need truth as much as we need food. The two are actually related: if we cannot truly distinguish nourishing food from poisonous, if we cannot distinguish the oyster mushroom from the beautiful amanita, the pure white "angel of death," we put ourselves by way of tragic suffering. Workers were injured building the Brooklyn Bridge because they did not know the truth of Boyle's law as it applied to diving. If the question of love is, indeed, the momentous and forced question I believe it to be, then we *need* truthful answers. Wrong answers acted upon produce painful consequences.

The Truth, conceived along traditional lines (as Kierkegaard describes it further on in the selection quoted above) is Truth *aeterno modo* or Truth *sub specie aeternitatis:* Truth in the mode of eternity, Truth from the standpoint of eternity. Paul Simon sings that that Truth is unavailable to mortal men, and I agree: one has to be eternal to know the Truth that does not change throughout eternity, and we are not eternal. But that does not leave us bereft of truth.

If you are a carpenter using a level, you are operating on the belief that the world is flat, that the plane designated as level here will be parallel to the plane designated by your level over there. That is a pretty good truth, but it is not as good as the truth that the earth is spherical, which is the belief that informs celestial navigation. Truer yet is the belief that the earth is an oblate spheroid, that eons of spinning has made it expand at the equator. Oblate spheroids, however, are smooth on the surface, and the earth is not. And so it goes. Not being immortal, we have to deal with partial truths. But some partial truths are truer than others, and I believe that it is prudent to base one's choices and actions on the truest truths you can find. That belief is prominent among the motivations that led me to philosophy: I wanted to avoid the risk of painful consequences that, more often than not, follow from acting upon truths that are not very true. You cannot travel far at sea with a carpenter's level . . . unless you hook it up with a device that can measure the angle from a fixed star to the horizon marked by the level, that is, a sextant: place too much belief in the carpenter's level alone, and you will worry about sailing off the edge.

There is truth, partial truth, in the idea of romantic love, as there is in its shadow, enduring love. But, as we now conceive those truths, they are irreconcilable, hence incapable of guiding us when we reach the fork in the upstream path. The endurance model tells you that you will regret it if you break your vow to Roger; the romantic model tells you that you will regret it if you don't. Impasse. How did we get here? And where do we go?

## BEYOND ROMANCE

We live in a time and place governed by an ideal of love that embodies a hidden contradiction. Romantic love wants the frisson of new love to endure forever. New and forever cannot coexist: you just can't have both; you have to decide, and both choices involve regret. To make eternal vows in the height of romantic bliss is to indulge in wistful self-mystification. To make the same vows based on a calculation of lifelong security is to embrace an economy that deprives us of *poiesis,* the creative poetry of life.

This book purports to take us beyond the partial truths that generate this dilemma to another partial truth, albeit a better one, a truer one; one that will produce less misery than we see about us now. It offers the hope of improving our happiness quotient.

## THE DILEMMA OF POLARIZATION AND PROHIBITION

The work begun here is the work of discerning love. My hypothesis is that love precedes the birth of the gods who have given or taken the names of love. Love inspired the gods and survives their demise. If love appears forlorn in our era, perhaps that is because it wants its next name. Love has been reified in the body of the mother, deified in the name of the father, and incarnated in the flesh of the son. There is truth in all these vicissitudes, also untruth. The task is to discern the truths and untruths with the aim of tilting the balance one way rather than the other. How would love appear if it were summoned in the name of finite fleshly bodies and freed of the conventional discriminations that polarize and rupture the bonds of human kinship?

The answer to this question lies in the summoning. My summons will take the form of responses: responses to these questions with which we begin. These are interlocking questions of affinity and alienation, kinship and prohibition, knowledge and ignorance, self and other, immanence and transcendence. I approach these questions with a style of thinking that gropes beyond the binary logic of Western metaphysics with the hope of preserving the great truths of that tradition by discerning them through the eyes of a new conceptual scheme.

This new conceptuality attempts to resonate with old concepts aimed at the same goal of understanding the world and its inhabitants and responding to them according to the intertwining of their lights and ours. It is a departure from tradition that takes its departure from the tradition.

Our tradition of romantic love is dependent upon the prohibitions emanating from its shadow, enduring love. Romance feeds on the prohibitions that constrain it. Romeo and Juliet love each other all the more because each is off limits to the other. There is a plausible argument to the effect that it is the prohibition that creates the intensity and excitement of romance: we want what we are not supposed to have just because we are not supposed to have it: the allure is produced by the veil and would attenuate without it. Plausibility, however, is not always a sign of truth, and this is a case in point. If prohibition is essential to desire, that must be because we have found it prudent to constrain desire. Which means that desire is the origin of prohibition and not vice versa. Which means that prohibition is not essential to desire, but a historically grounded accompaniment that has sedimented itself in religious constructions of the sacred and profane. The sacred is that which is sanctioned by laws grounded in the figures of divinity; the profane is that which is prohibited.

This religious sediment, apparent in some way in all cultures, is now taken by some as the origin of culture because it is the origin of the symbolic order constitutive of culture as such (under some definitions of culture).[7] Which means that, from within culture—the only viable locus for all of us— prohibition is essential to desire. The antinomy is apparent, and it stymies traditional thought.

Flesh blindly reproduces itself. Flesh blindly annihilates itself. Unmindful that it is doing so, flesh wills its own life and death. The intertwining of the figures of Eros and Thanatos intertwines itself with the intertwining figures of the sacred and profane. These figures detach themselves from the flesh of bodies and become autonomous in the flesh of words—which, institutionalized, produce more blindness, the second order blindness of conformity to convention reinforced by yet another blindness consisting of our need for acceptance. Love blindly constrains blind love.

My hypothesis is that it is the process of reifying symbols, detaching them from flesh, and granting them institutional autonomy that produces the prohibitions that have defiled desire into desiring defilement. If we paint love pure white, we will long for smudges: unhappy desire that has to bugger the priest to get truly off.[8]

The answers I seek lie beyond the semiological reduction.[9] Beyond or beneath the autonomy of signs forever severed from their source. The words that will heal the sickness of words are words that resonate with their source, touch their source, illumine their source in the mirroring of the flesh that is reversibility. I would neither lift all prohibitions nor affirm them in the mode of blind transgression. Rather, I would update the list by attending to the flesh, and attempting to illumine the reflection that separates flesh from itself, thereby granting it the pleasure and pain of touching itself. Maybe, for now, we shall find it prudent to touch each other through barriers of thin latex. Maybe that is preferable to buggering the priest.

Truth is one among many life values. So is love. In my view, they are inseparable. The thought of their inseparability is philosophy. The value of philosophy resides in the ways it gives us to name and think of things. Philosophical persuasion is consequential: bad philosophy produces bad action, bad consequences, unhappy lives. The philosophy that permeates our time and place produces manifest unhappiness, and that is a measure of its validity. We need better names for love than the ones we have.

# TWO

# ALETHEIA, POIESIS, AND EROS

## TRUTH AND UNTRUTH IN THE POETIC CONSTRUCTION OF LOVE

> Never seek to tell thy love,
> Love that never told can be.
>
> —William Blake

### THE QUESTION

> What's love got to do with it?
> What's love but a secondhand emotion?
>
> —Tina Turner

DOES THE TELLING of love constitute love? Or does love always elude the attempt to capture it in words? Is the history of love a history of narrative forms? If we understand *poiesis* to designate the generation of a narrative that, once espoused by a community, becomes a social form, then is love nothing more—and nothing less—than a poetic construct?

The attitudes regarding erotic love reported in Plato's *Symposium* presuppose a legitimacy to the love of boys, if the boys one loves have reached an age "when they begin to acquire some mind—a growth associated with that of down on their chins."[1] Foucault suggests that, although this relationship with boys was regarded as "problematic" among the upper classes at the time, if "it comprised . . . the elements that would form the basis of a transformation of this love into a definitive and socially valuable tie, that of *philia*," it could be regarded as "morally honorable."[2] Contrast this with our culture which, although it is beginning to legitimize homosexual relationships, regards sexual relations with pubescent children as criminal, whether these relations actually involve penetration or not.

Stendahl reports that courts of love were convened in France in the last decade of the twelfth century and that, at one of these courts held in 1174, the Countess of Champagne, answering the question, posed by a troubadour, whether true love can exist between married persons, judged that it could not. Stendahl goes on to recount the thirty-one articles comprising the "Code of Love for the Twelfth Century" as set forth in the works of André the Chaplain. The article given the preeminence of first place on the list states that "the plea of marriage is not a legitimate defense against love."[3] Our culture has developed more lenient attitudes toward adultery than those dramatized by Hawthorne in *The Scarlet Letter*, but it is arguable that the revelation of adulterous liaisons in the lives of such notable figures as Kennedy, King, and Clinton detracted from their public stature, that, for us, the plea of love is not a legitimate defense against charges of adultery. And we are more inclined to regard love as the only legitimate motive for marriage than to conceive marriage and love as incompatible.

Just as the definitions of love evolving through the historical vicissitudes of one culture contradict each other, so are there contradictions across cultures. Feminists of our culture who espouse a doctrine of radical tolerance in the name of multiculturalism are nonetheless disposed to undertake militant action against the practice of clitoridectomy in other cultures. In our culture the pleasure to be obtained from stimulation of the clitoris is held to be essential for a woman to experience genuine erotic love; in some other cultures that pleasure is held to constitute a danger for abiding love relations (as it was in an earlier phase of our own history).

These contradictions in the conception and practice of erotic love reinforce the postmodern case for nominalism and conventionalism, that is, for the standpoint that there is no reality corresponding to the name *true love*, that this designation is more like an honorific term applied to the social construct that happens to be privileged in a given place at a given time. If one asks about the genealogy of the construct, postmodern thought offers a series of replies. The quest for the origins of a normative construct is misconceived

(a) because origins are inaccessible, (b) because norms imply ends or final goals *(tele)* which reside as much in an inaccessible future as they do in an inaccessible past, and (c) because it is more accurate to regard genealogical accounts as narratives, that is, as chains of signifiers rather than as chains of causes. If one subsumes narrative under the general heading of *poiesis,* then love is a social construct produced by language, itself, rather than by the individual poet who happens to be its conduit.

Language spoke this way through Sappho:

> my feelings for you, my beautiful ones,
> will not change.[4]

And this way through Ovid:

> Helen . . .
> Weeps at the old bitch staring from her mirror.
> And who would rape her once or twice now?
> Time and Old Age eat all the world away—
> Black-toothed and slow, they seem to feast forever
> As all things disappear in time, in death.[5]

Why does language contradict itself when speaking through different poets at different times in different places? If it is intrinsic to the language of our passing era to differentiate the world through systems of binary opposition, to generate contradictions, and if the generation of contradictions is the mark of the absurd, then what are we to learn from our poets? What is the truth here?

What is the truth about love? Is it true that love is a social construct grounded in the speaking of language which produces absurdity? If truth, itself, is but one pole of an absurdity-producing binary opposition, how are we to assess the assertion that love is a social construct grounded in the speaking of language which produces absurdity?


## ROMANCE AND PROHIBITION

If it is true that the quality of our lives is affected by the manner in which one loves, by the narrative one enacts, then how might one choose—if one can choose—among the many narratives competing for our devotion? Or, finding little or no promise in the field of competition, how might one invoke language to speak in another way?

Something happens to human bodies at adolescence. Granting Freud the point that infants are sexual, it is nonetheless true that a qualitative change in human sexuality takes place during puberty and adolescence. We may also grant to Freud and the host of psychologists—behavioral, experimental, developmental, humanistic, etc.—who follow him on this issue the point that we tend to recapitulate the models imprinted upon us in infancy; still, it remains true that, during adolescence, we rebel. That rebellion may, indeed, amount to a recapitulation in the negative mode, but it may also take on new forms: every celibate was conceived, and to the distress of sociobiological theory, an unbroken chain of heterosexual reproduction can produce an individual who decides that he or she is exclusively homosexual. Theories based on the model of imprinting and recapitulation may reflect the backward-looking structure of causal explanation rather more than the data to be explained. Causes are retrospective, but motives are prospective in that they are pointed toward a future ideal. Is there, then, a promising prospect to be found—or made—by changelings in search of sexual identity and erotic love?

If we live at the end of the era of onto-theological metaphysics, ambivalently tossing through the wake of the second death of our god of love—if we are ready to exorcise, not the demon in the flesh, but the demonization of the flesh—then perhaps we are ready to embrace the flesh that makes words rather than merely incarnates a word already spoken.

Kierkegaard wrote words to the effect that no man ever wrote poetry to the woman he got. I know that to be empirically false, but I think it is empirically true that no one ever wrote an erotic poem before the age of puberty. What happens at puberty? Floods of testosterone and estrogen. Development of conspicuous secondary sexual characteristics—reedy voices and breasts, accompanied by zits—which, through the phenomenon Sartre called "the look," produce the self-alienating, self-generating capacity for reflective thought. Reflection, in turn, produces the mother of all binary oppositions: shame and lust. And the agon between shame and lust (i.e., the pleasure-pain of sexual desire) portends the history of post-Socratic eros.

Denis de Rougemont was not the first to comment on the fact that romantic love, still the model of love for our time, was a product of Christian culture, but his genealogy of romance is the most compelling account I know. What does this have to do with adolescence and the poetic construction of love? De Rougemont argues that "all European poetry has come out of the Provençal poetry written in the twelfth century by the troubadours of Languedoc" (75), that this poetry is the proximal origin of romantic love, that romantic lovers "love love more than the object of love" (50) that the love they love feeds on prohibition, and that "this obstruction is what passion really wants—its true object" (42).[6] Romantic love loves love, loves the emotional turbulence, and above all, loves the ideal projected upon the love object, an ideal that reflects the immanent fantasy of the lover rather than the transcendent reality of the beloved.

Departing somewhat from de Rougemont, I would add that the Christian transformation of eros into agape is predicated on the demonization of sexuality, incipient in Socratism, that provides the frisson-generating obstacle definitive of romantic love. Romantic love feeds on the unknown otherness or transcendence of the prohibited object and loses its passion once the prohibition is lifted.[7] This is why Bataille[8] regards the religious experience of the sacred as essential to erotic love. The sacred is the source of the taboo and the taboo is the source of the fascination: erotic love thrives in the ambivalent space created by taboo where the physically close love-object is rendered metaphysically remote by the consecrating prohibition.

Taboo and prohibition do not create sexual desire—animals manifest desire—but they do qualify it in the way that generates romanticism or eroticism. This is the truth of constructivism: if prohibition is a social phenomenon—the creation of a law (nomos) through a word (logos), perhaps Lacan's invocation of the name of the father (nom du père)—then the peculiar nature of the taboo will generate an erotic ideal commensurate with the prohibition. The lability of sexual objectification through the structure Freud identified as transference is well known: there may or may not be a general progression from mouth to anus to genitals, but it is clear that sexual interest can shift focus through a wide range of partial objects or fetishes, be they body parts (feet, breasts) or objects associated with them (shoes, brassieres, lingerie in general). There is a connection between fixation on partial objects and specific prohibitions—where the female breast is not hidden through the motive of shame we call modesty, it does not seem to become a fetish—but there are aspects of this connection that necessarily elude constructivist explanations.

## BIOLOGY, POETRY, AND PRAGMATICS

It is a matter of biological fact that the organs of reproduction among mammals are also the organs of excretion, and that human waste is a vehicle of disease. It is also a matter of historical or social fact that human waste and the processes of elimination have been eroticized and fetishized: de Sade delights in giving accounts of coprophagy, and there is a genre of erotic behavior associated with toilet functions known as "water sports." It is not only the restriction of sexual behavior to potentially reproductive acts that generates the list of perversions and prohibitions attributed by Foucault to Freud;[9] one must also acknowledge the sanctions that are generated from concerns about health and increasing empirical knowledge about such dangers as blood-to-blood or semen-to-blood contact and the ingestion of feces. The point here is that empirical fact has a bearing upon prohibition, hence an explanatory role in the understanding of erotic desire or love. Love is certainly not reducible to biology, but neither is it reducible to *poiesis*.

De Rougemont asserts that "happy love has no history—in European literature" (52). This is at best trivially true, that is, true only if one sanctifies the term *literature* and therefore refuses to apply it to such forms as Harlequin romance novels. Shakespeare was closer to the mark with Lysander's observation in *A Midsummer Night's Dream* that "the course of true love never did run smooth" (I, i, 132). Does the bump, the obstacle, the prohibition generate the truth of love? Does it test the truth of love? Or is it just somehow true that love always encounters obstacles?

The family is both a social and a natural unit among mammals. The rule of exogamy also straddles the distinction between the social and the natural. If one tries, as did Aquinas, to specify the norms governing sexuality, marriage, and the family under the heading of natural law,[10] one eventually confronts difficulties arising from the fact that the term *natural law* is an oxymoron. Law, as etymologists tend to agree,[11] is something that is laid down in a social or linguistic act, and the natural order is usually conceived as transcending human institution. Without providing the treatment this issue requires, let me just stipulate here[12] that, although human institutions are founded upon such natural givens as gravity and the biology of reproduction, nature allows for multiple determination, does not univocally demand one kind of institutionalization to the exclusion of all others, but does delimit the range of possible and probable forms of institution: royal families, for example, tend to die out at a rate that is proportional to degree of enforced incestuous proximity. In short, there is a primacy to natural origins, but a circumscribed plurality of social forms founded upon them.

Regardless how broad the scope of the family and loose the sanctions upon the law of exogamy, the two structures engender some degree of violence in the process of mate selection or love. There is necessarily a breaking of old and creation of new social forms, be they abiding families or transient affairs. That is one of the reasons for ritualization and attendant prohibition. Whether it is strife between the Montagues and the Capulets or values of

miscegenation in the heritage of an Alabama high school principal, the existing social order is disrupted by the novel formation generated by erotic liaison. Since it is a character of social order to be self-conserving, there is always
an obstacle to be overcome by lovers. To love is to disrupt for the sake of a
new union.

Disruption for the sake of union: another binary opposition. Like others,
this one is resolvable through the circularity of repetition as was dramatized in
the ancient Greek phallic plays: the young man's phallus supervenes over the
old man's phallic order, the bride is taken, and the cycle begins again. This is
ritualization, socialization: the generation of institutions that minimize violence through codification and repetition. It is, thus, intrinsic to love to be ritualized under social forms; although these forms vary, there are constants and
limits dictated, ultimately, by pragmatic constraint and the related constraint
upon imagination. Here is the domain of erotic *poiesis*.

## ALETHEIA

*Ich bin von Kopf bis Fuss auf Liebe eingestellt.*

—Marlene Dietrich

Here, also, is the domain of adolescence, the lived body, and truth. No erotic
*poiesis* before adolescence because the flood of estrogen and testosterone is
needed to fill the poet's pen. Eros and desire may, indeed, have filled the infant's soul, but the shame, born of reflexivity, needed to internalize the sanctions and externalize the object of desire does not come upon the scene until
the hormones flow and the secondary sexual characteristics emerge to pro-
voke the disgusting, enticing, erotically interested look.[13]

Changelings disrupt the social fabric simply by changing, becoming sexual. The rites of passage associated with adolescence are, indeed, constructions
that vary from culture to culture. We send our changelings to school, prefer-
ably boarding school, summer camp, or boot camp, to be initiated into the
practices that have to be mastered to gain adult autonomy and readmission to
the social order. Other cultures send their adolescents into the jungle or forest or desert for other modes of initiation, but there is a functional isomorphism in these rituals that is apparent across cultures. Infants and adults are socially stable in comparison to changelings. Changelings destabilize and
threaten social order: they are banished until they learn how to behave. And
there is always a specialized caste—call them shamans, priests, teachers, drill
instructors—charged with inculcating the society's basic dogmas in its youth

and training them to acceptable practice. Beneath the variable social construction is the natural process that motivates the institutional deployment of power and can serve as one of its measures.[14]

Changelings disrupt the social order; The social order restores itself through the institution of norms. The regulations coagulate around such myths or poetic constructions as natural law. Natural law ties sex to reproduction through institutionalizing love in marriage and the family whose own norms are structured by the telos of propagating the species. As they demand—or simply exercise—the sexual autonomy demanded of them by their own hormones, our culture's changelings remind us daily that poetic forms that fail to accommodate natural measures survive only in mutation: we are now teaching our youth how they might love without invoking the nemesis of unwanted progeny and disease.

Aquinas (1225–1274) taught that true love is possible only when consecrated by marriage. Twelfth-century courts of love had taught the opposite, that true love is impossible within the confines of marriage. Our culture is living through the chaos generated by the contradiction embodied in this binary opposition of romance: contemporary eros loves the prohibited object because it is prohibited, thus contemporary eros thrives on dissatisfaction. Is *this* true love? Is it the truth about desire, as Derrida has argued,[15] that desire lives in the *jouissance* of deferring the union that would spell its death?

Merleau-Ponty designated as "profound" the following remark made by Malraux about modern painters: "'although no one of them spoke of truth, all, faced with the works of their adversaries, spoke of imposture.'"[16] Something like this may also apply here. Despite our reluctance to define "true love" for all times, given its intimate connection with the processes of becoming, we are not quite so hesitant to identify inauthenticity in the erotic domain. The project of seduction depends upon deceit. Don Giovanni masks his identity from Donna Anna, Donna Elvira, and, one assumes, the remaining 1001 conquests he made in Spain alone. The masking was essential to the project of seduction because it protected him from having to fulfill his promises of undying love. Let Don Giovanni be as innocent as Kierkegaard said he was, let him believe every promise in the moment he makes it, the inauthenticity is simply doubled, the lie to himself merely facilitating the lie to the lady.[17]

There may be no single great Truth to be unveiled about love, no divinity who embodies an immutable True Love, but I believe that there are finite, mutable truths and lies intertwined in the erotic domain which can be articulated, as I have attempted to do here. Let me conclude with the thought that has been trying to articulate itself throughout this chapter.

The binary opposition between nature and construction, between biology and *poiesis,* generates mystification just because it is a binary opposition. One does not eliminate binary oppositions, not this one at least, by attempting to reduce one of the terms to the other, by privileging one of the poles, the linguistic structure, and refusing to consider its other, the biological structure. One might rather develop the aspect of truth *(aletheia)* that Heidegger described in terms of letting-be or listening *(Gelassenheit),*[18] and associates with freedom. Coupled with letting-be as its indissoluble correlate is a form of forgetfulness Heidegger designates as insistence, a projection upon beings, including the beings that are other persons, of categories that allow them to serve our purposes and reduce them to instruments overlooked in the process of utilization.[19]

Romantic love, the poetic construct that still defines love in our era, does not let the being who is loved *be,* but insists upon projecting upon the love-object an ideality constructed by our own muses and poets. One overlooks the flesh and blood person in the mode of forgetfulness known as transcendental constitution. Marriage is a threat to romance because the propinquity of one spouse forces upon the other an awareness of the person's reality as a living body with demands and purposes whose own insistence competes with the insistence of the projected ideal. The clutter in the bathroom obtrudes upon the vision illumined by candles.

Contemporary romantic love is essentially inauthentic insofar as the poetic construction collides with the desire to be loved for oneself. If the only form love can take is that provided by poetic construction, if there is no breathing person living his or her own embodied life until death do us part, only a misapprehension *(méconnaissance)* fashioned by my appropriation of some poet's construction of desire, then there is no love beyond romance, and I cannot love you because there is no you for me to love. The alternative is to write one's own poem to the person whose life and body have intertwined with one's own in a manner that reveals and enhances both. If the little death is inseparable from the big one at the end, if the love that intensifies the one assuages the pain of the other, that may actually be a natural fact enriched by a poetic vision.

# THREE

# NATURAL LAW
# AND SEXUAL MORALITY

## FRAMEWORK

THE VALUES UNDERLYING contemporary sexual morality[1] are as diverse
and heteronomous as the values underlying morality in general. The sources of
these values reflect the amalgam of religious, legal, intellectual, and social ideals
bequeathed to us by a long, rich, and multifarious heritage. There are, however,
de facto differences between sexual morality and morality in general. The difference relevant here has to do with consensus. Within the United States, the
laws governing homicide, theft, perjury, etc. are fairly consistent throughout
the land, whereas laws governing obscenity, prostitution, age of consent, etc.
vary from state to state, and it has been acknowledged by the U.S. Supreme
Court that standards of acceptable sexual behavior differ from community to
community.[2] Indeed, that variance in sexual morality has, itself, been granted
legal sanction in the federal laws now governing obscenity. This difference between sexual morality and general morality is also apparent at the global level.
I cannot argue the point here, but will simply assert it as a hypothesis, that
something like the Golden Rule, the appeal to universality, commands respect
worldwide in a way that no precept of specifically sexual morality does.[3]

There is no basic precept of sexual morality, no coherent structure of
thinking and esteeming that gathers us into a community of shared beliefs

and values. The disputes over abortion, birth control, divorce, homosexuality, and the like demonstrate the deep schisms in world culture and its larger subsets. Notwithstanding this heteronomy, there is a common thread running through the issues just cited. That common thread is natural law theory.

Those whose values commit them to opposing abortion, birth control, divorce, and homosexuality typically appeal to natural law to support their position. It is, they claim, contrary to the manifest intent of nature to subvert the processes clearly designed to foster propagation and sustenance of life by practicing abortion or birth control. Homosexuality contravenes the natural purpose of reproduction, and divorce undermines the bonding of natural parents required for the nurturing of the young. This reasoning is stretched further to assign negative moral categories to masturbation, cunnilingus, fellatio, anal intercourse, bestiality, and other sexual practices that do not lead to reproduction. Further extension of this line of thought produces condemnation of sex with multiple partners or non-dyadic sex, and sex with or among those too young, too old, or too incapacitated to perform the roles associated with bearing, nurturing, and rearing children. The list of prohibitions warranted by natural law theory extends to include incest, miscegenation, pre- or extra-marital sexual relations (i.e., promiscuity as such), prostitution, pornography, and erotic depiction in general. Natural law theory has also been used to support the doctrine of male superiority, application of different standards for sexual behavior among men, women, and children, and just about every other moral stricture brought to bear on human sexuality. The list given here is far from complete.

The list, however, is long enough and complex enough to make it evident that there are many ways of conceiving natural law and many areas of intersection and contradiction between natural law theorizing and other moral or ethical theories based on precepts that do not directly appeal to natural law (e.g., theories that ground themselves by appeal to human freedom and dignity, or by appeal to general welfare, equality, responsibility, reason, etc.). One might argue, for example, that sexual intercourse of all kinds should be restricted because promiscuity poses a hazard to the health and welfare of the community at large. Here a general ethical precept reinforces with natural law theory. In other areas, general moral precepts collide with precepts based on natural law theory: male superiority and double standards do not fit well within the ethics of equality.

The term *natural law theory* suggests that there is a coherent doctrine or at least a commonly accepted connotation to which the term refers. In fact, there is considerable disagreement about what natural laws are and what bearing they might have on human values. Consequently, it is incumbent upon me to clarify the constellation of ideas that I intend to designate with the term. The range of these ideas is broad, however, and cannot be narrowed without losing the impact of the meaning the term has acquired. I will attempt to be as precise as the subject matter allows.

The understanding of natural law theory to be developed in the next few pages defines itself in contradistinction to two opposed views: one I will designate as 'traditional natural law theory' and associate it with some form of theism; the other I will designate as 'constructivism' and associate it with a form of postmodern thought. The idea guiding my thought here is that the binary opposition between these polarized views is roughly equivalent to the familiar opposition between absolutism and relativism, and that the polarization by which they define themselves undermines the validity of both positions. My intent is not to mediate between the two views—that is logically impossible since they define themselves by mutual exclusion— but to seek the rich and ambiguous ground from which they have been derived.

In the process of developing the understanding of natural law theory that I think is relevant to morality in general and sexual morality in particular, I shall attempt to defend my belief that the distinction between them is ill conceived, that the very idea of a specifically sexual morality is a bad idea, that the precepts of sexual ethics draw their moral clout by basing themselves on general ethical principles, that viable sexual norms are derived from overarching norms having to do with pleasure and pain, obligation and responsibility, distributive justice, and the like: the difference between sexual acts that are acceptable and those that are not cannot be derived from the fact that the acts are sexual in nature.[4]

Postmodern thinking purports to reveal an aporia or deeply embedded inconsistency latent in the foundations of traditional natural law theory. The laws of nature can be regarded as descriptive and morally neutral (e.g., gravitation is a law of nature) or prescriptive and normative (e.g., natural law decrees that the organs of reproduction and excretion should be used exclusively for those purposes). Natural law theory in general— but particularly as it relates to sexual morality—depends upon an inference from the description of a fact to the prescription of a norm.

—The penis is an organ that fulfills the natural functions of reproduction and excretion..Therefore . . .

—It is contrary to nature to use the penis for other purposes.

If it is proper to constitute description and prescription as binary opposites, as standing in a relation of mutual exclusion, then this inference is prima facie invalid. Yet, it is arguable that such mighty institutions as the United States Constitution and Roman Catholic dogma rest in significant part on natural law theory, hence on some version of this inference.

What rationale might be supplied for the inference from description to prescription? The answer usually involves the related concepts of purpose (goal or *telos*) and design (form) which come together under the heading of function.

—Nature designed the penis to function in such a way as to fulfill the purposes of excretion and reproduction.

The concepts of purpose and design may be regarded as descriptive; but the fact described may also be regarded as pregnant with portent: if one can observe and describe some purpose fulfilled by a given design, one might find some warrant for conjecturing intent.

—Nature intends the penis to be used for excretion and reproduction.

Another premise is required to render this latent prescription explicitly normative. This is an exclusionary premise, which limits the function to the purpose observable in the design.

—Nature intends the penis to be used exclusively for excretion and reproduction.

From this premise one can validly deduce that any other use is contrary to nature.

Three separate issues collide in this inference: (1) the exclusive disjunction of fact and value, description and prescription; (2) the constellation of design-purpose-intent which subsumes natural function under some teleological rubric; (3) the exclusionary premise that restricts function to a given end or set of ends. I shall take up each of these, but not in the order in which they were presented.

TELEOLOGY: NATURAL, SUPERNATURAL, HUMAN

The natural teleology relevant to sexual morality falls in the domain of biology, the supernatural in the domain of onto-theology, and the human in the domain of politics and morality. These divisions are more than a little arbitrary: as I hope to show, the demarcating criteria break down under scrutiny.

The criteria at work in separating biological, onto-theological, and ethico-political teleology from one another center on the notion of final causality as a principle of explanation. I shall take Aristotle as spokesperson for natural teleology, but argue that his conception of the natural depends in essential ways on the supernatural and the human.

## Aristotle and Natural Teleology

I adopt here the interpretation of Aristotle's conception of natural law that regards it as derived from a biological paradigm.[5] Having repudiated the Platonic understanding of natural law as originating in the supernatural sphere of the eternal, immutable Forms, that is, in the sphere of the divine, Aristotle turns to nature in general and biology in particular to search for a ground and measure of lawfulness.[6] The science of biology, for Aristotle, is based on teleological explanation and, as such, is infused with values and norms.[7]

The issue of right-handedness provides an apt example. We observe the predominance of right-handedness, but does the greater strength of the right hand, observable not universally but for the most part, provide sufficient warrant for Aristotle to claim[8] that the right is generally superior? Aristotle's answer lies in a passage from *De Incessu Animalum*[9] in which he claims that "nature does nothing in vain." The underlying premise is that "nature operates for the sake of the end, which is good, so that what is needed for the end is beneficial, and nature provides what is beneficial . . . or needed for the end or good of the organism, which in this instance is its continued existence."[10] Further support for the general superiority of the right can be found in Aristotelian arguments that associate the right with the origin of motion (which enjoys the superiority of the mover over the moved).

The teleological argument that explains the general predominance of the right hand over the left is based on the biological purpose *(telos)* of serving the good of the organism, that is, what is beneficial or necessary for life. The reasoning just summarized proceeds from the empirically grounded premise asserting the predominance of right-handedness to the trans-empirical conclusion that asserts the general superiority of right-handedness. Bracketing the issue of its validity, the warrant offered in support of the inference is that "nature makes nothing in vain." This is clearly not an empirical assertion, but would traditionally fall under the general heading of metaphysics.[11]

To identify the assertion that nature makes nothing in vain as a meta-physical assertion is relatively uncontroversial, but when one attempts to analyze the import of that identification, one enters several debates. The debate of interest to me centers on the opposition between the postmodern categorization of metaphysics under the heading of onto-theology, on the one hand, and, on the other, the Aristotelian understanding of metaphysics as the endeavor to codify the organizing principles of scientific inquiry or reason at large. Postmodern thought characterizes Aristotelian metaphysics as onto-theological because Aristotle attributes intent to nature thereby betraying his essential dependence on a latent theology, a projection onto nature of cosmic intentionality modeled after the human but magnified to infinity.

At stake is the issue of teleological explanation and the constellation of design-purpose-intent informing Aristotle's understanding of nature. I see an ambivalence in Aristotle's standpoint: while it is true that his teleology depends on the attribution of intent-design-purpose to nature, it is also true that he seeks to distance himself from the Platonic appeal to a supernatural domain of Forms as the source of natural organization or worldly meaning. I do not think Aristotle resolved this tension. I do think that this tension remains unresolved to this day. It remains unresolved because, following Aristotle, an opposition between the natural and the supernatural, the a-theological and the theological, has grown up to obscure the quest that defines Aristotelian natural philosophy, that is, the quest to find meaning and value in nature.

This quest drives Aristotelian teleological explanation. It also drives Aristotelian hylomorphism—where a related ambivalence, a similar tension may be found. Aristotle argues for the fundamental coincidence of form and matter in nature, but he also offers separate etiologies for the formal and the material elements and separates the two in his taxonomy of causes. If form and matter are distinct in origin and if equivalences are drawn between the material and the natural, on one side, and the formal and the supernatural, on the other, then nature degenerates into raw matter lacking meaning, and that meaning has to be attributed to a supernatural process of informing or organizing worldly matter.

To claim, as I have, that Aristotle's conception of the natural depends in essential ways on the supernatural, that the two domains cannot be separated if sense is to be made of his teleological model of explanation, is simply to stress that aspect of his philosophy that recoils against the disjunction of matter and form, nature and telic organization. The project here is to follow the path of hylomorphism, the path of matter-pregnant-with-form or

autochthonous organization,[12] opened by Aristotle, but left untended by Western philosophy as it pursued a divergent path at the fork created by Aristotle's
ambivalence, the path of ontological dualism characterized by binary opposition between form and matter, supernatural and natural, fact and value, etc.

The teleology informing Aristotle's conception of natural law has a
human component that must be considered in conjunction with the natural
and the supernatural. Aristotle's assessment of competing political systems is
based on the criterion of human teleology. The best system is the system
that best serves the natural ends of humanity and the attainment of the
good life.[13]

To say, as Aristotle does in his *Politics,* that the state is a creation of nature,
and that humans are by nature political animals (I.1253a2–3) is to ascribe to
nature an intent in fashioning humans.[14] Here, again, the teleological principle is invoked with the premise that nature makes nothing in vain. The
human end of attaining the good life, which may be a matter of deliberate
human intent, is inseparable from the natural inclination to be political,
which, in turn, depends on the supernatural intent implicit in the claim that
nature makes nothing in vain.

The constellation of design-purpose-intent drives Aristotelian natural
law theory inasmuch as it allows Aristotle to draw inferences from what he
observes to conclusions with normative weight. That is, Aristotle uses paradigms drawn from biology and metaphysics to generate criteria based on teleological explanation by means of which he can assess competitive normative
theories and generate his own.[15]

## AQUINAS AND SUPERNATURAL TELEOLOGY

I take up Aquinas to make two main points, one having to do with his standpoint, the other having to do with the posture I adopt with regard to it.

1. The distinction between natural and supernatural teleology, although
thematically operative in both, can no more be sustained as a binary opposition in Aquinas than it can in Aristotle. The difference between them has
more to do with differences in the stance each takes with regard to the supernatural. They both use metaphysical paradigms to argue from empirical
premises to trans-empirical[16] conclusions, but Aristotle, preferring to retain
firm footing in the empirical domain, distances himself from the Platonic tendency to ground ethics in onto-theology, whereas Aquinas operates from
within the standpoint of faith and maintains that divine revelation provides a

ground of certainty that is qualitatively different from and superior to natural reason.

For Aquinas, there is but one true ground of law and that is supernatural teleology. Nature is the creation of divinity and it fulfills the divine purpose. Extrapolations such as Aristotle's regarding the teleology apparent in nature set forth under the heading of natural law can discern the ends of humanity insofar as they are discoverable by finite human reason, but the understanding gained thereby is incomplete, and the life based on natural virtues designed to promote those ends cannot be satisfying because humans were created for a supernatural end. Perfect beatitude requires faith as the fulfillment of the supernatural end and cannot be attained through the exercise of natural powers alone.

Since Aquinas regards natural law as a manifestation of supernatural law, there can be no real distinction between them: the relevant distinction is that drawn between the illumination of divine law provided by natural reason and that provided by faith.

2. I regard theology in general as founded on a metaphor that has outlived its credibility: god is the creation of humans rather than vice versa as supernatural law is an extrapolation from the scientific and political lawfulness derived from and applied to the finite domain of the human world. From my standpoint, infinitude is a name for the incomprehensible, apprehensible only in our awareness of our finitude, which serves the primary purpose of inducing humility and wonder, and is misused in the endeavor to substantiate positive cognitive claims.

The point I seek to draw from Aquinas here is that the ends apparent to natural reason point beyond themselves and are never completely satisfying. That is the reason for the human creation of the divine. The natural end of human life apparent to finite reason is decay and death. Faith regards death as the gateway to eternal happiness as reward for suffering the passion of finite life in the proper way. Finite reason finds the only source of happiness in the living of life, and anticipates death as the termination of the possibility of that happiness. Death brings complete satisfaction only through the extermination of desire, not its fulfillment. Finite satisfaction is therefore tainted by the realization of its own transience.[17]

## THE EXCLUSIVE DISJUNCTION OF FACT AND VALUE

Following Aquinas, the medieval tradition of Christian theology sedimented the subsumption of natural teleology under supernatural teleology so firmly that, with the Enlightenment, the discrediting of the latter led to the banishing of the former from the domain of orthodox science—until it became evident that orthodox biology could not do its job without the tool of natural teleology. Now, in the sphere of contemporary Continental philosophy at least, the deconstruction of the onto-theological foundations of science in general and biology in particular is attempting, through a more reductive radicalism than was imaginable to Enlightenment thinkers, to complete the purge of final causality, not by separating science from religion, but rather by classifying science as religion, that is, as onto-theology, and suggesting that the pernicious effects of Western religion (e.g., phallocentrism and the host of evils that follow from it) are recapitulated within Western science and rendered all the more devastating by virtue of self-dissemblance, that is, for being much less obvious.

I maintain that this historical progression is regressive, that it begins with the mistake Plato made that Aristotle did not quite rectify—the mistake of conceiving the supernatural as ontologically disjunct from human projection, that is, human teleology—that this mistake was compounded when Enlightenment thinkers decided to abandon teleological explanation rather than refine it, and that postmodern thinkers are inviting future thinkers to ignore their genuine insights by situating these insights in the context of an anti-science polemic against empiricism (conceived as a species of foundationalism) that further exacerbates the Enlightenment's overreaction to the Platonic mistake.

This mistake can also be described as the failure to distinguish between the finite ends of human teleology and the infinite ends of divine perfection. Final causality is a misleading term for human and natural teleology. The logic of goals and purposes *(tele)* is properly conceived as open-ended. The positing of closure at infinity—i.e., perfection—is a way of misunderstanding both the human world and the natural world surrounding it. It is an instance of the onto-theological fallacy: a paradoxical reversal of thought that extrapolates cosmic intent from a finite human model . . . and then fashions a moral code based on the subsumption of human ends under divine finality.

The Platonic mistake which Aristotle perpetuates rather than corrects is instantiated in a use of the craftsmanship analogy[18] that attributes to nature the deliberate human intent manifest in human activities. In the first book of the *Nicomachean Ethics,* Aristotle establishes a teleological framework for his ethical theorizing: human activities are to be assessed on the basis of the end or good to which they are directed. Happiness is the name given to the final end, "that for whose sake everything else is done."[19] Happiness so conceived is described as "lacking in nothing," as "final and self-sufficient," and as "the end of action" (1.1097b15–22). To specify this end more concretely, Aristotle raises the question of the function of humanity. "Have the carpenter . . . and the tanner certain functions or activities, and has man none?" (1.1097b29–30). He then applies the craftsmanship analogy: just as the end of the craftsman is to attain "eminence in respect of goodness" in the performance of his function or craft, so is it the end of humanity, the "human good," to perform its function well. The unique function (or specific difference) constitutive of the essence or definition of humanity is "activity of soul which follows or implies a rational principle" or "activity of soul in accordance with virtue" (1.1098a8–18).

The analogy commits the onto-theological fallacy by reasoning from finite, circumscribed human functions to a function assigned to humans by nature. As shown above, Aristotle argues in the *Politics* that nature designs humans in such a way as to achieve the end of happiness. Here, in the *Nicomachean Ethics,* that end provides a measure for moral evaluation of human activities. The finality of that end is trans-finite: it is "self-sufficient" and "lacking in nothing." These terms belong in the domain of the self-caused cause or *causa sui,* that which needs nothing in order to be; they have departed from the domain of human finitude where purpose and design are driven by lack and need.

The rectification of this mistake does not lie in abandoning teleology, but in delimiting teleology to the domain from which it was initially extrapolated. Guided in this manner, I would rephrase Aristotle's question. Is it the case that, as craftsmen, we are driven nonarbitrarily by certain intentions toward certain ends, but that, as humans, we have no intentions which incline us nonarbitrarily toward certain ends and away from others?

Happiness is as felicitous a term as any other to name the conceptual space that designates the harmonious fulfillment of human desires. It is the task of philosophy to work at the project of filling that space. It is the mistake of onto-theology to conceive that space as filled by a trans-finite purpose which we must try to discover through nonempirical intuition or faith or interpretation of scripture guided by divine hands. But it is equally a mistake of deconstructionism to conceive nature and empirical circumstance as irrelevant to the task of filling that space or as cryptonyms for an antecedent onto-theological filling of that space. Nature is relevant to human teleology, to human intentions, needs, desires, and values: not nature as the book from which divine intent can be read, but nature as the source of organic life and all that sustains and delimits it.

The distinctions between the human, the natural, and the supernatural are human distinctions, to be sure, but they are drawn in response to a world that transcends humanity. Everything human is natural, but the converse does not hold. Deliberate intent must be restricted to that domain of natural causality known as human: when intent is applied to nonhuman aspects of nature, one commits the onto-theological fallacy of conceiving the world as an artifact constructed by a cosmic artisan.[20]

The natural world includes the human world because we are natural entities, but it transcends the human world in space and time as it transcends our ability to understand it. Under this thesis, human culture is just as natural as the culture of an ant colony, and anything that takes place in human culture is just as natural as anything that happens in any other natural domain—whence follows de Sade's challenge to natural law morality that nothing that happens in nature—bestiality, cruelty, incest, and so forth—is contrary to nature. The natural world also includes the supernatural world, if one accepts the thesis that the supernatural is an artifice of human culture. Given our natural needs, it is a nonarbitrary project to pro-ject a world yet to be contrived in which those needs are met. This ideal world projected as a future world is supernatural in the sense of divine only if one commits the onto-theological fallacy; its transcendence is better conceived in terms of the no-longer and not-yet of natural time.

The inference from fact to value must be made—if one forsakes the absolutes of onto-theology, on one hand, and rejects the abject relativism to which antifoundationalism commits itself, on the other—simply because there is no other ground for value. The naturalistic fallacy is a fallacy only if the natural world we observe is devoid of value. And this is the case only if an antecedent commitment is made to separate facts from values and provide separate etiologies for their provenance.[21] Make that commitment and G. E. Moore's pronouncement that we must look beyond the natural world in order to ground our values follows inexorably. I take this to be a compelling reason not to make the commitment. The point here is that description is not value-neutral. Describe the penis as an organ of pleasure (as an erogenous zone *pace* Freud), and the argument that opened this paper would arrive at a conclusion that would conflict with the one restricting the uses of the penis to reproduction and excretion.

The truth of natural law theory is that natural entities (including the human body) lend themselves unequally to human goals. It is not contrary to natural intent to try to use the penis to pound nails—because nature has no intent in designing the penis as humans do in designing hammers—it is just stupid. It is also unwise, but not unnatural, to insert an unprotected penis into an anus because the pleasure obtained is far exceeded by the risk. The issue here is not a question of intent on the part of nature; it is the issue of natural limits or natural constraints upon human freedom.

## THE EXCLUSIONARY PREMISE

We speak of natural organs or organisms as being designed for given purposes. We also speak of them as having evolved certain forms to fulfill certain natural needs within the constraints of natural circumstance. The difference here is properly conceived as the difference between the paradigms of onto-theological creationism and naturalistic evolution theory. Not unmindful of the problems attendant upon it, I shall simply acknowledge that I have adopted here a variant of the paradigm currently known as evolutionary biology: as should be evident by now, I regard it as human arrogance to construe our culture as supervenient upon the natural world rather than emergent from it. History cannot be reduced to biology, but it is inconceivable apart from biology.

Freud has been taken to task for arguing that anatomy is destiny—even though he contended that the destiny portended by gender differences is malleable and subject to the vicissitudes of racial and family history, cultural influence, and even personal decision. The laws of psychology are misconceived if they are taken as grounded in nature exclusive of culture or culture exclusive of nature, for the two are inextricably intertwined. It is, I think, undeniable that the fact of being anatomical portends the inevitable destiny of death and the host of values that respond to that fact. The factual or biological aspect of the nature–culture continuum provides a basis for assessing the values that emerge in the human world. For example, I would claim that the values associated with the projection of a life after death are far less appropriate to the fact of death, which limits finite human becoming—far less truthful—than the values associated with authentic acknowledgment that individual human lives are coterminous with the lives of individual human bodies: the values of the latter preclude the values that produced *autos-da-fé* during the Spanish Inquisition.

The thesis seeking to articulate itself here is that of a reversibility of nature and culture in which culture emerges from nature and returns to inform it. One reflects on death in order to choose among the options available in responding to it; the natural fact of death forecloses the option of immortality, but opens possibilities that range from martyrdom to health food addiction. When some options gain cultural supremacy and others are rejected, further limitations are placed upon human freedom: suttee is now illegal, but in former times it created serious restrictions upon Indian widows in responding to the deaths of their husbands.

We are embodied natural entities. As such, we are constrained by biology and physics: we need food, water, air; we are held down by gravity. Culture responds to these constraints with various cuisines and technologies designed to distribute water to deserts and air to divers. Recently, we have learned to counteract gravity with surgical tucks. More to the point, we have learned to alter our cuisines and technologies to reflect what we have learned about the biological effects of fat in our diets and pollutants in our environment. The laws we enact in our cultures respond to the laws we find at work in nature and can be assessed in accordance with the measures provided by our own natural ends of health and happiness.

Nature, as we understand it, is constituted by our interests, that is, by our culture; but culture is constituted in response to the natural environment with which it has always had to contend. It is not accidental that we have always been interested in earth, air, fire, and water: we have no choice but to contend with these elements. How we contend with them is the issue. Fire heats our dwellings and also burns them down: there are natural constraints upon our uses of fire. This is the domain of the exclusionary premise.

Under traditional natural law theory, every natural element is conceived as fulfilling a purpose for which it was designed, and uses contrary to design are excluded, prohibited by taboo in human culture. There have always been places where fires may be lighted and other places where they may not. There are divinities for all the elements, and those divinities demand propitiation, obedience to their laws. The sublation *(Aufhebung)* of the deities—taking religious symbols to be human creations—which I advocate (on grounds that there are better ways to respect the elements), does not diminish the force of the laws they symbolized, it rather calls for greater degrees of delicacy and depth of understanding. My general point is that human teleology, based as it is on natural needs, commits us to respond to natural laws. But that response is grounded in our projects and designs rather than any deliberate intent attributable to nature or its putative creator.

The exclusionary premise restricts human behavior in accordance with human teleology, not divine teleology. The natural law of gravity does not tell us that it is contrary to nature for humans to fly, but it does set limits to the means and deliver brutal consequences when the means employed are inadequate to propitiate its demands: when the flight attendant says that we will be on the ground shortly, she or he is always telling the truth—it is a natural fact, a fact permeated with value.

Our natural needs generate nonarbitrary projects in the fulfillment of which we turn to nature. The exclusionary premise tells us what nature will and will not provide, and at what risk, what expenditure of time, labor, and ingenuity. What is contrary to nature is what we have not yet learned to coax from nature in ways that are consonant with our own desires and fears. We are always in the process of learning what is contrary to nature: it may, for example, be contrary to nature to have 7.1 million defecating human beings occupy the forty-eight square mile island of Manhattan. I suspect that it is, but tend to think that this is a matter of sanitation technology and its limits rather more than one of divine intent.

To argue, as I have here, for the reversibility of nature and culture is not to posit them as separate and discrete domains that interact or intersect, but neither is it to posit a homogenized and undifferentiable unity. The model I advocate is that of a spectrum delimited by bounds of possibility that stop short of pure nature on one end and pure culture on the other. The notion of a nature in itself apart from human cognition is a limiting point of human cognition—as is the notion of a symbolic domain with no ties to the sights and sounds of which symbols are made and through which they are communicated. One can, however, discriminate phenomena such as death and disease, which have cultural significance but resist cultural manipulation, from other phenomena, such as art and morality, which have ties to nature but are more susceptible to human contrivance.

## NATURAL LAW AND SEXUAL MORALITY

Aristotle struggled with the opposition between the universality imputed to natural law and the particularity or variance of culture-bound morality. The struggle continues. The human body may be regarded as a natural constant across culture and history or as an artifact that varies with culture and epoch. In my view, it is wrong to set up the opposition, mistaken to polarize in either direction, and more accurate to say that biology constrains cultural variance, but does not univocally dictate a given praxis. No culture that I am aware of has left the human body unaltered and unadorned, but there is wide variance in the ways in which different cultures mutilate, pierce, paint, coif, and train their bodies. Different praxes produce different consequences. Romans may have learned too late that lead oxide whitens the face, but kills the body. Chinese aristocracy abandoned the practice of binding the feet of their infant daughters. Circumcision still appears to provide some health benefit, but I hope that clitoridectomy will not survive into the twenty-first century. Eye shadow, however, is forever, and I suspect that men will adopt it as gracefully as we have taken to cologne and hair spray. My point here is that there are natural limits that eventually delimit the range of practice. Cultural plurality and diversity may be regarded as a huge anthropological experiment to discover which sets of mores are more felicitous than others.

I am not asserting a categorical imperative that commands absolute respect for human bodies as Kant asserted his imperative based on the absolutization of Reason. I am asserting an open-ended and emergent set of values that might be conceived as hypothetical imperatives.[22] The antecedents are fuzzy in character and variable in force; they constellate around terms such as happiness, well-being, health, prosperity, and the like, all of which are multideterminable, but subject to natural constraint. If you want to be happy or healthy or prosperous, etc., then you had better eat your vegetables, give up cigarettes, exercise regularly, use condoms, work hard, buy-low-sell-high, reduce your viewing time, recycle, and interview potential sex partners carefully and before the act. In short, I am adopting some classical Aristotelian virtues, such as *phronesis* and *sophrosyne,* as well as some newer ones, such as authenticity and nondemonic eros. The major change I propose is that of responding intelligently to what we know of natural regularity instead of exercising blind obedience to the gods that have been constructed to symbolize those laws. It is not an intent of nature that constrains us, it is our intent that is constrained by nature. If you look at the sun, you will go blind; if you want to observe the eclipse, use a filter.

As it is with one's eyes, so it is, I think, with one's genitals. Delightful though it might be to some tastes during some phases of life to maximize the number of sexual partners, the number of ways of generating frisson, and the frequency of that generation, this project, if carried out imprudently, is naturally bound to culminate in more pain than pleasure, more misery than happiness. We do not need a god to tell us that promiscuity is evil and threaten punishment. We need to know that sexual intercourse is the best way that nature has stumbled upon to transmit germs from one body to another. It is also a pretty good way to promote intimacy, pleasure, and affection—or alienation, pain, and rancor. Sexual mores have always been guided by the *telos* of happiness to minimize the threats to individual or collective well-being. These threats are grounded in both nature and culture, that is, under my model, they are grounded in some intertwining of nature and the response to nature on that part of nature that responds to itself.

I am advocating a morality predicated on the attempt to understand the biology of human sexuality and respond appropriately,[23] that is, in accordance with the hypothetical imperatives devised to accommodate the natural constraints that delimit human behavior. It is a morality of consequences that depends on knowing how to produce the effects deemed desirable—and avoid those deemed undesirable—in that variant of human teleology that follows from one's own definition of happiness. As noted above, I do not take happiness to be a completely specifiable term, but neither do I regard it as empty: I think that pain, hunger, disease, oppression, poverty, ignorance, premature death, and so forth are, in general, natural threats to happiness.

Mystification is anathema to knowledge—which is why I repudiate traditional natural law morality. Mystification always entails separation of values from their grounding factuality. There is a paradox here. Divine intent is deemed necessary to bridge fact and value, to make natural circumstance relevant to human behavior—but the interposition of the bridge disguises a more intrinsic connection. It is better to avoid promiscuity because one knows it involves the risk of disease and unloved progeny than because one is obedient to a god whose motives are not to be questioned. What one does in the name of the father is not something one does on the basis of personal responsibility. Mystification and infantilization are traditional means of manipulation that have contributed to the neurosis and misery apparent in contemporary erotic praxis: we witness the purveyors of mystification poisoned by their own concoctions and know that the preachers of chastity illumine our lives by exemplifying true perversity.

In sum, we have many things to learn from nature that are relevant to the quality of our lives. One of them is that nature is not driven by intent. Another is that nature informs our intents. A third is that our intents are better served the better we understand the ways in which the natural world constrains them. It is a frailty of postmodern thought that it resists this learning.

# FOUR

# SEXLOVE

---

## MARGINALITY AND RECTITUDE

THE VALUES OF SEXLOVE in American culture have sustained rapid and messy change during the half century I have been awake. Change produces wonder, unease, questions. What has provoked these changes? Are there patterns discernible in them? What do they portend?

Let me begin with some before and after snapshots. Back then, Ingrid Bergman conceived a baby out of wedlock and was ostracized, but, more recently, Madonna's annunciation was a media event. Irish gays and lesbians did not band together to demand the right to participate in New York's Saint Patrick's Day parade. School officials did not attempt to distribute condoms to minors in order to minimize teenage child-bearing; in fact, condoms were labeled "sold for the prevention of disease only." Divorces produced broken families; single moms did not herald their status as qualifying them to run for congress. Erstwhile paramours of adulterous presidents did not display their pubic hair in centerfolds, and neither did anyone else because such revelations could and did lead to fines and imprisonment instead of fortune and fame. Blaze Starr wore a merkin. Abortion was unilaterally treated as a sin and a crime. Prostitution was illegal everywhere. The publisher of *Capt. Billy's Whiz Bang* did not build a mansion on the proceeds of his sales. And if he had, the mayor of Chicago would not have attended his parties. Swingers did not have their own publications. Lavishly appointed gentleman's clubs did not flourish throughout the land; men snuck into rundown Gaiety burlesque houses in the seedy part of town.

Women were not admitted to Brown University, and the men who were did not have to ask for explicit permission to kiss their dates. Pinups were painted on the fuselages of B-29s, and no one expressed outrage. Calendar girls were scantily but effectively clad, and on the walls of every automobile repair shop and barracks. The term *sexual harassment* did not appear in federal statutes, and someone's body had to be touched before the censure became official and punishment meted out. Bosses who dated their secretaries were considered foolish, but they and their parent organizations were not fined for misdemeanor. Georgie Porgie was a nursery rhyme, not a national *cause celebre*. We will probably never know whether candidates for the Supreme Court bragged to female subordinates of their sexual prowess and physical endowments, but if they did, congressional inquiries would not have been held. And they certainly would not have been televised. Federal moneys were used to block the importation and sale of *Lady Chatterley's Lover;* they were not used to fund art expositions in which a photograph of anal fisting was hung. And the magazines at supermarket checkout counters offered recipes for tuna noodle casserole instead of formulas for achieving multiple orgasms.

What explanation could do justice to this motley array? Can we account for changes in media content by citing developments in media technology? Can we explain the breakdown of family values by appeal to increasing affluence of the middle classes, the rising proportion of women in the workplace, the discovery of antibiotics and the pill, the erosion of religion, foreign influence, downfall of the *pater familias,* drugs, cars, rock and roll? Taken singly or collectively, such putative causes beg the question. The question they beg is always the same question: why did these historical events precipitate just these changes in the mores of sexlove rather than others? Gutenberg opened the way to pornography as much as to religious warfare: why did one revolution take place rather than the other? It went the other way with the Internet: why?

A hypothesis: there is a qualitative difference between the divisiveness surrounding the values of sexlove and the divisiveness surrounding the values informing other pressing issues of our times. Everyone wants peace; we just disagree on how to achieve it. Everyone wants a strong economy; we just disagree on how to distribute the wealth. Everyone wants to improve national standards of health, education, and social welfare; we just disagree on the means to these ends. We want a healthy environment and a sound ecosphere; we want to eliminate crime and promote justice; we want each newborn to grow up healthy, wealthy, and wise. There is consensus with regard to goals; the divisions arise at the level of strategy.

What do we want in the domain of sexlove? What is the ideal state of erotic beatitude? We all want fulfillment. We can recognize peace, prosperity, physical health, and, perhaps on occasion, mental illness. Could we identify erotic fulfillment if we stumbled upon it?

The answer here, I think, is that once we could, but now we face new difficulties. The standard apparent in former times, the measure that was tacitly affirmed even when it was contested, is the nexus of values that constellates around the social nucleus of the family: what are now called family values. The family so conceived has one mother and one father; they are the natural parents of their children. They are monogamous. They engage in reproductive sexual behavior. The marriage that institutionalizes their relationship explicitly excludes sexual relations with others. In the ideal union, each partner has precisely one sexual partner throughout the course of his or her life. There may never have been an instance of this ideal, but it was the governing paradigm nonetheless.

The conceptual foundation of this ideal is natural law theory. Natural law theory maintains that sex is designed for reproduction. The explicit telos is propagation of the species. Monogamy is indicated by the need to nurture the young. Natural law theory is reinforced by satellite arguments that demonstrate the superiority of this social form in minimizing the dangers inherent to sexual intercourse. Exclusive monogamy minimizes the threat of sexually transmitted disease, fosters the orderly transmission of property within bloodlines from generation to generation, and reduces to one the number of social upheavals involved in mate selection and the reformation of social unities. Natural law theory also reinforced a patriarchal system of governance within the nuclear family and the society at large.

Natural law theory is now being challenged on several fronts. The concept of natural law depends upon what Kant called the "physico-theological proof" for the existence of a divinity whose intent is apparent in the design of nature. Kant argued that such a proof is impossible, and most contemporary intellectual leaders agree. Even among theologians, few contend that the existence of divine intent in the natural order of things is demonstrable on rational or scientific grounds. Natural law theory is based on supernatural beliefs grounded in religious faith rather than the findings of natural science. This has the effect of polarizing discourse and dividing the advocates of family values and natural law theory from the critics. The issue of sexlove values fuses with the issue of the relation between church and state, and the question becomes whether to ground values in political processes or religious commitments. That is a debate whose antecedents stretch back indefinitely. If it is to shed light on the peculiar nature of contemporary phenomena, it must be specified in a way that is unique to our times.

A second hypothesis: notwithstanding the powerful arguments in favor of the view that the values of sexlove have always been grounded upon an antecedent political reality having to do with the localization of power in one sector or another—or perhaps in consonance with these arguments—there has been a significant change brewing which is now forcing a crisis. This is the change from naive to reflective politics. There is nothing new in advocacy and the use of political power on the part of individuals and affinity groups to promote their ends. The novelty that marks the contemporary era is the thematization of political processes as creating communal values rather than responding to them.

Marx argued that politics was founded on economics. One brought about political change by raising the consciousness of a given community to awareness of its socioeconomic status and the interests implicit therein. In the Marxist view, political values are dependent upon an antecedent economic reality.

Nietzsche presented a conflicting view. He argued, in effect, that the socioeconomic reality was founded on something more basic, the social-psychological constellations of power and the structure of resentment. One brings about political change, not simply by thematizing the values implicit in an economic reality, but by altering (or reversing) the values that gave rise to that reality.

Both viewpoints are extrapolations from the Hegelian notion of sublation or the dialectical process of negating a negation, but whereas Marx replaced Hegelian *Geist* (mind or spirit) with matter as the ground and driving force of historical change, Nietzsche replaced it with will. The motive force of will for Nietzsche is transpersonal and open-ended: will seeks power, its own self-augmentation. The figures of will, the ends adopted, the projects undertaken, are determined by the interplay of the creative individual freedom of Overmen *(Übermenschen)* and the submissive group dynamics of groups of Undermen *(Untermenschen)* or herds. In both cases, leadership is required to bring about political consensus as the vehicle of change, but the Marxist leader is bound to the end of egalitarian distributive justice, and the Nietzschean *Übermensch* is bound only by personal freedom. That is to say (according to contemporary interpretations with which I disagree), bound by nothing at all.

If one accepts this understanding of the Nietzschean model and super-imposes it—contrary to Nietzsche's own profound elitism—upon a political structure of social democracy, the result is something akin to the agonistic relativism of contemporary sexual politics. Absent the constraint of a governing paradigm such as the ideal of patriarchal monogamy grounded in natural law theory, the democratic ideal of political equality tolerant of benign diversity opens the way to the free-for-all now reigning in the agon of sexual politics. Every value creates an oppressed minority. If Bataille is right that every taboo betrays (and intensifies) an antecedent desire, then every prohibition generates oppression for the class of people who share that desire. The correlate to this is that the more general the prohibition, the larger the group of the oppressed, hence the more powerful. Since the ideal of patriarchal monogamy excludes the desire of most of the populace—an inference I base on the empirical observation that few people live in accordance with that ideal—it generates the most rancor and grants a moment of political solidarity across a wide spectrum of otherwise conflicting sexual ideologies.

To comprehend the confusion rampant in contemporary sexlove values, a third element must be brought to the fore. I do not take this as a hypothesis, but rather as a grounded truth: the truth that our era is still governed by the Christian demonization of sexuality as such. Sex is a bodily phenomenon that links humans to animals, transience, decay, and death. It is opposed to everything holy, everything spiritual, pure, and immutable. Isolated unto itself, the value of sex is entirely negative—its pleasures, intense but fleeting, obfuscate our minds by obscuring our proper ends—and its sole vindication lies in the only service it can render to eternity, the propagation of the species. Mortal conception is maculate, the original sin of finitude and becoming, the failure to be divine.

With the atrophy of natural law theory, propagation no longer suffices to vindicate and constrain sexlove. What, then, does? Pleasure might vindicate sexlove, as Freud argued, in the sense of explaining its motivation, but it does not seem to provide any intrinsic measure to the species permanently in heat. Indeed, the pleasures of sex, unlike other bodily pleasures, seem to draw us beyond every constraint, to feed our hunger for novelty and intensity: unlike hunger, sexual appetite seems to search for prohibitions to fulfill its desire for transgression.

Here, then, is where we are. We cannot conceive an ideal of erotic beatitude because any such ideal generates norms and prohibitions that oppress a minority. It is true that we are at one, collectively, in opposing rape, incest, and child molestation.[1] Collectively, we are prepared to enforce constraints that would oppress rapists and pedophiles. This general agreement on the negative aspects of sexlove betrays a positive commitment to consensuality, the rule of exogamy, and the protection of fragile innocence. But this is far from providing the basis for an ideal of fulfillment that would serve to measure the relative value of different erotic lifestyles. It does not establish guidelines, as natural law theory did, to judge the merit of homosexuality, masturbation, promiscuity, pornography, extramarital liaisons, relations with animals, group sex, and the various sexual practices lumped under such generic terms as perversion and sodomy.

The demise of a popular ideal of erotic fulfillment grounded in natural law theory deprives us of a specifically sexual morality, that is, a set of values that pertain primarily or exclusively to sexlove relations. Rape and child abuse are, I think, properly seen as violations of general ethical precepts prohibiting us from harming others, and can be condemned without need for a specifically sexual morality. The vacuum left by the atrophy of natural law theory explains the sexual heteronomy characteristic of our times. Gutenberg did not foster a wave of pornography as the Internet has because the constraint of natural law theory was more robust in the fifteenth century than it is now or is likely to be in the twenty-first century. I would maintain that the dying of the divinities that ground the norms of natural law produces such golden ages of "decadence" as ours whenever it occurs in history: nothing can produce a unitary ideal of sexlove except the idea of a cosmic design, that is, nothing but some form of divinity. Conservatives have that exactly right: only old time religion can restore the traditional nuclear family to its former glory as the sole model for the fulfillment of sexlove. But, for this long standing opponent to onto-theology, that price is too high to pay.

It is also not necessary to pay that price. The absence of a specifically sexual morality leaves us with only general ethical precepts to guide us, but in my view, they are sufficient. Indeed, as I argued in the preceding chapter, the absence of a specifically sexual morality constitutes a step in the direction of moral enlightenment insofar as it demystifies our ethics and brings us to greater awareness of the principles that inform our attitudes and drive our judgments and decisions.

We are living through an age of rapid transition with regard to the values of sexlove. Other words for rapid transition include chaos and violence. These are troubled times, filled with the insecurity attendant upon all paradigm shifts, all upheavals in established norms. It is difficult to sort out which norms to bulwark and which to discard. Here are my diagnoses, prescriptions, and prognoses.

The absence of a specifically sexual morality opens the competition to valorize any form of sexual practice that does not prima facie violate general ethical precepts. There are advocacy groups openly promoting all the forms of sexual practice I listed a moment ago.[2] There are also advocacy groups seeking to abolish these practices. The competition will be resolved on the basis of the viability of natural law theory, for that is fundamentally what is at issue.

This competition is playing out on the field of a politics of tolerance, that is, the political milieu of a social democracy freeing itself from the constraints of religious commitment to natural law theory. Any norm enforced that cannot be shown to violate general ethical precepts—precepts that prohibit doing harm to other individuals or the social entity at large—any such norm is increasingly being identified as arbitrary and oppressive, as marginalizing some subset of the population that is doing no harm. This identification is the foundation of political correctness: the thesis that it is wrong to harm those who are different if their difference constitutes no threat is itself an instance of general ethical precepts and defensible as such. In the sphere of sexlove, it enfranchises individuals to express their sexual proclivities, even if those proclivities run contrary to natural law, with the sole proviso that nobody is to suffer real harm except the moribund divinity.

The politics of tolerance, however, is now circumscribed by another prohibition that is confusing the issue of the values of sexlove. That is the prohibition I have labeled as the demonization of sex. This wholesale negativity with regard to sex informs natural law theory, but is distinguishable from it, since natural law theory advocates sexual behavior of a certain kind. The demonization of sex is founded on the sundering of body and soul, coupled with the denigration of one and the elevation of the other, and operates through a symbolism that designates sexuality as evil. Its effect is to marginalize sex as such.

We are still living in an era in which maginalization of sex *is* rectitude. Titillate ourselves as we do in the media, we are still true to our puritan heritage; the primary precept at both ends of the political spectrum remains the same: just say no. Indeed, I would argue that the proliferation of commercial sex betrays profound dissatisfaction in our private sex lives. We want it all, but are deeply fearful of letting the force flow through us. In no other dimension of social engagement is hypocrisy so rampant and so visible. Bill and Hillary are appropriate icons: just don't ask and please don't tell.

In our times, the demonization of sex has found an ambivalent ally among the advocates of political correctness. If sex is evil, then to initiate sex with other persons is harmful. If the burden of initiation falls upon the bodies afflicted with testosterone, then those bodies are prone to harmful acts of oppression and must be restrained by law. When the enforcers of rectitude demand consent of all parties to sexual engagement, they are doing no more than underlining the prohibition of rape and can be faulted, if at all, only for being overzealous and insensitive to the nuances of mating rituals. When they censure consensual relations among adults, they make two mistakes. One is to reinforce the demonization of sex, which harms everyone who engages in sex and especially those whose preferences do not conform to natural law theory. This is contrary to essence of political correctness as I have just defined it, and amounts to ideological inconsistency.

The second mistake is to confuse the politics of the patriarchalism associated with the symbolism of natural law theory with the politics associated with the pragmatic ramifications of the natural or biological properties of testosterone. In consensual relations, the burden of initiation is a burden because initiation risks rejection and that vulnerability constitutes a diminution of power. Rapists are a common enemy to both men and women. It would be difficult to determine the ratio of the number of men harmed in protecting women against rape and other violence to the number of women harmed by the perpetrators of such acts, but Helen survived the Trojan war and lots of men did not.

The same symbolism that required the conception of the Christ figure to be asexual demanded that Mary's role in it be less than consensual, that her son die a virgin, and that his priests be celibate. This symbolism preordains the model of romantic love, that is, the model of love that feeds on indefinite deferral and withers with consummation and fulfillment.

My diagnosis is that we all suffer from the demonization of sex. My prescription is to sublate the symbolism that associates sex with evil. My prognosis is optimistic. Americans have no exclusive franchise on pragmatism, but current as well as past history supports the association of our traditions with a pragmatic outlook. I am optimistic because I am hopeful that our pragmatic heritage is robust enough to supervene over our puritanical heritage. When we confront teenage pregnancy with condoms rather than moralizing and condemnation, when we respond to AIDS with breakneck research and compassion, when, in short, we solve the problems of sexuality pragmatically through research and education rather than symbolically through mystification and guilt, we demonstrate our ability to develop a sexual morality based on practical wisdom or prudence *(phronesis)* rather than obedience to figures of the divine designed to promote our welfare by keeping us in the darkness of superstition.

We are on the brink of the realization that a politics of tolerance based on general ethical precepts will, indeed, produce diversity in the arena of sexual praxis—as it has in other domains—but that this diversity is a threat to none and maximizes the freedom of all.

To conclude this reflection on the felicity and upheaval consequent upon the demise of natural law theory and its onto-theological foundations, I would like to acknowledge a debt that those of us in the heterosexual community owe to our brothers and sisters in the gay liberation movement. Gay liberation depends on two agons with natural law. The first is obvious: homosexuality is incompatible with natural law theory insofar as that theory ties sexual morality to the reproductive male-female dyad. Gays and lesbians are fighting that fight and, I think, winning the battle for sexual liberation across the board, that is, winning the war that will allow us all to be both sexual and proud.

The second agon is more subtle. In some quarters, it is currently politically correct to deny to biology any constitutive or limiting role in sexual praxis. The idea here is to transcend biologically based sex role norms associated with natural law theory. I think that is a good idea. The bad idea is that biology and our knowledge of it have no bearing on the issue of sexual morality. That idea is bad just because it is false, and to operate on error usually produces more misery than good. Gay men, confronting the plague of AIDS rather more acutely than the heterosexual community has yet had to, know this idea to be false. Gay men are on the side of the growth of biological science because their lives depend on it. And gay men are changing their sexual mores in light of the knowledge we have acquired so far.

When I flew from my home in Pennsylvania to present these thoughts to a group of scholars in Alabama, I entered a huge human conspiracy to defy the law of gravity and the natural fact that we are born without wings. We who engage in this conspiracy do so at some risk and with great circumspection. We also do it without shame. We are a pragmatic lot and for the most part motivated pragmatically to keep from doing harm to ourselves and one another. That is where our strongest values originate. Biology tells us a lot about what to do and what not to do with the organs with which we were born; it also allows us to calculate risks in such a way as to maximize pleasure and minimize pain. The natural world of which we are a part is a ground of our being, a measure of our knowledge, and a constraint upon our behavior, although it functions ambiguously in all these ways. Gay men and lesbians are showing us that natural law theory is bankrupt theology, an appeal not to nature but to the supernatural. Gay men are also demonstrating that scientific knowledge of worldly natural law is truly liberating. Political determinations of what is correct would do well to accommodate scientific determinations of what is true. Not because natural fact betrays divine intent, but rather because the knowledge of natural fact promotes human freedom just as natural fact itself circumscribes it. It is prudent to know as much as one can about the consequences of various forms of human behavior, and to act in accordance with that knowledge. This is as true in the domain of biology as it is in physics. In the natural world, *phronesis* is the foundation of all morality, sexual morality included.

# FIVE

# ROMANTIC LOVE

## INTROIT

THE ANCIENT GREEKS tell two stories about the coming into being of Eros. In one account, love is the oldest of gods, the first to emerge from primal chaos, and the one responsible for the creation of world order. In the other, Eros is among the younger gods, a fair and delicate creature who needs a peaceful environment in order to exist, but disrupts it with random darts of love.[1] In my view, these two apparently competitive accounts are compatible and mutually reinforcing: love must be seen as both primordial and a new arrival on the cosmic scene.

Past, present, and future are dimensions of time that flow uninterrupted from one mode to another, but each has its own characteristics that set it apart. We know the past in detail, but cannot change what has already happened. We know the future only generically—we know that certain kinds of things will happen, that there will be weather, politics, and fluctuations in the stock market—but we do not know concretely what determinate shapes these events will take, although we can try to anticipate them, even to influence how they play out. One dominant characteristic of the present is its capacity to engage and envelop us. The present is now, it is urgent, it is realer than past or future. It is the context of our moods, our sense of reality, and it governs our thinking in moments of decision and action. Lessons from the past and forebodings about the future certainly play a part, but only as they insinuate themselves into the decisive moment. This characteristic of the present generates temporal myopia, an unobtrusive arrogance that accords the horizon of the present in which we live a privilege it may not deserve. We differ in age, gender, cultural heritage, and so forth, and have some awareness that others look at the world through different perspectives. Indeed, it is a fact of life that others force us to this awareness; they demand respect and a measure of humility to accommodate our differences. This tempers our arrogance, our egocentricity. The constraints on our temporo-centricity, however, are not enforced in this way: we *all* live in the present.

The ideal of love that governs the present time is romantic love. In the essays I have written on the subject, I have adopted the consensual view of European scholars that romantic love had its inception among the noble classes in twelfth-century France and was shaped by the social and religious thinking of that time and place. I continue to think that this narrowly focused snapshot of romance is exquisitely revealing, perhaps more revealing of romantic love than any other picture that could be put in a tight frame. But as I probe the romantic ideal to uncover its latencies—the power that makes it so robust and pervasive despite its conspicuous flaws and the disasters it invites—I have learned to recognize its features in times and places far removed from the court of the Countess of Champagne. The rape or abduction of Helen by Paris recounted by Homer in the *Iliad* has romantic tendrils that reach back into the murk of prehistory. The same could be said of the *Pillow-Book* of Sei Shonagon.

Romance is the name of the god of love that reigns in the present, and it was Christened for the congregation of our era just as the scholars say. In cosmic time, the godling of romantic love is a newborn, but this parvenu is also as old as Father Time, a glint on the scythe he carries, a response to human finitude and the passage of time that leads us all from darkness into darkness. Romantic love is a peculiar way in which we answer to the call of transcendence; it is one of the ways we respond to the awesome appeal of what lies beyond us, the way that now has us in its thrall. Romantic love is an unmindful invocation of catastrophe. Romance is vertigo, the swoon into an infantile dream. Romantic love is not our only erotic option, and it is certainly not the best one. We are so caught up in the present, however, that we take the form of love that now prevails, romantic love, as the only form, as love itself.

Romantic love is a swerve in cosmic time, a phase in the development of humanity comparable to adolescence. It is a passage that we may have had to make, given our global history and its interdependencies, but there are other ways we might have gone and other ways that we might now go. The love-hate continuum that has ever ruled over our relations with each other and ourselves can express itself over a wide spectrum of psychological structures and social forms, and these patterns can vary in degrees of intensity, gratification, tumult, and tranquillity. This variance in love style is apparent to cultural historians, but it is also discernible within our own culture as individuals mature and pass through different phases of life. The emotional and cognitive forms of human relations among grandparents are different from those apparent among parents, those involved in mate selection, children, and infants. The variance in love styles within each of these age groups is also evident. There are choices that can be made, options that can be sought or avoided.

It is doubtless true that we do not live in a free space of infinite possibility. Sexlove is highly regulated by law, custom, cultural expectation, family circumstance, and the like. We internalize the values that circulate about us like the air we breathe, and we take them in with as little thought as we draw a breath. When the air turns noxious, however, as now it has in many places, we begin to pay attention. Such is the case with the values of sexlove that we have tacitly adopted and allowed to govern our lives. I will leave it to others to document the sexual malaise of our time; it is tedious work because the list of ills is long. AIDS, of course, but also chlamydia, herpes, and all the other sexually transmitted diseases. Unwanted lives being yanked into the world or aborted in huge numbers. Rape, molestation, commercialization, depersonalization, harassment, and public humiliation. Name your poison. The one that strikes me as particularly emblematic is the ambivalence of values that turns our leaders into hypocrites. The private lives of our statesmen cannot stand scrutiny, and neither can the lives of our spiritual leaders, including our athletes, military heroes, and other celebrities. Not to mention the clergy. If, as Aristotle argued, tragedy consists in the fall of persons of great magnitude from happiness to misery and makes them "worse . . . than the men of the present day,"[2] then we have more tragedies in a decade of evening news than Sophocles and Aeschylus could have depicted in their lifetimes. Perhaps it has long been thus, perhaps the ridicule is in the eye of the TV camera. I leave the historical point moot; the collision between public values and private lives, however, is rampant on both sides of the TV screen and brings misery upon us all. Perhaps we are privileged to have our noses rubbed in it. Maybe we are now in a position to do something about it.

There are those who argue that it is impossible to achieve erotic fulfillment in a cultural climate rife with political and social injustice. First we must change the air, then we can breathe. The metaphor makes my point: it is impossible not to breathe. One does what one can under the circumstances. Hide in a closet or carry a banner in a parade,[3] there is no way not to be engaged in love-hate; genuine indifference is not an option in the spectrum of human relations (or it is pathology in its starkest form).

Is the romantic ideal of love responsible for the erotic malaise of our times? My answer to this question will emerge throughout the course of this chapter, but it may be well to give a preliminary sketch here at the beginning. Hitherto I have argued that the deep source of our troubles lies in the demonization of sex that begins with Socrates, consolidates in Medieval Christianity, and sustains itself through a kind of metaphysical inertia or perpetuation of values despite attenuation of belief in the underlying religious doctrine. Romantic love feeds on the sexual ambivalence of this tradition: it is aimed toward ecstatic unification and affirms sexuality as the means, but in its quest for a purely spiritual union it negates the flesh of sexual desire and posits the body as the matter that separates us from one another without acknowledging that our bodies also allow us to come together. I continue to believe that this is the case, that romance is the unhappy form that love must take in a milieu governed by the demonization of sex, but here I want to temper my critique and seek a primordial truth of love that manifests itself through the distortions of romantic illusion.

## A GENEALOGY OF ROMANCE

The past is murky, but origins are discernible. Not absolute origins: they require some sort of creator god who is cause of itself and all things that follow, and what is named in the term *causa sui* is a classical contradiction in terms that can be celebrated as a mystery of religious truth or rejected as a form of anthropomorphic projection and self-mystification. The origins of which I speak do not have to be retrieved from relics and runes, but are evident in the present. Organic beings are born; they grow, reproduce, decay, and die. Like all things, we come into being and pass away. We seem to be more acutely aware of this than other beings; we are reflective. Reflection on our transience is the source of philosophy, literature, religion, and their derivatives. It is also a main source of love: *eros, philia, agape,* and their derivatives. The source or origin named here is primarily psychological, although it manifests itself historically and can be traced in relics, runes, and ruins.

In classical terms, to know a thing is to know its causes and effects, why it came into being, and its contribution to cosmic destiny. The principle of sufficient reason is one expression of the desire to know things in this way: for a thing to be, there must be a reason that suffices to account for its being. Reflection is characteristically narcissistic; it is concerned with itself, wants to know itself, and gives rise to the questions of provenance and destiny. The first truth of reflection is the ignorance it betrays in its interrogation. The first truth of reflection is awareness of transcendence, that what we seek lies beyond us, else we would not be seeking it. The second truth, which bubbles to the surface of awareness long after the first, is that we must have some sense of what lies beyond us, else we could not begin to look for it or hope to recognize it if we found it. The third truth takes longer still to formulate itself: this is the truth that the transience, finitude, or temporality that is the source of the interrogation precludes arriving at an answer that is final and absolute, yet nonetheless affords a growing awareness of the thing we cannot but understand since we *are* it. Alpha and omega can never be known, but the progress in understanding the processes of birth and death is indisputable.

Socrates is generally acknowledged to be the thinker who brought the essentially narcissistic flavor of reflection to the forefront of philosophy. "Know thyself" was his Delphic motto and Socratic ignorance his wisdom: he knew that he did not know, and in that knowledge demonstrated his awareness of transcendence. He articulated the first two truths of reflection mentioned above.[4] Whether it is Socrates or Plato who is to be held accountable for obscuring the third for better than two millennia is a question I leave for scholars better equipped than I to answer, and will content myself to argue that it did get obscured in the Platonic dialogues, and that in that occultation lies the germ of romance.

In the *Symposium,* the classic work on love that is cited by nearly every important writer on love in the Western tradition, Plato sketches a theory of human development that mirrors the analogy of the divided line in the *Republic.* Life is a quest for permanent possession of the ideal in which truth, beauty, and goodness coincide. The motive force of this quest is Eros or love, the striving for transcendence driven by desire for what we do not possess but do glimpse in a sort of prescience as that which will answer our need and make us happy. In the *Symposium,* Plato emphasizes the beautiful aspect of the triadic ideal, and says that we begin life fascinated by images of beauty, fleeting appearances. Some do not pass beyond this stage of thralldom to passing fantasies; perhaps these are the artists Plato criticizes in the *Republic* for dwelling in fascination with things that are thrice removed from reality and evanesce. For Plato, permanence in time is the essential feature of genuine reality, and images are destined to fade. Others, however, respond to the call of Eros and grow out of this stage into the next, where the object of desire is a physical object, something that lasts longer than a fantasy, perhaps a human being whose physical being radiates beauty. Those whose lives are structured around the quest to possess beautiful persons dwell in this second phase of development.

The beauty of human bodies is tied to flesh, and flesh decays. Its transience betrays its lack of reality, and some of us are led to seek a higher manifestation of beauty in things that are more enduring than the physical beauty of objects. The quest is for a vision of the form that makes beautiful things beautiful. The transition here is from an earlier sense of the Greek word *eidos,* the visible physiognomy of a thing or the face it presents, to a later one, the idea or form that allows us to see the thing as what it is. It is by virtue of the idea or form of dog that we can recognize Rover as a canine; similarly, it is by virtue of the *eidos* or idea of beauty that we can recognize Helen as beautiful. Those who abide in this domain are attracted by ideas rather than things. They are closer to reality because ideas do not pass away as things do, but are more permanent in time.

At this point in the dialogue, Plato writes that Diotima (the wise woman from Mantinea who taught Socrates about love) issues a warning. She tells Socrates that he may not be able to understand what she is about to say. So far, her teaching has remained in the finite realm to which mortals have access, but the true object of love, the ultimate reality, does not change at all. To attain permanent possession of this eternal object, one must become immortal.

> What may we suppose to be the felicity of the man who sees absolute beauty in its essence, pure and unalloyed, who, instead of a beauty tainted by human flesh and color and a mass of perishable rubbish, is able to apprehend divine beauty where it exists apart and alone? ... Do you not see that in that region alone where he sees beauty with the faculty capable of seeing it, will he be able to bring forth not mere reflected images of goodness but true goodness, because he will be in contact not with a reflection but with the truth? And having brought forth and nurtured true goodness he will have the privilege of being beloved of God, and becoming, if ever a man can, immortal himself.[5]

The end of the quest symbolized by the figure of Eros is immortality, coincidence with immutability or absolute reality, achievement of ultimate transcendence. This requires departure from human flesh, this "mass of perishable rubbish," and entering a realm of pure ideality, pure spirituality—the spirit or mind or *psyche* being "the faculty capable of seeing" the absolute wherein truth, beauty, and goodness coincide (although it must detach itself from the flesh that tethers it to finitude in order to attain this purity).

As soon as he has articulated this theory, Plato illustrates it in dramatic action. Alcibiades, a golden youth of Athens and an embodiment of physical beauty, bursts into the symposium and confesses his unrequited love for the notoriously ugly Socrates. He tells how he sought to seduce Socrates and win his love, and how he was rejected. Socrates is a philosopher driven by the highest form of Eros to seek ultimate reality and is living his life as a preparation for death, departure from his finite body, and entrance into the realm of pure ideality. He has long since transcended the physical desire that Alcibiades, in his ignorance, is trying to awaken in him. Thus, Socrates becomes the symbol of the highest development of love, the sublimation or *Aufhebung* of *eros* into *philia*.

Where in this Platonic teaching are we to find the germ of romance, that mystification of the quest for transcendence? The short answer is easy to state: the germ of romance lies in the detachment of the idea from the flesh, in the polarization of the two senses of *eidos,* physiognomy and form, that leads to positing them as mutually exclusive. The Platonic program for human development requires us to take leave of our senses in order to bring our minds to perfection; it requires us to depart from our bodies in order to free our spirits to live in absolute ideality. Here is the thought from which the ideal of romantic love will be generated.

## ROMANTIC LOVE

Romantic love is the desire to appropriate an ideal, to possess perfection, to consummate a union with the beautiful object that betokens sheer pleasure. The object of romantic love can also be defined as love, itself: the romantic lover is in love with love, in love with the ecstatic high that comes in the early phases of a romantic liaison. What the romantic lover seeks is the *experience* of love; the love-object is merely the means of producing this experience. These two definitions coincide: the beautiful object is conceived as such because it produces exquisite pleasure. The contradiction that lies at the heart of the romantic quest is the opposition between the ideality of perfection and the reality of the bodies engaged in the experience. One aspect of this contradiction has already been noted: ideals, especially the ideal of perfection, are held to be timeless and unchanging, but bodies dwell in the domain of transience, and the physical beauty associated with youth is fleeting. Beyond this contradiction, however, there is another which may be even more devastating to the romantic project.

Our bodies are the source of our identity. We come into being when our bodies are conceived or born, and we cease to be when our bodies die.[6] The actions that define our histories, including our speech acts, are bodily actions. Our bodies are not merely vehicles through which some noncorporeal spirit manifests its intentions; our minds—our intelligence, memory, desire, and character—are distributed throughout our flesh, and could not function without it. It is a longstanding philosophical mistake to conceive our minds and bodies as disjunct and mutually opposed; they are inextricably intertwined, two aspects of the same reality. The crucial point in the present context is that our bodies are the means by which we enter the social milieu. We recognize each other through our bodily appearance and understand each other through our bodily comportment. We are our bodies, including the traces that other bodies have visited upon ours and the traces our bodies deposit in the world as marks of its passage. It is as bodies that we are and are known. In that broad sense, all our knowledge of each other is carnal knowledge.

Carnal knowledge is usually understood in a narrower sense as sexual intercourse, as the knowing of each other that takes place when we sense each other through the broad spectrum of our body's perceptual capacities. To touch another's body, to feel its flesh and sense its peculiar being, is to encounter another person and learn something of who that person is. Although we can, and sometimes do, attempt to minimize the personal contact in sexual relations, the very means we employ to avoid that contact betray the fact that carnal knowledge is knowledge. Here lies the contradiction in the heart of romance.

The project of romantic love is to possess an ideal, but bodies are not ideal. Plato knew that. Plato knew that bodies decay and thus could not be perfect. Plato sought perfection and taught us to follow Socrates' example: to eschew the flesh, the "mass of perishable rubbish," and seek perfection in a realm beyond, a realm of sheer transcendence to be found on the far side of finite human embodiment. Socrates would rather die than embrace the body of Alcibiades. I have spent decades arguing that Socrates made a bad choice, that the ideas and values informing the example left to us by Socrates are misguided and the cause of widespread suffering. Socrates did, indeed, deliberately choose death, and Alcibiades fell from honor into disgrace. I think they would both have led happier, more fulfilled lives, had the wisdom of Socrates reached the third truth of reflection mentioned earlier, the truth that human finitude precludes possession of absolute ideality on this side of the grave, and that on the far side there is nothing.

Nonetheless, there is nobility in the Socratic choice, something that attracts us to it. Similarly, we are attracted to the nobility in the romantic quest. It is the same nobility: το καλον.[7] Socrates and the romantic lover are both drawn to something higher, something better, than what they see around them. They want—desire—something more. This is the quest for transcendence, born of dissatisfaction and the sense that there is something more to be had. This quest for transcendence marks the point of intersection between the *philia* that drove Socrates and the *eros* that drives the romantic lover.

Transcendence. The term is overdetermined; it bears a host of meanings, meanings that generally refer to what is beyond us, but there are as many names for the beyond as there are for divinities both sacred and profane. The goad is need, want, desire, or finitude in general: our sense that we lack something that is required to make us whole or happy or fulfilled. In my view, it is this need that has led us to create our gods and goddesses as symbols of the wholeness, goodness, and perfection we so conspicuously lack. We seek union with godhead as the means of completion, and conceive this quest for union as a spiritual quest, that is, as a quest to embrace and embody ideality through the highest aspect of ourselves, the aspect we designate as mind, psyche, spirit, brahman, atman, soul, etc. To succeed in this quest we typically are called upon to go through some self-transforming ordeal, a trial that proves our worth, brings out the best in us, and prepares us for the union. Self-transcendence, going beyond ourselves, is required to reach the transcendence we seek.

Transcendence and self-transcendence: these are the marks of love, be it love for another human being *(eros)*, for wisdom *(philia),* for humanity as such *(agape),* or for god *(theosebeia).*[8] Romantic love embodies transcendence and self-transcendence; it participates in that deep truth, but does so in its own unique way.

Romantic love might be viewed in a preliminary way as the deification of the love object. Here is the theme of overestimation (Freud) or crystallization (Stendahl) coupled with the attempt to define and vindicate oneself through the amorous gaze of the fascinated other (Sartre).[9] I attribute perfection to my beloved; my self-dissimulating desire grants to her a perspective that both sees me as I am and affirms me absolutely. If this mystified attribution of perfection is mutual, I find in her eyes the vision of myself that makes me whole and complete. I deify my beloved in order to become the god I must be in order to fulfill my quest for transcendence.

The unfortunate fact that we remain finite poses a problem for all human quests for transcendence, be they religious or amorous in nature. If the transcendence sought is conceived as an absolute, as Plato did, then the problem encountered is the incommensurability of the finite and the infinite, the lack of a common ground on which mortal humans can join with the immortal and unchanging. Different religions offer different solutions that run the gamut from mediation by saints and prophets to mystical union in some form of ecstasy. Christianity, with its doctrine of the Trinity, calls upon the faithful to believe what they cannot understand, the mystery of the coincidence of finite man and infinite god in the figure of Jesus of Nazareth. Romantic love solves this problem in a way that sets it apart from other quests for transcendence and defines its own peculiar character.

Whatever we can reach, touch, understand, or join together with ourselves cannot be transcendent because that contact presupposes that the object is no longer beyond ourselves. Anything a finite human can possess must itself be finite, hence not transcendent. To confer the status of absolute upon a finite object is idolatry. As I have just suggested, romantic love is a form of idolatry, but one with a unique twist—the twist that gives romantic love its identity. In deifying the beloved, the romantic lover at the same time places a barrier between himself and the object of his desire. He keeps his quest alive by strategies designed to preclude the contact with and carnal knowledge of his beloved that would reduce her to finite proportions and destroy her transcendence. The beloved, for her part, is complicit in this prohibition and seeks always to remain aloof, elusive, unattainable, mysterious, in any case, unpossessed.[10]

The classical example—upon which I shall not dwell, having treated it extensively in other work[11]—comes to us in the songs of the twelfth-century troubadors in the south of France. They sang of love necessarily unrequited, the prohibition against sexual culmination being the structure that gave romantic love its ethereal ideality. The reality of the time, at least for the aristocracy who adopted this form of love, was governed by Christian values of absolute fidelity in marriage and an economic structure that used marriage as a means of consolidating family wealth. The young bride was given to the older groom, a man of means, in order to unite the families and augment their power. The groom got the girl and her dowry, and was not constrained by vows of fidelity as was she. The bride got a man twice her age and economic security. What she did not get was an appropriate lover. It was in this context that the Countess of Champagne, delivering a judgment in a court of love convened in 1174, makes the following declaration.

> We say and affirm . . . that love may not extend its rights over two married persons. For lovers grant each other all things mutually and freely without constraint of any motive of necessity, whereas the married are in duty bound reciprocally to submit to the will of the other, and to refuse each other nothing.[12]

Love and marriage are seen as mutually exclusive or at least opposed in principle: marriage is governed by duty, but love is free, constrained only by the lady's virtue. Her husband has exclusive rights over his young wife's body, but her soul is free to seek the love it desires. She is wooed by troubadors and young men of her own age preparing to seek their fortunes on adventures such as the Crusades. She grants them her favors, but the favors granted were fetishes, perhaps a scented handkerchief, that the young men carried next to their hearts as they jousted at home or plundered abroad. The successful ones returned, older and richer, ready now to take young brides of their own.

This is the stuff of which romantic poetry is made. The barrier of conjugal fidelity intensifies the yearning, but beyond this it allows the lovers to create their own fantasies of the love object. One loved the vision of the brave youth or wistful lady that one nurtured in one's dreams. One could do that freely because there could be no body contact, no carnal knowledge of the person involved on the other side of the relationship. And if, by fate or overpowering emotion, the barrier was breached—as it was by Lancelot and Guinevere, Tristan and Isolde, Abelard and Heloise—disaster and ruin were sure to follow. Furthermore, when Tristan takes Isolde away from her royal husband and off to the Forest of Morrois, when they breach the barriers of her marriage vow and his vow of fealty to the king, they create a new barrier: when King Mark finds them asleep in the forest, they are separated by Tristan's sword, a symbol of chastity. The point is that the intense experience of love they sought could not survive without the barriers that kept their fantasies alive by preventing them from knowing one another.[13]

Here, as in Plato, we see a spiritualized form of love which forsakes the *eidos* of the fleshly physiognomy for the *eidos* of the ideal vision. The transcendence of the beloved is preserved by willful ignorance of the flesh and blood reality of one's partner. The price is high—romantic love must remain unrequited or fall into ruin—and there is no way to negotiate around these terms: gods that can be touched are no longer godly, but fallen idols. Whence follows the dilemma that devastates romantic love:

> If I possess my love,
> she is not what I long for;
> if I do not possess my love,
> my love is unrequited.

Once one learns to recognize this structure, one finds it cropping up everywhere in the literature of love. For Freud, the primal love object is mother, but the father's prohibition, the taboo against incest, precludes me from possessing her. Hence, for every love object or mother-surrogate, if I can have her, she is not the mother figure: my desire is predicated upon her transcendence, her unattainability. For Sartre, the project of love is to possess a freedom as a freedom: for her love to be fulfilling to me, she must give it freely, but what is given freely can also be taken away, and the fear of loss produces anxiety. The lover's quest is to secure through possession the love that is freely given: a manifest impossibility that recapitulates the familiar dilemma. If it is free, it cannot be possessed; if it is not free, it is not what the lover seeks. Postmodern erotic pessimism offers another variant of the same structure: the satisfaction of desire is the death of desire. If you fulfill my desire, I no longer want you; if you do not, I go unfulfilled. One preserves the frisson of desire through strategies of indefinite deferral and unconsummated foreplay or *jouissance*. There are significant differences among these accounts, to be sure, but they remain variations on the same theme, the theme of romantic love: transcendence attained is transcendence lost.

## BEYOND ROMANCE

The full spectrum of contemporary erotic malaise cannot be reduced to the dissatisfaction that the structure of romantic love invariably produces. Romantic love is but one of the dead ends to which the demonization of sex leads. Nonetheless, it does explain the ambivalence characteristic of our times, the oscillation from deep cynicism to romantic yearning: we know we cannot have what we want and that produces cynicism, but we cannot keep ourselves from yearning for it anyway. The ecstasy of new love—the renewal of self in the embellishing eyes of the fresh lover, the familiar stories and gestures and ploys of endearment redeployed before an appreciative other not yet weary of them, the sexual fervor one had almost forgotten—lures us on to cast ourselves into another whirlwind with the forlorn hope that this time it will not just add to the wreckage. We recapitulate the turmoil of adolescent mate selection, but this time with more lives involved. This time a spouse is rejected, not just a former lover, and one's children lose the security of the familiar home as the taken-for-granted horizon of the only lives they have known. One has but one life to live and one's time and market appeal are running out. One has been duped and disappointed. This is not the way it was supposed to be. There must be more. So we make another desperate grab for transcendence.

The pattern is as dismal as it is prevalent. The promise of true romance sells everything from perfume to vitamin pills. It furnishes lyrics for operas as well as popular songs and plots for stage, screen, and novels. *Cosmopolitan* could not exist without it, and neither could *Playboy*. As a culture we are shoveling our lives into a hole that cannot be filled. There has to be another way.

And there is. But we are searching for it in the wrong place. The new wave of thought trickling its way down into popular culture with the promise of something new, different, and better calls itself postmodernism. It is heralded as what comes after the modern times we have found so chaotic, neurotic, and generally unpleasant. From my vantage, however, this new wave is but a back eddy of an ebbing tide, an old form of sophistry refurbished to con a new herd of marks.

Semiological reductionism, the strategy I take to be foundational for postmodern thought, trades on the belief that the meanings we have for ourselves and that others have for us are but symbolic constructs grounded in the cultural forms they, themselves, generate. I will not recapitulate my critique of this movement here—it will continue to emerge throughout this book—but it is important to see how it intersects with the structure of romantic love. If our identities, yours and mine, are idealities constructed of signifiers, if there is no palpable reality we can reach, then love can only be romance. If I cannot embrace you, I am left to my fantasies, and you provide only the occasion for living them out. If you cannot draw me out of my fantasies and present yourself in the flesh, if you cannot manifest yourself as a reality that transcends my familiar conceptual matrices, then the transcendence I seek in you can be at best only a meaning I project upon you rather than a reality I experience through you, that is, a false transcendence, a mystification.

Love in the postmodern age recapitulates the self-dissemblance of the romantic conceit—the projection of absolute transcendence onto the object of desire—but it proffers a theoretical justification that serves only to compound the mystification. I am condemned to love unrequited because there is no way I can touch or reach or know the object of my love: the way is barred by the web of signifiers through which I construct the meanings that all things, including my beloved, have for me. I cannot perceive you, I have only my perceptions of you. Postmodern lovers hold hands and lament that they cannot really touch one another. This is, of course, half true: I cannot know you, as the Christian god purports to, in your ownmost ipseity, but am limited to finite apprehensions bounded by space, time, and my own projections. It is, nonetheless, profoundly stupid deliberately to ignore the other half of this truth: I cannot but know you when I see you, feel your anger or your pain, enter the space scented by your breath; your embodied presence obtrudes, it demands recognition and response. I can open myself to the reality you present and attempt to know you, or I can close myself off to protect the ideality I cherish. The first option is love; the second is romance.

Genuine love feeds on the carnal knowledge of the beloved, but this knowledge kills romance by dispelling the fantasy that is the true object of romantic fascination. Fantasies are by nature thin, lacking the rich texture that comes from the complex relationships among worldly things. To begin to know another person is to realize that she outstrips my knowledge, exists in a web of relations that has little to do with me, has a history I have not lived, sees from a perspective that is not my own. The quest for carnal knowledge of another is necessarily endless, since she is ever changing and becoming. Her identity is emergent and elusive: this grants to love an indefinite span of exploration, capable of filling a lifetime. The poverty of fantasy, however, portends rapid exhaustion; hence boredom is a constant threat to romantic love. My fantasy is a pale reflection of a possible reality, a nexus of thoughts lacking adumbration, an idea that withers if not fed by input from worldly fecundity. Dream lovers are fantastic creatures that cannot transcend the imaginations that created them. And like all dreams, they cannot withstand the light of day: perceptual reality obtrudes and displaces the image, leaving the romantic lover with a sense of having lost something he can barely remember, and with nothing left to do but court another vehicle to carry his fantasy.

The *ressentiment* of postmodern love amounts to a pout: the absolute is forever out of reach and nothing less will do. The best response to a pout is a laugh, and there is mirth aplenty to be found here. Postmodernism at its best is a prolonged postmortem on the god who, in dying, demonstrated that he

never was, except as the projection of an infantile wish. Does one emerge
from this investigation with tears of remorse, pouting from the loss of an illusion, having achieved nothing better than a shift from one form of infantility
to another? There is no absolute love,[14] therefore there is absolutely no love.
The value I demand is an absolute value: knowing there is no such thing—
knowing that the very demand is misconceived—I am *nonetheless* bereft of all
value. The laughter is in the nonetheless, and in the kindergarten illogic of the
argument contrived in the postmodern rhetoric of baroque virtuosity.

There is no absolute love, but there is finite love.

The absolute is not the measure of love, as Christians and postmoderns
believe. Love feeds on desire and lack, that is, on finitude. A loving god is a
contradiction in terms. Plato saw that. And then forgot it.[15]

The absolute is peace, serenity, plenitude, stasis, immutability. Absolute
transcendence is incapable of self-transcendence: perfection cannot grow beyond itself; its only movement is to circle narcissistically back into itself.

The categories of love are the categories of becoming: striving, yearning,
changing, growing. Love is the force that takes us beyond ourselves toward
each other and the selves that emerge through that relation. It is dynamic,
restless, questing, and moving always beyond itself to find itself in that very
movement.

Plato argued that love as finite desire differs from its object, the permanent possession of the good that constitutes immortality. How can the gap
between finite and infinite be bridged? The logic here is inexorable: the fulfillment of desire is the death of desire; the culmination of love is death of the
body. This is the thought that will mature through phases of the Christian
mysticism of death into the romantic ideal of indefinite deferral culminating
in the *Liebestod*.

Irony: Derrida's postmodernism recapitulates the same structure that informs the quintessential modernist thinker, Hegel.[16] The mistake that permeates this tradition is the Platonic mistake of conceiving the object of human
transcendence in terms of an immutable ideal generated by an infantile rejection of the reality of death. Irony compounds: death anxiety generates death
worship.

In the case of love, to burst the illusion of the absolute is to clear the way
toward the reality of human transcendence. The object of finite desire is finite
and worldly. The object of finite desire is another person . . . and the other
person one grows to be in relation to other persons. It is a movement away
from infantility, not a nostalgia for the sense of oneness mistakenly attributed

to gestating intrauterine life by Ferenczi and others in fits of idyllic reverie incommensurate with their own scientific knowledge. Even Aristophanes should have known better: it is not the lot of humans to be at one with themselves; the end of life lies on the way to its end, not beyond it. This is a brute fact of temporality and becoming.

Love is primordially tied to ends, ends as goals and ends as terminations. Love is a quest: desire is a form of goal orientation that is endemic to living organisms. Coming into being and passing away, the life phases of birth-growth-reproduction-decay-death, the body's will to live and its equally implacable will to die betray a telic structure or purposiveness manifest across the full spectrum of life from the simplest to the most complex of cells. Sexlove is, indeed, the oldest of our gods.

But this aboriginal force is subject to its own self-transforming nature: love is also our youngest god. A god whose *eidos* is ever changing, ever renewed in shape and expression. When cells become sufficiently complex, when reflection obtrudes, there arises the possibility of choosing to direct desire in one way rather than another, to pursue this end rather than that. There also arises the awareness that this very project of striving betrays our lack of oneness, perfection, wholeness. To live is to be on the way to another phase, to be incomplete in that way. This is the third truth of reflection, the awareness of which I am seeking to foster here. The youngest god whose physiognomy is forming itself through our awareness of our limits and our possibilities is the one who sees that the transcendence we seek lies in the seeking, that the end of desire is to recognize its own truth.

The quest for transcendence that drives sexlove belongs to the domain of becoming that is definitive of finite reality. It is a philosophical mistake traceable to Plato's eleaticism, his fascination with the immutable *eidos* patterned on the ideality of numbers, that leads us to posit permanence and unchange as the criterion of reality. The *eidos* as idea is parasitic upon the *eidos* as perceptual physiognomy: to reverse this ordering, as Plato did and postmodernism continues to do, is to get it exactly backward. The quest for transcendence is pointed toward the elusive more that we sense is there to be found. Pursuit of that something more entails growth and change, development and becoming. This is the reality that is genuinely definitive of human existence, and the longing for stasis, peace, rest, and permanence is just that, a longing, a desiring, a quest tied to becoming and change. It is a misguided quest, this quest for quiesence and death, but it is a quest all the same. Its mistake lies in the contradiction upon which it is founded, the contradiction of seeking a life of peace after a life of turmoil when peace and stasis is exactly what life is not. Whatever form of rest may be beyond the life of becoming is not life because life is becoming.

The something more afforded by life is to be found in the finite realm of worldly reality. The something more that is sought through sexlove is the self that is more than one's own self, the self that will bring me to be more than I am now. The term I have adopted for this intertwining of transcendence and self-transcendence is, as noted earlier, the Greek word το καλου. It names a constellation of thought, which will be the focus of chapters 8 and 9.

The next phase of the argument, to be developed in the chapter that follows this one, updates the critique of romantic love and its ties to postmodernism by analyzing one of its contemporary manifestations, cybersex. The guiding idea is that sexlove in the domain of virtual reality is a culmination of the romantic ideal, the extreme that concretizes the romantic quest and illumines its basic structures, its promise, and its futility.

SIX

# VIRTUAL BODIES/BODIES OF FLESH

YOU MEET ON-LINE and chat. You exchange photographs. You talk on the telephone. You feel that you are well acquainted, although there is still much to learn about each other. When, finally, you meet, you instantly realize that you do not know one another. The person you recognize from the photograph is a stranger. The perceptual reality displaces the virtual reality, banishes it to a never-never land whence it can be recalled but never recollected: the memorial trace of the virtual persona has been obscured by the fleshly presence; all that can be retrieved is a thin cipher whose adumbrations are abstract, feeble, incapable of resonance and reassurance. The person here in the flesh is someone about whom you have some knowledge, not a person you know. The knowledge you have will have to be reoriented, recontextualized, adjusted to fit the person you are now beginning to know.

You may not want to meet in person. It may be that you have chosen to come together in virtual space because that venue allows you to be fantastic lovers, allows you to construct fantasy variations of yourselves that may be younger, more attractive, more daring than you really are. You may act out the ideals that guide your everyday efforts to become more than what you are, and attempt to realize in cyberspace the dreamy personae that outstrip your mundane capacities. On line, you are Stonefox; in the supermarket, you merge into a crowd of gray. And he is Dionysus after a day of selling life insurance. You cannot meet because the flesh would dispel the fantasy and the love you crafted on-line would evanesce.

Movement can take place in virtual space—on a videotape, in a digital movie—and movement expresses style. Style is also apparent in the dynamic flow of words, whether typed or spoken. Style is the prime vehicle of identity because style, the how of movement and expression, facilitates recognition and grants it a degree of confidence that static attributes cannot match: I can know the color of your hair and eyes, your height and weight, your age and gender—all the characteristics that can be printed on an ID card—I can even study your photograph . . . yet still have difficulty picking you out of the crowd. But if I have spent some time in your company, seen you walk and gesture, I can find you quickly at the airport—even if I could not remember the color of your eyes, and maybe even if you had colored your hair and lost weight.[1]

Husserl argued that eidetic variation takes its departure from perceptual modes: imagination is parasitic upon and constrained by the perceptual noema. Derrida argued the contrary: the perceptual noema is recognizable as such because it instantiates an ideality conditioned upon iterability. Husserl's standpoint is finally inconsistent with his overriding commitment to transcendental idealism. Derrida's position is consistent with a thoroughgoing transcendentalism, but its difficulty in accounting for the genesis of signifiers stems from the same problem that beset Husserl, the problem of accounting for the genesis of ideal forms. Original repetition[2] is a deliberate oxymoron that names a refusal to pursue the question of origins. Both Husserl's inconsistency and Derrida's refusal can be overcome by combining transcendental projection and sedimentation with an empirical understanding of perception that allows us to learn from experience.[3]

The virtual bodies that come together in cyberspace are constructed through signifiers. As such, virtual bodies are parasitic upon fleshly bodies and constrained by them, but fleshly bodies betray a style that constrains their behavior in the very act of expressing their intentions. The fleshly bodies of Dustin Hoffman and Meryl Streep are recognizable in the virtual bodies of the characters they portray; Hoffman may, indeed, become Tootsie and Streep Sophie, but it is Streep's Sophie that she becomes, and Tootsie's face is a female variation of Hoffman's physiognomy, his *eidos*. Still, the personae that are evident in the roles they play may, themselves, be conceived as roles, as virtual identities carefully constructed by the actors and those who tend their images. When Streep steps out of Sophie, she remains Streep, but who is at home at the Streep residence when Meryl relaxes her professional demeanor and steps out of that role, too? Who could answer this question? Her mother, her friend, her lover, her child, her analyst, her makeup person, her dog, her teacher? Maybe even herself?

The answer, I think, is all of them and none of them. Each one could give a partial answer and none could give a final answer, although some answers might be less partial than others. Meryl Streep transcends all her adumbrations. God knows who she really is . . . which is to say that nobody knows: the ideal unity is just that, a total comprehension vouchsafed to none, although some approach it more closely than others. Note, however, that the question has changed as it developed. Who is that playing the role of Sophie? Meryl Streep. Who is that playing the role of Meryl Streep? Same answer, but the question is a different kind of question.

There is a sense in which one can play a role that has been constructed around one's own virtual persona. Most of us are aware of maintaining an ideal before the gaze of others and our own conscience, superego, or ego ideal. There are things one wouldn't do in public, even things one wouldn't do in private—even though it is possible to do these things, even though there may be a vertigo of possibility whose appeal toward the unthinkable may be frightening, even though the unthinkability of the unthinkable may reside in the delirious possibility of the thought. One can ask about such public and private personae[4]—Who is that playing the role of Meryl Streep?— but such questions presuppose an answer to a prior sort of question. An instance of the prior question has already been seen: Who is that playing the role of Sophie? It might also have been: Who is driving that car? Who is swimming in lane three? The prior question asks us to designate a human bodily identity; the subsequent question asks about that person's persona or character, history, values, typical forms of behavior, etc.

The distinction between these questions has been drawn in myriad ways which have traditionally oriented themselves around such binary oppositions as physical body versus soul or psyche, *esse* versus *essentia,* or (now) fleshly body versus virtual or textual body. There is a growing consensus among contemporary Continental thinkers that such binary oppositions are misconceived because the two domains overlap. I, too, hold this view. There is also widespread belief that the distinction I have drawn between designating a bodily identity and describing that person's character or persona is misconceived, not only because the two domains overlap, but because all answers to the question of carnal identity are ultimately reducible to questions about personae: no distinction can be drawn here because both sets of questions ultimately ask about social constructs that, as such, are indistinguishable. In the example at hand, there would be no distinction between the use of the signifier "Meryl Streep" to answer the question about who played the role of Sophie and its use to ask the question about the person playing the role of Meryl Streep. I challenge the reductionist aspect of the constructivist view.

After a long acquaintance on-line, you meet in person. You recognize Dionysus easily. You have studied his photograph or digitalized image, this is the appointed time and place, and there in his hand is the rose he promised to bring. Despite this, there is a doubt that will not be there when you meet again. His voice is the voice you have heard on the telephone, but he is talking too fast, dithering, filling the uncomfortable space with matters of no consequence; the person on the telephone was sure, deft, relevant even when indirect. Perhaps his eyes are embarrassed, wary, dancing away from yours. This person is, indeed, Dionysus, but he is not the persona you had anticipated. At this moment, when the virtual world and the mundane world are colliding, when the ideality you constructed is being displaced by the reality that transcends you both, he is undergoing the sort of change of aspect that happens when the duck changes into the rabbit.

Suppose, in the midst of all this, the waiter appears with a telephone. A problem at the office. Dionysus listens intently, then responds crisply, decisively. He nods to the waiter to take the phone away, and resumes the conversation seamlessly. Once again, you are disoriented as yet another change of aspect takes place: a new, unsuspected dimension unfolds. Same person. New persona. His business self ripples back over Dionysus's social self and shows it in a new and different light.

The term *virtual* as it is used in such locutions as "virtual reality" or "virtual body" means something like imaginary or existing only in signs and symbols as opposed to existing in fact or in reality. Hence virtual reality and virtual body are oxymorons: unreal reality or imaginary flesh. "I was virtually blinded by the flash bulbs" means that I was not really blinded and will be able to see again shortly. The oxymorons become philosophically puzzling when taken up in the light of the transcendental standpoint, the standpoint from which the meaning of reality derives from the projection of immanent or imaginary forms. If Dionysus sees you as attractive, projects upon you categories of beauty grounded in his desire, then, for him, you are attractive. If a culture sees cigarette smoking as sophisticated, then, for that culture, it is elegant and soignée to light up. If you choose to live in a text or in the culture to be found in cyberspace, then, for you and for the others dwelling in the cybersocial domain, the worlds constructed out of signifiers, pixels, and digits are real. Or so a pure transcendentalism would have it.

In the erotically charged atmosphere of an adult BBS, in the cyberspace crafted to provide the instant gratification of dreams, reality obtrudes. Just as it does in dreams. Stonefox wants to know if Dionysus is married. (Dionysus married? Don't be silly! / I'm not being silly. You ducked that question on your bio. You're married, aren't you?) Dionysus wants to know how much Stonefox weighs, how tall she is, where she works. And when Serpent logs on, the greetings include queries. Is this Lady Serpent or her husband? Which half of this swinging couple who share the same on-line alias (or user ID) has his or her fingers on the keyboard right now?

A newbie, Gorgeous, appears and wants to know how to whisper, how to speak privately to just one other person rather than having the typed words be visible to all present in the channel. The question is answered, but several people have already checked and Gorgeous has not filled out the biographical questionnaire. Everyone wants to know whether Gorgeous is male or female. Gorgeous declares her femininity and begins to flirt outrageously with the males. Something in her manner isn't quite right. In a very few minutes Gorgeous is inundated with challenges. A pop quiz on what every woman knows but most men don't. Gorgeous comes up with the right notes, but the melody is off. She's simply declarative when she should have been evasive. She is defensive rather than playful. In the brash hyperspeed of cyberspace, the confession is quickly extracted: Gorgeous is a TV. So far just a TV, not yet a pre-op. Everything falls into place, and Gorgeous is accepted for what he/she is without rancor or recrimination. Just wanted to get that little thing straight.

If you can't speak geek, that's noted. If you can, you're typified. If you drop too many whispers, you won't be trusted. If you take too long to say it, nobody wants to hear it. If you have fat fingers, you're either drunk or stupid. And if you garble all over everybody because you haven't disabled call waiting, people get annoyed.

If pointed replies are sharper than they are funny, egos get wounded. Dionysus kisses Stonefox lightly on the cheek. Stonefox tosses her cookies on Dionysus's feet. Dionysus sulks. Then zaps Stonefox into a human McNugget. Stonefox buries Dionysus under a deluge of macros, prepared in advance for such occasions and deployed with a few quick key strokes, which cast aspersions on everything from his taste in ties to his fondness for used kitty litter. Dionysus gets mad and ugly. Dionysus gets dumped by the sysop.

Teddybear is horny as hell and wants to hot chat with any female at all. His invitations go unanswered. And some kindly soul tells him in a whisper that it isn't done that way: the board is full of randy males, twenty or thirty for every female, and the ladies exercise restraint and discernment. There are cybermountains to be climbed, cyberseas to be swum, and Venus never was readily attainable to all comers. Teddybear has to learn to be interesting.

In the reduced cybersphere, protocol has tighter form than in a singles bar. You have to say it for it to be visible. (Fox: you are cruel. Grin.) But it only takes a few hours to get the hang of the thing. Because you already know most of the rules without having to be taught. Because Husserl was right: fantasy worlds are all variations of the *Lebenswelt*.

Suspicions run high. If you aren't a dweeb, why are you here—instead of making it in the real world? If you're a regular, you probably don't have a life of your own, or the one you have is one that you're trying to escape.

If you're here, you have a credit card, some education or training, access to if not outright ownership of a computer, discretionary time, and private space. You are at least eighteen years old (or maybe it's twenty-one). You have some interest in love and sexuality, even if you say it's only a research interest. And there is some reason why that interest has led you to this place rather than to a church social, singles bar, or philosophy and literature conference: some reason why you sometimes prefer to meet people in cyberspace where your body is not visible and your true identity can be protected.

None of this is virtual. It has to do with fantasy, with imagination and possibility, but it is real as opposed to imaginary. You can't pay for on-line time with an imaginary credit card. You can pay with somebody else's card—for a while—but if you get caught, the jail they send you to is real. Virtual reality is constructed in the perceived world, the real world of things we can touch, feel, and see with our fleshly bodies. This is all empirically testable. Watch what happens to virtual reality in an electric storm. When the system goes thud in the night, the person whose user ID is Zeus does not simply turn off the storm.

And . . . finally . . . if you are here, *you* are here. You bring your intelligence, your values, your desires, your vulnerabilities; in sum, your style. You want to be loved for who you are.[5] And the truth about that comes out sooner rather than later. Nobody who took the time to get to know her was surprised to learn that IowaMary logged on from a laptop in a hospice bed. Saddened to learn of her passage, but not surprised when the details came to light after the fact. It was consistent with her style, the perspective that emerged from the electronic traces she left, the values that informed her way of dealing with masculine importunity, her idiosyncratic admixture of urgency and remotion.

Still: when, after months or even years of on-line banter and romance including sulks as well as hot chat, Dionysus and Stonefox meet each other at one of the regularly scheduled get togethers, they find themselves confronting intimate strangers.

Why do the denizens of erotic cyberspace always institutionalize opportunities to meet in the flesh . . . when they have chosen that space to protect the identities that will be busted if they show up in person? Why do the masks typically come off in the process of the ball? What is this bivalence of bodily identity and virtual persona whose pathological form is schizophrenia, whose ordinary manifestations oscillate between ambiguity and contradiction?

Contemporary ID cards might well have been designed by John Locke. He conceived human bodily identity in terms of continuity of the physical body from its origin at birth.[6] This is but an extension of his more general principle that "*the principium individuationis*[7] . . . is existence itself; which determines a being of any sort to a particular time and place, incommunicable to two beings of the same kind" (*Essay*, 441–442). But Locke quickly distinguishes between the man and the person, identity in the case of the latter requiring consciousness of its continuity.[8] This distinction between body and self, between man and person, allows Locke (as a similar distinction allowed Descartes) to preserve the elevation of the thinking human soul above the mere physical organism of the animal, but at the price of creating problems of continuity of consciousness (hence personal identity) between sleep and waking, madness or drunkenness and sanity or sobriety, acts forgotten and remembered, etc.: "Socrates waking and sleeping is not the same person" (*Essay*, 460), and although we may punish a man for what he does when mad or drunk, "in the Great Day, wherein the secrets of all hearts shall be laid open, it may be reasonable to think, no one shall be made to answer for what he knows nothing of . . ." (*Essay*, 463–464). The identity of the person is not reducible to the identity of what Locke called the man, that is, the human fleshly identity.

Notwithstanding all the difficulties attendant upon Locke's manner of drawing this distinction between bodily identity and personal identity—not least of which is the privilege accorded to the first-person viewpoint in the determination of the self or person—there is an element I would preserve, indeed, have preserved in the distinction made above between bodily identity and virtual persona. Saying that Streep played Sophie (or drove the car or swam in lane three) names her carnal identity. The question asking who she is when she steps out of the role of Sophie or out of the more or less contrived public role of Meryl Streep is a question about her various personae that presupposes a prior knowledge of her corporeal identity.

This distinction can be maintained without encountering the problems besetting Locke and his successors in the empiricist strain of the Cartesian tradition if one (a) acknowledges that both identity and persona are abstractions from the lived body (that is, if one refuses to conceive body and mind as ontologically disjunct), and (b) if one does not reduce intentionality to consciousness or the reflective cogito (that is, if one acknowledges that flesh is purposive and manifests its own kind of intelligence and reflexivity).

The following diagram is designed to illustrate the relations between the two competing models traditionally regarded as mutually exclusive.

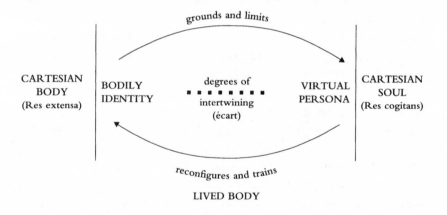

Diagram of Reversibility Model

The Cartesian model conceives body and soul (or mind or self, etc.) as standing in the binary opposition of mutual exclusion; it denies the possibility of carnal reflexivity, intelligent flesh, bodily intentionality, etc. The reversibility model takes the Cartesian categories of *res extensa* (thing extended in space—material bodies) and *res cogitans* (thinking thing—mind, spirit, soul) as defining limits by asserting the impossibility of pure instantiations of either: there can be no disembodied soul, and the only human bodies devoid of intentionality are dead. Cartesian bodies, like Cartesian souls, are linguistic constructs, mistakenly reified, which have no worldly counterparts. Within the limits defined by these poles of impossibility are degrees of corporeal reflexivity designated as living bodies. At one end of the spectrum are forms of bodily identity that ground and limit the manifestations of style here described as the virtual personae at the other end: the two always intertwine, but in differing degrees. One can never leave one's body behind, even in cyberspace, but there are differences in the degree to which it obtrudes, differences in its manner of self-revelation or self-concealment, differences in the ways in which it enables or hinders us in executing the projects in which we engage, and so forth. In short, there is a distance or fission or *écart,* grounded in the reflexivity of human flesh, that separates flesh from itself and allows it to view itself as an other, take up attitudes toward its actions and possibilities, and transform itself in modes of self-transcendence.

One broaches the limits of intelligibility to say that a dead body manifests style: style is an adverbial term referring to manner of action or behavior. If, as I have suggested, one's persona is grounded in one's style, then, although dead bodies may have bodily identities, their links to any personae are either historical or metaphorical: the credit for the dignity he exhibits while lying in state belongs more to his mortician than to Lenin; it is his legacy at work, not Lenin, not the ambiguous intertwining of his carnal identity and his manifold personae, that manifests a loose unity grounded in his fleshly style. Lenin's persona may have lived on in some metaphorical sense, but not in his dead body, even though that dead body is properly identified as Lenin's.

It is a mistake to argue that the style inhabiting one's personae is separable from one's lived body, except as an abstraction. Meryl Streep can play neither Sophie nor herself without her body. No more than Ralph Jones, the insurance broker, can play Dionysus or Jane Doe can play Stonefox without taking themselves, their lived bodies and their styles, along into cyberspace as they generate eidetic variations of themselves under their user IDs or aliases or virtual bodies. Their fleshly bodies ambiguously inhabit their virtual bodies in somewhat the same way as Streep's fleshly body is virtually present in the films from which it is literally absent.

The style of the lived body subtends the distinction between bodily identity and virtual persona, but the bodily identity is not reducible to the virtual persona because the persona lives on for a while in the virtual domain when the body dies. The point here is to deny binary opposition between "lived" and "body" while insisting on the distinction between the living body and some of the predicates that may properly be assigned to it. Style resides in flesh, but flesh and style transcend one another in different ways. One's bodily identity grounds and limits one's style, but the virtual personae that manifest your style allow you to reconfigure and train your carnal identity. You can dance because you have a mobile body, but you can't dance well if your body is sick or overweight. It is your virtual persona as a dancer that brings itself into being by training your body to move in graceful rhythms and reconfigures the habitus that informs the way you move.

This brief excursus into cyberspace has a direct bearing on the evolution of sexlove and the choice among competing love-styles open to us in today's culture. The adventures in sexlove now taking place in cyberspace are brand new variations on an ancient theme.

Stonefox and Dionysus fall in love with the virtual persona each has constructed of the other just as Romeo and Juliet fall in love with the fantasies of each other they have constructed. Stonefox and Dionysus are held apart by the computers that bring them together as Romeo and Juliet entice each other across the social divide that prohibits carnal knowledge. The restrictions of the social medium through which they interact frees them for flights of imagination. This is the structure of romantic love. One loves love, one pleasures oneself through the fantasy of the beautiful other whom one imagines mirroring back the enhanced vision one projects across the barrier that keeps mundane reality at bay. In the case of Pyramus and Thisbe, romance fed on the chink in the wall that held them apart; in the case of Stonefox and Dionysus, the computer screen kept them safely distant while dangling before them the tantalizing fruits they constructed for themselves and each other.

If knowledge is a condition for genuine love, if you cannot genuinely love someone you do not know, then the dependence of romantic love on the barrier to carnal knowledge leads one to wonder if the term *romantic love* is not yet another oxymoron. This question will come up again. For the moment, however, I want to ponder the counterthesis, the thesis that romance is an introit, an entirely fitting structure to employ in the opening moves of the mating game.

There are two plain facts of erotic life that seem to be unconnected, but which come together to enfranchise romance. The first is that love makes one vulnerable: if one offers oneself and is rejected, it hurts, and the greater the exposure, the more of oneself one declares, the more it hurts. The second fact is that the conceits of self-enhancing posturing—everything from cosmetics to downright duplicity, from wonderbras to presenting oneself as what one palpably is not—are nonetheless revelations. Posturing is behavior and all behavior reveals. To brag is to betray what you would like to be; to primp is to manifest your ego ideal; to play a studied role is to rehearse for the show of a future self.

The idealizations of romantic love thrive on barriers and reticence; they promote imposture and duplicity; they are overt forms of self-protection and covert forms of self-betrayal, and, in the best case, they promote transformation and self-transcendence: one must prepare oneself to deliver what one pretends to be. If I adopt the demeanor of power, assume the macho stance, then I must call upon all my resources to meet the unexpected threat that confronts me in the presence of the other whose favor I am courting. If I entice her to love the man I pretend to be, then I must become that man if I want her to love me. But if she rejects that pretense, I can console myself that she did not reject me, that her rejection reflects only a miscalculation in my choice of personae through which to offer myself for her approval.

Love depends on alterity, on that form of transcendence. Self-congratulation is thin; one wants the affirmation of an *other* person. The necessity for alterity, however, brings with it a dark side, a shadow that always looms behind when we face the light of approval. No love without vulnerability, no great love without great vulnerability, no vulnerability at all without latent resentment: hostility is always on the horizon, ready to flare up at a slight. It is a mistake to take this penumbra of darkness as a sign that one's love is faint or malformed: love and hate intertwine and cannot be separated. That upon which one's life depends is potentially a deadly threat, and threat is the source of hatred. One cannot drink deeply without living with the risk of dying of thirst.

This should not be a troubling thought, because we have been contending with it from birth: the great good mother is also and necessarily the evil witch. To bring this thought to thematic awareness should, rather, be comforting: it provides solace to know that the hostility we occasionally feel is a measure of love's intensity rather than its failure. It is also true that this intensity has diseased as well as healthy forms, the difference in quality being ultimately a matter of reality perception and personal strength.[9]

Positively viewed, romance is a prelude to sexlove, an opening gambit, an intense period of hope and despair, an invocation of higher powers: foreplay. As such, it always has a sequel, a next act: the crescendo culminates, and the music takes on a different tempo. The mistake of our age is to mistake the prelude for the symphony. Unending *jouissance* is exactly what mature love is not. It is also impossible. To mistake the thrill of romance for the mark of genuine love is to prepare oneself for disappointment. It is also to deprive oneself of deeper satisfaction. The next course could be richer, indeed, is richer for those who prepare themselves for it. The sadness is that so many starve at the banquet table for lack of the ability to discern nourishment.

The point of the venture into cyberspace was to demonstrate the volatility of romantic idealization. The displacement of constructed idealities by perceptual reality, the abrupt change of aspect when Stonefox and Dionysus finally meet each other face to face, is an inevitability. The romantic interlude in the chat rooms of cyberspace always and inevitably comes to an end. Either it exhausts its limited possibilities, atrophies from iterations of the same, starves itself into boredom, and goes off in search of fresh meat . . . or it takes the leap into the 3D world and is displaced by reality. Those are the only two possibilities. What is narrowly true of cyber romance is broadly true of romance as such: sexlove cannot sustain itself on idealities alone. If the barrier remains in place, the fantasies die of repetition; if it tumbles, they are chased away by the unveiling of the flesh. The barrier is at best a temporary measure, a prophylaxis against vulnerability, a safety harness to wear while we develop our strength, an encumbrance to shed when we are ready to touch and be touched. Overestimation is volatile: it always evaporates or changes.

When romantic lovers finally come together, they do so in death. The repetition of this theme in romantic literature is emblematic. Thisbe drops her veil on the way to the tryst, the lion nuzzles it leaving it bloody; Pyramus finds it, assumes her dead, and kills himself. Thisbe finds his dead body and kills herself on the spot. Isolde the Fair sails off to heal the ailing Tristan. As her ship approaches, it hoists a white sail of hope. Isolde of the White Hand, moved by jealousy, reports to Tristan that the sail is black. He expires in despair. Isolde the Fair, finding him dead, lies down beside him and joins him in death. Juliet takes the sleeping draught and feigns death to avoid marriage with Count Paris. Romeo, unknowing, hears of her death, hastens to her tomb, poisons himself, and dies. Juliet awakens, finds Romeo dead, and kills herself with his dagger. Et cetera. The romantic novels of more recent vintage solve the problem without so much blood: the novel always ends when the last obstacle has been overcome and the lovers are united at last; the sequel to romance is left untold. Kierkegaard states the point succinctly: "When two beings fall in love with each other and begin to suspect they were made for each other, it is time to have the courage to break it off; for by going on, they have everything to lose and nothing to gain."[10] The culmination of romance is terminal. Or so it is viewed by romantics, by those who can see no further.

The same phenomenon of displacement—the radical change of aspect when the fantasy object is revealed through perception and carnal knowledge—provides a compelling disproof to the forms of constructivism now deploying semiological reductionism. It is, as I have happily acknowledged, half true that your meaning for me is colored by my history, my desire, and all the host of influences on how I interpret the world. My intent here is to emphasize the importance of the other half of that truth, the truth that your palpable presence displaces those projections that are incompatible with it. If I could only see through the lens of projection and interpretation, if my eyes could not force me to acknowledge what my prejudices would prefer not to see, then the perceptual displacement experienced by Stonefox, Dionysus, and all the other cyberlovers who venture into 3D could not take place. That it invariably does take place, that the visions generated by digitally encoded signifiers always fade before the fleshly presence, shows the one-sidedness and reductionism operating in the constructivist theses.

If you are a male TV masquerading as a woman in cyberspace, it is conceivable that you could succeed in the deception and enter a serious on-line relationship with a male who thinks of himself as straight. It is improbable, but let us hypothetically assume that Gorgeous entices such a male into accepting him/her as a woman and forming a romantic attachment that acquires increasing strength through their encounters on-line, maybe even in telephone conversations. The time of reckoning is, nonetheless, waiting on the horizon. Either they refuse to venture beyond cyberspace, in which case the relationship fades into the boredom of repetition without new stimuli, or they decide to meet in the flesh. The 3D encounter cannot fail to change the way that Gorgeous's lover perceives him/her. The lover may accept the change, might welcome it, may have even longed for it through latencies of which he was only dimly aware, but the woman he knew in cyberspace will be displaced by the TV he meets in 3D.

Romance always has to encounter transcendence. There is always a beyond.

To see beyond romance, however, another vision-clearing exercise is in order. Freud's mark on the discourse of sexlove is permanent, pervasive, and confusing. Every one of his major theses has been seriously challenged by one intellectual heavyweight or another. He has been celebrated as a liberator of women. He has also been condemned and ridiculed by feminists. Yet nobody would contest the fact that his influence on the twentieth-century culture of sexlove is unrivaled. The core of his theory is the Oedipus complex. Like the romantic model of love—with which it has close ties—it touches on fundamental structures of human existence, magnifies some, distorts others, and leaves us in a quandary. The next chapter sets forth a coherent and comprehensive account of the role of Mother in the genesis of human sexuality, correlates it with themes presented in earlier chapters, and prepares it to fit into the gestalt of sexlove this book attempts to construct.

SEVEN

# MOTHERLOVE AND SEXLOVE

## TWO PROBLEMS IN FREUD'S ACCOUNT OF LOVE

THE ESSENCE OF the Oedipus complex lies in the plausible assumption that Mother is the first love-object. This is a mistake. Mother is not a love-object, because infantile experience is not articulated along the axes of self-other, inner-outer, subject-object. The infant's perspective is unaware of itself as a perspective. Indeed, that unawareness of itself as a perspective is what defines infantile consciousness, whether it lives through a newborn or an adult body. Mother is a separate object only from the standpoint of an adult observer; for the infant, Mother is a global presence whose being is not yet distinct from the infant's own being. Individuation has not yet come into play; it is only a portent existing in the demand of the transcendent world to have its articulations acknowledged.[1]

Infantile amnesia limits phenomenological investigation of the quality of early experience. One can only observe the behavior of infants and speculate. These speculations, in turn, are corrupted by projection of adult qualities where it is exactly the departures from the quality of adult experience that we seek to understand. Freud regularly refers to the infant as an ego or subject when, according to his own theorizing, the ego is relatively late in developing. He classifies the instincts associated with self-preservation and survival as ego-instincts and treats them as primordial. This dualism of self and other governs Freud's thought throughout; it confounds his understanding of love and obscures otherwise compelling insights.

Freud characterizes the earliest phases of life as primary narcissism, remaining unmindful that the metaphor he has chosen is that of reflection, specifically reflection that presupposes the self-alienation of recognizing oneself in an external object. The very idea of narcissism depends upon a separation of subject and object which allows the subject to find herself in an object —an external reflection—yet this separation is an achievement that lies before the infant, something about her de facto condition that she will have to learn through painful experience. Separation involves the coming to awareness of having a perspective, a process that begins at birth, reaches a height of intensity at adolescence, and starts to regress with senility, never having reached completion.

According to Freud, the teleology of pleasure seeking is driven by the goal of reenactment and repetition: one seeks to return to earlier occasions of pleasure to recapitulate them. The earliest intentional behavior he attributes to infants is the turning of the head to recapture the vision of the mother's breast that will position her nipple in reach of the infant's mouth. This model of explanation predelineates the Oedipal structure of adult love: one seeks to recapitulate with adult partners the quality of pleasure imprinted in infancy. With Mother one has the unique and never-to-be-repeated experience of the confluence of ego-instincts and sex-instincts: the goals of primary narcissism, pleasure and survival, are coincidentally fulfilled by Mother's warmth and nutrition, the pleasures of her soft, enveloping body and her breast. Mother is, thus, the primal love-object, the paradigm that governs our erotic striving, the memory we seek to retrieve through latter-day surrogates. The quality of her love, present in the past obscured by infantile amnesia but operative in the ceaseless proliferation of associations and derivatives going on in the unconscious, is what we seek to make present again.

This is a tragic view of love, tragic because doomed to failure, and doomed to failure because success cannot be conceived, much less achieved. Could one, *per impossibile*, find the perfect surrogate, she would be prohibited by the law of exogamy, a law psychologically enforced by impotence or frigidity. But, of course, the perfect surrogate cannot be found: no woman can be primordial Mother; even one's own biological mother would fall short, just because she is now, despite her eminence and privilege, a person among persons, and no longer the polymorphous global presence Mother is to the infant. The quest for the primal love-object is blocked by stronger forces than the incest taboo; it is stymied by the very process of maturation that brings it about: to have reached the phallic stage is already to have passed beyond the possibility of living through the primordial identification with Mother. Every attempt to repeat this experience is regressive in the double sense of violating the reality principle and longing to revert to infantility.

Note the structural isomorphism between Freud's Oedipus complex and the double bind of romance. Romantic love founders on the dilemma of transcendence: either I am unfulfilled because I have failed to possess my beloved, or if I succeed in possessing her, I no longer love her, unattainability being a condition of love. When the transcendence of the beloved is the transcendence constitutive of Mother, the transcendence accruing to her by the primal prohibition against incest and reinforced by her global superiority, the dilemma retains the same structure, only the specifications of transcendence change. If I find the perfect surrogate, my love is forbidden; if I do not find her, I live without the love I seek. In both cases, romantic love and Oedipal love, to cross the barrier of transcendence, to achieve intimacy with the love-object, is to confront erotic shipwreck because in both cases the prohibition is held to be constitutive of desire. Finally, in both cases, the dilemma of transcendence arises from a faulty conception of transcendence, one that sets transcendence and intimacy in a relation of mutual exclusion.

Genuine transcendence resides in an alterity that is revealed through intimate knowledge rather than constituted by barriers to that knowledge. Maturation beyond the stage of Oedipal attachment consists in learning more about Mother. One is not frightened by castration anxiety into suppression of love; one is nurtured into a mature form of love of which infants are incapable. This is a form of love that shares with erotic love the quest for affirmation through self-transformation, but seeks that affirmation through strategies of independence rather than those of fleshly intertwining. By the time that desire is full-fledged and explicitly sexual, that is, by the time of adolescence, that is, by the time that real social and physical dangers generate genuine prohibitions, the good Mother has already weaned the child and taught it to look beyond the nest for its satisfaction. It is not the fear of castration enforced by Father so much as it is the empowerment to contend with the world provided by both parents that drives the maturation process.

Unbridled sex-instincts, Freud tells us, are sadistic: not sadistic in the sense of seeking to inflict pain on the sex-object, but sadistic in the attempt to dominate and control.[2] Whence, then, arise the tender emotions associated with mature forms of sexual expression? What motivates the transformation of narrowly sexual aims into love? Freud defines love in several ways at different points along the course of his own developing thought: love is aim-inhibited repetition; love is "the relation of the ego to its sources of pleasure";[3] love is "primarily narcissistic, is then transferred to those objects which have been incorporated in the ego, . . . and expresses the motor striving of the ego after these objects as sources of pleasure;"[4] love is subsumed under Eros, the life instinct, which seeks higher forms of organization through binding and unification. The problem of accounting for the genesis of the tender emotions of love from the sheer pleasure seeking of sex-instincts may be subsumed under the greater problematic of sublimation, the channeling of raw instinct into culturally higher forms. As Ricoeur points out, sublimation presupposes a vision of ends, a teleology drawn by final causes, which Freud's energy-based economics is at a loss to explain.[5]

Tender emotions: this paltry phrase names the difference between rape and love. Eros manifests itself in all the strategies of manipulating the other in order to achieve one's own frisson: attempts to dominate, suborn, and deceive; efforts to purchase, possess, and use. Eros also motivates acts of generosity, self-sacrifice, and loyalty; moments of valor, creativity, and deep pathos. Every account of love from Plato to the present aims at understanding the nature, genesis, and portent of these tender emotions, be that understanding couched as a reduction to unconscious biological causes or, at the other extreme, as an elevation to supernatural heights of a mystical principle of cosmic unification. Freud embraces the gamut: Mother is the source of love, and her title is as celestial as it is biological; she cannot be conceived apart from the confluence of nature and nurture.

But how is she to be conceived? Specifically, how does she evoke the tender emotions that bind testosterone to *poiesis?*

So far, I have argued that Freud's explanatory paradigm, based as it is on an economy of dualism, goes astray in two ways: it fails to understand the syncretic quality of infantile experience by presupposing a self-other separation which has to be overcome through mediations across an ontological fissure, and it compounds this failure by conceiving these mediations as driven by a retrospective mechanism of repetition and reenactment which leaves the telic and creative aspects of desire, named as sublimation, strictly unaccountable.

## SYNCRETISM AND THE GENESIS
## OF ETHICAL CONSCIOUSNESS

To understand love is necessarily to understand its antithesis—if, that is, love and hate are opposites, a binary system constructed around the fulcrum of a negation. For Freud, the fulcrum is the dualism between the external world and the internal organism. Hate originates in the exogenous domain of worldly stimuli that generate pain by building tension and give rise to flight, movement away, repulsion or, in the extreme, aggression and attempts to destroy. Love's origin lies in narcissistic organ-pleasure, release of libido from endogenous sources, which attracts us to ourselves and motivates us to repeat the motions through which we please ourselves. Mediating across the negation that separates outer from inner is Mother, the object of a primordial identification. At his best, Freud describes this identification in terms of the logic of syncretism and indistinction of perspectives,[6] but his metapsychological commitments to an explanatory paradigm based on dualistic economical principles change the logic of syncretism into the logic of mediation: Mother becomes the external object that must first be introjected through transference of narcissistic investments or cathexes, and subsequently externalized and alienated through the mechanism of repression based on enforcement of the law of exogamy through the castration complex.

Departing now from Freud, I would venture the hypothesis that the enigma of the tender emotions is illumined by the structure of identification or, better, syncretism. In primordial indistinction, self and Mother merge, and polymorphous infantile sensuality permeates the continuum wherein the boundaries within the triad of self-Mother-world are indistinct and overlap. The organism's project of survival is not lived as self-interest, as the term ego-instinct suggests, but rather is diffused throughout the syncretic continuum as a global telos. Even on the part of the adult Mother, it would be mistaken to regard the project of the infant's survival as a mediation between self-interest and altruism; it is closer to the model of symbiosis wherein the interests of the two organisms merge into ambiguity and indistinction.

This community of interest lived at the pre-thematic, pre-reflective level subtends the existential value of golden rule morality and constitutes a founding moment of ethics.[7] The thematic attribution of interests or desires like unto one's own to others at the reflective level, coupled with the pathos of respect for the self-interests of a self who is not oneself, forms the basis for the analogizing apperception or recognition that, in turn, founds ethical consciousness. Ethical consciousness is reflective, a relatively late acquisition that presupposes development of perspectival awareness or recognition of community across discrete individual bodies and their separate interests. The origin of this reflective awareness cannot be explained by appeal to analogy—which always begs the question of the ground of the identification it seeks to explain—because the analogy is itself founded upon the pathos of syncretism.[8]

Here, in my view, is the elusive truth of the Oedipal structure, a truth obscured by the two mistakes mentioned above and the symbolism that perpetuates those mistakes by concretizing Mother into an individualized imago. Mother is not Jocasta, not Mary, not Madonna: Mother is a diffuse and enveloping global presence from which individual personae emerge through a process of differentiation and psycho-physical maturation.

Here, also, is the equally elusive truth of Freud's controversial thesis of infantile sexuality. The infant-Mother-world syncretism is sensual. It is incipient sexuality: its sexual moment is present as a vague portent, but is not thematic. Sexuality proper requires a passage through the psycho-physical changes of puberty, and it is mistaken to read the resultant structures of thematic desire backward into infancy. It is just as mistaken to regard infant and Mother as dwelling in asexual intimacy. They dwell in a sensuous domain permeated with the primal qualities of pleasure and pain: milk and feces flow and ebb; bodies intertwine, separate, and come together again in a primal dance configured by uneasy desire driven by the mobile dialectic of primary and secondary processes. The pleasures of the nipple presuppose the pains of hunger, engorged breasts, and cellular level awareness of becoming, transience, approaching end.

Mother and infant must lose each other for the infant to find its self and Mother to retrieve her self; they must separate from each other in order to survive as mortal individuals. The germ of differentiation drives the entire process of gestation and informs the symbols of organic becoming, the symbols through which we conceive life-death-life, love-hate-love.

## MOTHER AND LOVE

How shall I pursue love if I am not capable of recognizing it? How shall I find my love if I am not capable of recognizing her? Freud tells us that our inchoate knowledge of love and its object is primordial and tragic: in the mode of self-deceptive repression we betray through denial what we cannot consciously acknowledge, that our desire is forlorn, destined to wistful mourning and neurotic displacement, barred from realization by biological necessity and the imperatives of culture. The tragedy is mitigated by renunciation, redirection, resignation, in a word, sublimation. Socrates, Christ, and Buddha are the world-historic symbols of the transcendence of eros in the direction of pure spirituality. Transcendence is possible by virtue of transference. Desire must be mobile, free to move from object to object, able to attach itself to different kinds of objects, capable of transforming itself as it ascends through the chakras, the stages of the cross, the levels of the divided line.

What is the magnet that attracts eros and draws it through phases of self-transcendence toward higher levels of self-realization? The appeal to which Socrates and his kindred archetypes responded is the finality of peace, the stilling of desire. The best among us move from union with Mother's flesh to union with Father's spirit. From non-self to self to non-self again. The goal is release: release from desire, release from flesh, release from *samsara,* the cycle of rebirth. Success or failure is determined by ethical categories: *arete* (excellence) and *sophrosyne* (temperance), redemption from sin, reduction of karmic debt. Oedipus goes willingly to his death, having paid the debt of his desire, illumined by its end, guided alone by his inner eye—leaving his sons to recapitulate the agony of his passion and pride, chaste Antigone alone being capable of discerning the inner truth of the death of the flesh.

This narrative is vindicated exclusively by the appeal of an afterworld founded upon the psychodynamics of fear and *ressentiment.* That is to say, it cannot be vindicated. Where does this leave love?

There is another appeal. This is the appeal of a fleshly other to be recognized in her otherness, and to be affirmed in the reversibility of flesh and the merging of its desire.

How shall I pursue love if I am not capable of recognizing it? How shall I find my love if I am not capable of recognizing her? If I recognize love in the mode of nostalgia for an immediate and unconditional fulfillment of all my desires, then I am in vain pursuit of a past that truly was never present, and my longing to recapitulate that infantile quality of experience is genuinely regressive. It is recognizable in my tantrums when my rights of absolute and exclusive possession are threatened, and equally recognizable in my boredom with the object possessed and secure. Yet, we are properly guided by reminiscence: it need not lead us into nostalgia or preconfigure desire as a compulsion to repeat.

Gestation is separation. It is division and formation of new unities. The passages of individual maturation are inevitably marked with the pain of transition. Mother expels me from her body, weans me from her breast, spurns the gift of my feces, and rejects me as a suitor. She educates me to self-sufficiency by withholding her nurture. She forces me to attenuate my demands and accommodate her own. She turns me toward the world, and leads the way out of the bower, distributing her care to my father, siblings, and other members of the community whose needs, demands, and offerings rival my own. She prepares me to balance immediate sensuous gratification with deliberate calculation and negotiation. As she withdraws from me, she becomes more distinctly herself and less an extension of my barely formulated wishes. Mother is an emergent agonist, the vehicle of the introduction of negativity—disappointment, refusal, retribution—into a world in which it had been no more than a heavy portent. Mother punishes me, uses violent means to enforce a will contrary to my own, thus enabling me to recognize my will as my own.

It is Mother who socializes me. Although she may invoke the name of the father, she does so for her own purposes, mediating the law through her own desire, which alone gives consistency to the pattern of exceptions. The period of latency is ill named by Freud—who also stresses the hypothesis of repression beyond credibility with the figures of castration. This is the period of initiation to the world, the third term of the syncretic triad that now defines itself and establishes its own autonomy with its peculiar systems of impartial rewards and punishments, pleasures and pains. Infantile desire is not so much repressed as it is articulated, thematized, and distributed among objects and persons, each bearing its own implacable logic of demands and offerings, which feeds back into the differentiation of desire.

Puberty extends infantile sensuality into thematic sexuality, which, in turn, introduces a new quality of reflection and alienation. Secondary sexual characteristics are public. They define the changeling as sexual in the eyes of a world in which sexuality has been demonized and imbued with shame. Shame is a disease of reflection: the adolescent learns to see herself through the alienated perspective of those who know her secret and regard it with an admixture of scorn and greasy prurience. This is when the narcissus flowers: challenged from the outside by the look of the other and undermined from within by the unwelcome changes distorting her familiar body, the identity of the changeling becomes her mania. Public and private personae develop and collide: she locks her door and grooms herself for and against scoptophilic appreciation and intrusion. Above all, she forms intense bonds around the axes of identification and betrayal. She acquires a perspective aware of itself as such, threatened and attracted by difference, longing for affirmation across the distance of otherness. She wants a friendly mirror in which to find herself. She wants friendly flesh through which to feel herself, to explore and exploit the powers and pleasures newly afforded her. She does not want to be hurt or violated or betrayed or defiled. Neither does he.

Do they want Mother? They do not want their mothers, the concrete maternal figures with proper names who overflow with admonition and sanctions. But they do want community, intersection of perspectives, a space where pathos is secure against the hostile and threatening other. Recognition of this space in the social topography of adolescence is guided by reminiscence. I can sense the resonances of community, recognize the perspective that intersects here and now with my own, experience the outside of my inside because I have dwelled in such a place in a previous lifetime. If I have not enjoyed the warmth of syncretism—or, rather, to the extent that I have not—I am lost, and the quest to find myself in the eyes of another, at best overwhelming, is undermined from within.

We do want Mother, need Mother. More accurately, we need the enabling that Motherdom has or has not nurtured within us in a prehistory faded beyond recall, but lingering on in the qualitative penumbra of our daylight hours. We need to be able to recognize love when it is present in ourselves and others, to discern within ourselves and others the marks of genuine pathos. This is the etiology of what Freud called the tender emotions. It is the horizon of care that binds community. It is the foundation of ethical consciousness, our primordial directedness toward reciprocity. It is also the engine of vengeance.

But . . . is this not a formula for nostalgia, compulsion to repeat, and regression to infantile modes of being-with? Is this not the source of demand, the insatiable quest for unconditional nurture, unqualified affection, undistracted attention? It can be and, perhaps, often is; but it need not be. The distinction needed here is provided by Freud in the array of concepts centering around fixation and unfinished business. Gestation is separation, and regression is the failure to depart on time. The issue is maturation, adjustment to the challenges and claims of otherness, acquisition of the reality principle as a way of living. What may be unfinished is the process of weaning, and the fixation is a refusal to relinquish the simple pleasures of infancy and take on the complex pleasure-pain of loving others differentiated from oneself. Ethical consciousness is not only the recognition of genuine care; it also involves reciprocation, even initiation, of care.

The uninterpreted half of the Oedipus story is Jocasta's wounding and abandonment of her son for the sake of her own self-interest, an act as extreme, excessive, and destructive as her welcome of the young, limping, regal champion into her bed. In both cases, she should have known better. The good Mother is absent from this scene. Oedipus was not weaned with care, and he recapitulates the excesses of his infancy in his manhood. At the end of the Theban trilogy, Oedipus is finally vindicated by his gentle transition out of his body into death, not because it is a passage to pure spirituality, but because it is emblematic of his growing ability to deal appropriately with the transcendent reality revealed through his relentless quest for truth. The truth of Oedipus does not lie in the story of a universal longing for Mother; it resides in the story of a noble and painful recovery from a wretched childhood.

In my reading, the story of Mary's son is tragedy unmitigated by self-transcendence: the infant of the virgin, the product of immaculate conception, dies into assimilation by Father never having known woman, never having reciprocated the touch of that other. Infinite, disembodied wisdom treated this preadolescent androgyne as badly as Socrates treated Alcibiades, and for the same reason: denial of embodiment as ground of morality. It is this denial that constitutes the wretched childhood of Western civilization.

## LOVE-HATE

What of the sexual dimension of ethical consciousness and care?

The first thing to be said is that sexuality is intrinsically charged with value: desire essentially informs good and bad. The classical denial reaffirms the truth. "All is fair in love and war." Fairness is at issue from the start. The statement is true for infantile consciousness, the consciousness that saturates our history of both love and war. It simply condenses the thesis of infantile sadism, the will to master the frisson-producing presence, a pervasive will oblivious to otherness and separate amscans[9] informed by pathos it has not yet learned to perceive.

Thematic sexuality is a differentiation of infantile sensuality that does not exist for itself before puberty. When, during adolescence, it does emerge with the evolution of reflection, shame, and the capacity for cataclysmic organ-pleasure, it emerges into a context permeated with the Hegelian quest for recognition and identity; it is configured, one way or another, as much by that context as by the somatic context established by the flow of hormones and the intense pleasure potential of the maturing genitals.

Freud argued that, during puberty, polymorphous pleasures consolidate in the genitals and unify under the telos of reproduction. I think he was led astray by unexamined presuppositions derived from theistic natural law theory, but was nonetheless in touch with a fundamental truth, the truth that it is definitive of consciousness to unify its themes while attending away from the horizons that encompass and inform them. My thesis is that the thematic genitally focused sexuality that emerges at adolescence emerges within a horizon structured by the quest for affirmative recognition of identity, a quest that supervenes and encompasses any latent impetus toward reproduction (or contribution to gene pool) as it encompasses and informs the overt project of pleasure seeking. In a word, sexual desire, when it emerges as such, is incorporated within the project of love, which has been gestating from the start: it is not mere coincidence that, through mutual reinforcement, the two entelechies converge, actualize, and peak at the same time.

This analysis of affirmative recognition would be incomplete and potentially misleading if I failed to take up its correlate, the dark side of sexlove, and consider its relation to ethical consciousness. Ethical consciousness is pathos for the other. The proper metaphor is reversibility rather than unification: reversibility preserves identity and difference, but allows for transference, reciprocity, corporeal empathy. I can feel your pleasures and pains through the reversibility of flesh, feel them at the level of fleshly sentience rather than infer them analogically. I am attuned to this from the start by the imprinting of the primordial syncretic experience. I am vulnerable to your pathos: my identity feeds on it and nurtures it. I can open myself to this experience or erect defenses against it. These options are not exclusive: the fact that we are encased in separate gloves of skin that simultaneously keep us apart and allow us to touch each other opens a continuum of modes of intercorporeity—of proximity and distance, vulnerability and defense, cathexis and anti-cathexis, openness and closure—bounded by the limiting points of unification and oblivious indifference.

Mother taught me sensuous intimacy and pleasure. Mother taught me rejection and pain. The world reinforced these lessons. Freud was correct in holding that hate is an externalization of pain. Beyond that, however, hate is the externalization of bad: it is the projection of moral negativity upon a proximal other. I neither hate nor love across the distance of utter ignorance of the other's existence. The intensity of love and hate is directly proportional to degree of intimacy, and intimacy always portends both. The child who throws a tantrum in the supermarket and screams its hatred of Mother for all the world to hear is at the same time proclaiming its love. Astute mothers hear it that way. And astute mothers also hear the proclamation of love following the gift of the brightly wrapped candy bar desperately sought as a genuine, but highly conditioned, expression of sentiment: denial might have evoked rage. Infants are like that.

And so are infantile adults. It was William Congreve who wrote at the turn of the eighteenth century that

> Heav'n has no rage, like love to hatred turn'd,
> Nor Hell a fury, like a woman scorn'd.[10]

At the end of the twentieth century, O. J. Simpson lifted Congreve's sexist bias. The general truth is that vulnerability produces lability. The defenses dropped in the glorious moment of declaration that ends the pain of isolation do not dissolve, but recede like a virus to sally forth renewed when my own true love betrays my faith, just as my best friend did in high school. The more she was ensconced in my world, the more pervasive her scent in the furniture of my life, the more her absence radiates from my field of presence, and the more I lament her passage through my days. The retrospective anti-cathexis is intensified by shock and surprise, as Freud discovered, and in the erotic domain it takes the form of an iterated compulsion to blame.

When erstwhile lovers, embittered by betrayal, come together to negotiate possession of children and communal property, the items on the table quickly become fetishes for lost self-esteem. I can relinquish the pleasures of her body when her eyes harden and mirror disgust where *lust* once beamed, but I cannot forsake the self I once sought in those eyes. The project of retrieval is determined by moral categories: I want, above all, to have been good and right and decent. I want it all to have been her fault.

If, as Freud suggested, my penis is my alter ego, the fetish of my identity, then to sheath another where I came into my own, is to cut me off from myself. It is not only from Father that my fears of castration are born. Father does foreshadow my own inevitable demise: that is the truth of the phallic plays recapitulated in the myth of Cronos and Ouranos. I am, if anything, even more fearful of the one I love.

As Hillary Clinton knows, with her man's women spread all over front pages and centerfolds, self-esteem does not consolidate exclusively in the penis or its symbolic extension. Castration is a false concretion, another residue of Freud's penchant to condense a horizon within an overdetermined symbolic theme. The fact is that, when we love, we love with our whole selves, that love regularly survives the wilting of the penis, that the phallic alter ego is properly a transient phenomenon of adolescence, in short, that it is not loss of a body part that we fear when we give ourselves over to love: it is the threat to the totality of our being, the real threat of ontological rejection, that produces hatred and its derivatives (jealousy, deceit, battery, spite, etc.).

The possibility of rejection gives meaning to acceptance as the possibility of negation valorizes affirmation. The promise to love is a wistful reminder that desire and its demise transcend volition; it is an incantation against the precarious nature of love, an appeal to magic to secure our love against the vagaries of fate. As our sleeping bodies monitor the world with the goal of prolonging sleep against disturbance ambivalently coupled with vigilance to awaken to danger, so do our loving bodies monitor each other's behavior with a vigilance that cannot be suspended. Freud's own logic forced him to concede that ego- and sex-instincts cannot be conceived in isolation from each other: the reality principle forces mature lovers to acknowledge and compensate for the conditions beyond their control that govern their erotic fate. This is the difference between infantile syncretism and the mature love of separate identities whose affinities reinforce each other by virtue, not in spite, of the separation that grants them individuality.

Freud was uneasy about asserting an isomorphism between the capacity of an instinct to reverse into its opposite apparent in the vicissitudes of sadism-masochism and scoptophilia-exhibitionism, on the one hand, and love-hate, on the other. The binary terms—activity-passivity, self-other, inner-outer—that seem to map so cleanly onto the first two pairs of opposites, do not accommodate the love-hate-indifference structure so easily. The reason for this should now be apparent: in love, the self-other relation is not a binary relation of mutual exclusion.[11] Alterity operates in the gestation of the self defining itself through the intimate alienation of reflection. And that alterity is derivative upon the alterity of the other's look, which sets the process of reflection and self-identification in motion.

The self that is generated through the reflective process is mediated through the other's desire, to be sure, but that is only half the story—and to leap from that half truth to the Lacanian conclusion that all sense of individual selfhood is mystification or *méconnaissance* is itself a mystified understanding. The other half of the truth is that the self of the other's desire never entirely fits me. I may be drawn to fulfill the other's desire, may work at that project in varying degrees of deliberation and conscious awareness, but that very effort presupposes an awareness of difference between the self I sense myself to be and the self that I would have to be to fulfill the other's desire. The foundation of both the selves in question is my body, and its malleability to desire has limits.[12] I may reject the persona projected upon me by the other's desire. The pathos of ethical consciousness, incipient in the syncretic phase and problematized during adolescence, demands mutual recognition in a dialectical process that, unlike Hegel's, involves a positivity grounded in our bodies and the world we inhabit. Mother's elbow, from some angles, may resemble her breast, but it will not give milk. And I must eventually learn that the gift of my feces may smell like shit to mom.

Love and hate are not, therefore, distinct and mutually exclusive structures; it is rather the case that they mark the positive and negative limits of a continuum of care in which the possibility of rejection always haunts the ontological assurance of affirmation. The proper term to employ here is not ambivalence—it is pathological excess to will the destruction of the love object—the proper term is ambiguity: to be the source of my affirmation is also and necessarily to be the potential source of my despair. It is intrinsic to life to end, and the same is true of love: both life and love, as phenomena of becoming, incorporate an awareness of transience. Freud defined hate as externalization and alienation. A more encompassing definition would see externalization and alienation as but two strategies in the more encompassing project of self-preservation.

As I have argued throughout this work, it is mistaken to conceive love under the figures of union and loss of individual identity: the separation of our bodies entails a separation of selves that, far from being overcome in love, is a necessary condition for it. We cannot live without our discrete bodies, nor can we love without them. The death of your body may herald the end of my life, even though I survive your death physically. Among elderly couples, the death of one frequently marks the beginning of the decline of the other because the most important ground for the affirmation of life has been taken away. But it is also true that all the other grounds for affirming life remain, that the organism is imbued with a will to live that protects itself against the threat of the loss, through death or rejection, of the beloved.

Were love separate and distinct from hate, mating rituals would not be rife with circumspection and vigilance. The phases of affirmation, declaration, and commitment are always interspersed with moments of testing, withdrawal, and challenge. The latter betray our awareness of love's potential for damage. A slight is magnified out of proportion because its portent is heavy. If you were late in arriving, if you made a gesture of affection toward another, if you forgot to call when you said you would, my reaction is typically an order of magnitude greater than the short term effect of that event in my world. A minor inconvenience and I am livid. My anger is a measure of my fear that your disservice signifies a disparity between us in degree of affection or commitment. In heterosexual relationships, this problem is compounded by differences in perspective based on differences in the way sex roles and physiological structures intertwine. For example, the post-coital male is sometimes wont to suffer attenuation of interest and affection when his female counterpart wants gestures of the opposite sort.

The early phases of mate selection are intense and mercurial. They test the ability of the lovers to respond appropriately to real and imagined threats arising from differences in perspective. The differences in perspective will never disappear, that is a false promise of the unification models of love, but what may develop among successful couples is a growing ability to tolerate, understand, and even to affirm the alterity upon which the affirmations of love depend. It is your difference from me that endows your affirmation with weight and gives me what I could never provide for myself, a vision from the outside. There is no way to eliminate the dark side of the alterity upon which love depends.

Mother guides us in learning how to respond to alterity in a series of distancing events: birth itself, then weaning, then toilet training and discipline in general, then all the gestures that nudge us from the nest out into the world. At her best, Mother prepares us for mature love; she does not beckon us back to oceanic engulfment. We do not seek to find her in a mate, just because she never was the model of an individual mate. By the time she becomes an individual, she is no longer primordial Mother. For the developing individual, each new love is truly the first love. One never knows whether he or she will be our last love, but that is always our hope.

## FAMILIARITY AND TRANSCENDENCE

The dark side of alterity is inseparable from its bright side. Alterity is transcendence and transcendence is bivalent: what I do not know of the other both attracts and repels me. We have seen that it is the otherness of the other, the fact that she embodies a perspective that does not coincide with my own, that nurtures my quest for self-transcendence: I want to vindicate my being in those eyes that see me as I cannot see myself. We have also seen that the look of affirmation can change into the scorn of rejection, that there is negative as well as positive recognition. What has not yet been developed is the category of indifference.

I espouse the Heideggerian thesis that care is general, that it is impossible not to care about the persons and events that touch one's life, that to deny one cares is typically just that, denial. True indifference can only be founded upon ignorance (or, again, some pathology). Statistics of one kind or another inform me that, somewhere in the world, a child is molested or dies of malnutrition or consumes some life-threatening substance for the first time every so many minutes. If it happens within my sphere, I care. If it happens in some place that is merely a global location to me, my ignorance fosters indifference and my concern is abstract. How, then, could indifference be a psychic posture relevant to the intimate domain of sexlove?

Among the axes that structure the domain of intimacy, the one that is relevant here is the axis of intensity-familiarity. As we have seen, familiarity is a threat to romantic love because it erodes the barriers necessary to maintain the fantasy and sustain the intensity of desire. If, through the inroads of intimate contact, the veils fall away and I see you in the flesh, if your unveiled body becomes a familiar object in the space I occupy, if your stories have been told and retold, if your penchants and perversities have worn lines demarcating danger areas in our communal space that I have learned to avoid automatically, then—at the very best—the steps of our dance through life are sure-footed, synchronized, safe, and serene. We don't step on each other's toes, but the blaze has burned out of the tango.

The counterthesis has also been presented. The more rigid and confining the barriers, the smaller the space enclosed, the more stifling it becomes inside. If the faces milady turns to me are invariably coy, if macho man remains forever distant and aloof, their repertoires are quickly exhausted: repetition and boredom are sure to ensue.

Familiarity kills romance. The novelty-preserving barriers also kill romance. Either way, it dies. This is but another variation of the dilemma of romantic transcendence, another articulation of its essential frailty.

The truth of romance, obscured by its misconception of genuine transcendence, is that Salome's allure does not reside in her veils; if she were ugly and repellent, like a Gorgon, we would want her to keep her veils and remain hidden. But when Salome dances, we anticipate the moment of unveiling: the frisson is in the fresh revelation of her beauty. The truth that romance fails to exploit is that Salome has—or could have—indefinitely more than seven

veils, that beauty, the object of desire, has nothing to fear from revelation because there is always more to show.

As temporal beings, we are ever-changing, always transcending ourselves
toward an emergent identity. Self-transcendence is a fact of life; it becomes a
challenge, however, when we consider the dimension of value, the better and
the worse. Birth-growth-reproduction-decay-death: does the cycle of becoming entail degeneration? Does life necessarily terminate in corruption?
Plato, as we have seen, is ambivalent on this point. The body decays and must
be discarded like rubbish. Hence, we are not our bodies, but the spirit that
dwells temporarily within and seeks release to reach its perfection. The horror
of becoming is that flesh inevitably decays. And yet the portrait of the dying
Socrates Plato presents in the *Phaedo* is not a picture of corruption, but one of
nobility. Plato defines courage as knowing what to fear, and he tells us that
what we should fear is not death, but shame. Shame is our response to having
performed an ignoble deed. Nobody can force us to behave in an ignoble way
if we would truly rather die. That is the point—or at least one of them—of
Plato's portrait of the dying Socrates.

Does one need to posit an immortal soul to explain Socrates' courageous
and noble death? Or can one's last act, like the last act of Oedipus, be the fin-
ishing touch in a life of self-transcendence which has no sequel in an afterlife?
My standpoint on this has already been adequately articulated: the vindication of life lies within life; to appeal beyond it is to tell oneself a lie that, as
such, cannot be noble. Or effective. The shift in thinking called for here is to
understand aging as an open-ended process of growth rather than one that
peaks qualitatively in late adolescence and then enters a protracted period of
decay. If one regards the mind as a bodily phenomenon, it is not clear that the
last phases of life are qualitatively the least. Swimmers and skaters may peak in
their teens; politicians, money makers, artists, and scholars do not. Nor, I
think, do human beings in general.

Self-transcendence is a fact, but it may be vectored up or down. If beauty
is the object of desire, if beauty is best understood in terms of nobility (το
καλου), and if there is no limit to human endeavor in that direction, then one
need not fear that revelation of the emergent self necessarily results in the
familiarity that breeds contempt. Indeed, the familiarity that poses a threat
to love is not a product of overexposure, it is the result of a failure to see that
stems from taking persons and things for granted. To take a person for granted
is to see that person through the lens of a habitual constellation of meanings formed in the past, informed by our own needs, and reinforced by

unawareness of itself. It is a way of not seeing, a tacit insistence on reducing another person to a convenient set of categories. When those who matter to us change, it is unsettling: in general, we prefer the comfort of familiarity to the discomfort of adjusting our perceptions to the new reality and making correlative changes in our typical patterns of response. We send our spouses off to therapy in hopes that they will return fixed, restored to the norms that fulfill our unthematized expectations. When they return engaged in a process of self-transformation that demands recognition and readjustment on our part, we feel betrayed. What has been betrayed, in fact, is a taken for granted structure of ritualized coexistence that has gone stale. The familiarity that breeds contempt is but an extension of the same structure of projection and fixation on immanent categories, the same structure of not knowing the other, that operates in romantic love.

Mother—and Father, too—are familiar persons, but with them the structures of familiarity work differently. We ought to be able to take them for granted, and to foster that security is one of their obligations. The child's knowledge of its parents is intimate but not, as I have argued, the carnal knowledge of intertwining. There is an asymmetry: the measure of equality that applies to erotic lovers and friends does not apply here. Parenting has its rewards, but it is essentially altruistic, even self-sacrificial, and increasingly so as we move further away from an agrarian culture, when children no longer play a positive role in the family economy. Transcendence and self-transcendence play a major role in the child's relation to its parents, to be sure; they are our original teachers, mentors, therapists, and judges who work to foster our growth toward maturity. This teaching and nurturing, however, presupposes a distance, an inequality in range and quality of experience: they are supposed to know more; they are supposed to model a quality of behavior we seek to emulate but cannot, at any given moment, be expected to match. I can begin genuinely to know, appreciate, and respect my parents as parents only when I have struggled through the ordeals of rearing my own children. My knowledge is, thus, intrinsically retrospective. It is a sad fact of becoming that I typically cannot convey to my parents, because they have already died, the understanding of the magnitude (or, in negative cases, the poverty) of their generosity that comes upon me as I look to their example to guide me with my own progeny along paths my parents walked before me.

Mother is, therefore, not the sex object that Freud said she is.[13] She is not a sex object for the structural reasons grounded in the nature of human existence, the biology of reproduction, the psychology of nurturing, and the sociology of basic family life. Father may be jealous of her time and affection, but he and I are not rivals in the erotic dimension. His desire and mine are configured differently. This should become increasingly apparent in the next chapter when we take up the question of what a sex object is, and develop the notion of carnal knowledge along lines yet to be explored.

# EIGHT

# SEX OBJECTS
# AND SEXUAL OBJECTIFICATION

## DEMONIZATION AND DECONTEXTUALIZATION

### THE PROBLEM OF OBJECTIFICATION

THE PROBLEM ADDRESSED is that of ambivalence in contemporary treatments of erotic interest. If one person is the object of another's desire, has the first person been objectified by the second? Does sexual interest entail sexual objectification? Is sexual objectification intrinsically degrading? If all erotic interest involves objectification of some kind, is it therefore intrinsically degrading in some way?

There are two separate and conflicting discourses concerning sexual objectification on the contemporary scene. The first originated with Freud and was revised by Lacan. In this discourse, sexual desire is conceived as object-oriented. As Freud conceived it, libidinal energy can be invested either in the ego (narcissism) or in another object, but, in either case, desire is a transitive relation that is necessarily object-directed. When Lacan takes up the object relation, he conceives it as intrinsically susceptible to *méconnaissance*[1]—which I interpret as a form of reflexive mystification that arises from the internalization of projections—but still conceives it as an *object* relation.

The other discourse is one in which objectification is taken as an undesirable characteristic of some forms of sexual interest. To be a sex object in this discourse is to be mistreated; the mistreatment consists in being reduced from human to object. Expressed in the terms made famous by Martin Buber, the point here is that sexual interest in "I-It" relations involves objectification and is undesirable, whereas sexual interest in "I-Thou" relations is preferable because it does not involve objectification. "I-It" relations are subject-object relations, and "I-Thou" relations are subject-subject relations.

There is a theoretical problem created by these two discourses. In one discourse, objectification is deemed essential to desire. In the other discourse, objectification is deemed deleterious to desire. This problem is not immediately solved by the distinction between subject-object relations and subject-subject relations. In subject-subject relations involving two persons, there is a principle of otherness or transcendence that separates the two subjects:[2] in some way, the desiring subject is different from or other than the desired subject. In traditional terms, if I desire you, then I am not you. And if I am a subject for myself, then you must be an object for me. Not necessarily an "it," maybe a "thou," but in no case are you the subject for me that I am for myself.[3]

The question is then how one can acknowledge that sexual desire presupposes objectification, but still maintain that objectification is a negative that should be overcome. Clearly, some way must be found to distinguish between kinds of objectification. And this distinction must be one that has practical application: it must allow us to discern concretely sexual practices that objectify in a degrading way from sexual practices that necessarily involve objectification but do not degrade. If this distinction cannot be made, then objectification cannot be used as a measure of sexual degradation. Thus, Sartre, for whom all concrete relations among human beings involves the objectification of "the look," is committed to an abject pessimism: there is no possible erotic interaction that is not founded on the dialectic of a sado-masochistic struggle for domination.

This question is crucial in many issues now engendering fierce controversy. The focus here is the debate concerning pornographic versus erotic depiction of sexual activity. Any depiction of a person involves objectification: the graphic or verbal representation is an object, not a person. But some depictions arouse ire simply because they are held to be objectifications (e.g., the depictions in magazines such as *Playboy* and *Penthouse,* the depictions in most, if not all, X-rated films, the depictions in hardcore literature, etc.); and other depictions are taken by most to be benign even though they necessarily objectify (e.g., the depictions in classical painting, the depictions in films by directors such as Ingmar Bergman, the depictions in literature by Lawrence, Joyce, Nin, etc.). If we knew what we meant by "objectification," we might be able to be more articulate about what we find objectionable.

There are several ways of understanding sexual objectification. As the term itself suggests, there is a root problem in all the psychological, epistemological, and axiological accounts of objectification: that is the problem of understanding how the object of sexual interest can be more than an object, i.e., how the object that arouses desire can be experienced also as a subject, as a person. This root problem is an ontological problem, a problem of the ontology taken for granted in most contemporary theorizing in which the only subject one can genuinely experience as a subject is oneself. Since Kant, it has been a commonplace in the discourse of morality that one should treat other human beings as subjects and not merely as objects, but our Cartesian heritage does not allow us to conceive how this is possible at the theoretical level, or understand how to achieve it at the practical level.

This chapter is an attempt to translate ontology into practice. In other published work,[4] I have addressed the problem of objectification and set forth an ontology that makes it possible to conceive human relations in terms other than subjectivity and objectivity. It is a matter of thinking of human relations in terms of bodies rather than consciousnesses. If one understands sexual interest at the level of corporeal intentionality, the way is opened to understand what has hitherto been designated as sex object in another way, i.e., as a desired body.

In the discourse of traditional ontology, the depiction of persons intrinsically involves reduction. To be a person is conceived as being essentially a consciousness or soul that accidentally inhabits a body. But only bodies can be depicted. To depict the body is necessarily to omit the soul, hence objectification (rendering the body-soul composite as only body) is reduction and debasement: the essential and noble element is necessarily left out.

In my discourse, the depiction of a body in such a way as to manifest its desirability does not necessarily entail reduction. If a person *is* a living body, then to depict the person as such is not to debase that person.

Once the objectification intrinsic to depiction is neutralized, the question of modes of objectification can be addressed. What kinds of objectification are held to be debasing, and why are they regarded in this way?

## CONTEXTUAL IMPOVERISHMENT: THE CASE OF *DEEP THROAT*

My contribution to this debate centers on the notion of contextual impoverishment. I maintain that the distinction between the "objectification" of pornographic depiction and the "beauty" of erotic depiction can be understood as a difference in degree between the unidimensional enframing of one treatment and the multidimensional enframing of the other. This treatment of the phenomenon of context can then be extended to include the anticipations of the participating witness: the object of pornographic or erotic depiction cannot be isolated from the posture, situation, and desire of the person participating in the revelation as its witness.

Gerard Damiano's film, *Deep Throat,* achieved a level of notoriety that led to its being viewed by many people who do not typically select X-rated films as a source of entertainment. I have chosen it as my primary example because I think few would contest classifying it as hardcore pornography, and because I hope its notoriety maximizes the chance that those I am addressing here will have seen it or, at least, heard something about its content.

The film opens with credits running while Linda Lovelace drives toward the home she shares with a female friend. When the credits finish, she enters the house and announces her presence to Helen, her roommate. Helen calls from the kitchen, "Honey, I'm in here." The camera follows Linda into the kitchen. From the doorway we see from Linda's perspective. Helen is seated on a countertop, legs wide apart, nude from the waist down. A man seated on a stool in front of her is engaged in cunnilingus. Helen asks Linda for a cigarette and, in the process of lighting it, asks the man whether he minds if she smokes while he is eating.

Decontextualization is apparent in several aspects of this scene. The most striking is the visual shock of the sexually explicit scene in the kitchen—for which the viewer has had no preparation. In this, as in most of the sexually explicit scenes throughout the film, there is no depiction of courtship or even negotiation. The viewer is confronted with a variety of sex acts without introduction to the characters involved, their relationship, or the circumstances surrounding their sexual engagement. The names of most of the males are never mentioned. In fact, in the next explicit scene, the men are identified by numbers rather than names.

Decontextualization is also practiced in the framing of the sexually explicit shots. During these scenes, the camera spends most of its time focused on genital areas or the women's breasts. There are facial shots to register the pleasure or passion of the actors, but relatively few portraits integrating the genitals of the players with the rest of their bodies. In general, the roles played are anatomical, and the anatomies presented are fragmented. By contrast, the transitional scenes, which function to carry whatever there is in the way of story line or dramatic development, are filmed in traditional ways. Since it is the purpose of these scenes to provide context, they reveal character through the gestural language of integrated bodies.

In *Deep Throat,* as in most X-rated films, the sound track of the explicit scenes is frequently dubbed over with music. There is little in the way of dialogue apart from the groans, moans, and ejaculations associated with both the genre and the activities depicted. When words are spoken, they are highly conventionalized ritual phrases—"I love it."

The story line of *Deep Throat* is archetypal. The kore,[5] a princess figure defined by youth, beauty, dissatisfaction, and unspecified yearning, is courted by a host of suitors. She tests them for their ability to provide the unknown element that will fulfill her desire. Each is rejected, despite the magnitude of his offering, and the princess descends into the dark night of despair. She seeks guidance and finds it in the person of a doctor, the archetypal old man or sage possessed of esoteric learning, who discovers the nature of her desire and reveals it to her. He initiates her, and she is transformed, reborn in a festival of light. The wise man, however, cannot be her prince: he is too old and he bears the stigma of the one who took her innocence.[6] Linda must find her own consort, and this man must prove himself in a trial that brings about his own transformation and awakening. The male ugly duckling makes the transition to princely swan when he and Linda make the mutual discovery that his unwieldy sword fits her sheath. Ecstasy ensues.

This is a romantic story that has been exploited by everyone from Hesiod to Hollywood and all the intervening troubadours. It verges on kitsch just because it trades on our prescience that the obstacles to happiness will be overcome.

The power relations in the story are clear. The locus of power resides in the kore's locked and hidden treasure, her undiscovered ability to produce pleasure in herself and an appropriate mate. She is the locus of power, but the power or manna initially masters her. The male figures are also in service to this manna, and must discover their own powers of wisdom and swordsmanship by penetrating the darkness and breaking the lock. The sage remains relatively unchanged, but is saddened by the necessity of relinquishing his discovery. Princess and prince awaken into conscious awareness and increased mastery of the power that resides within them.

One might argue that the kore figure loses her power in the moment of its revelation, and that the power of the prince's sword augments. Or one might argue that the fecundity of the queen mother commands the service of the sword. Leaving moot the question of the sequel, I think it is incontestable that, within the moment framed by the story, the awakened, but as yet unsatisfied, princess controls her suitors by her power of selection. It would be different if she were raped of that power, but that is another story, not the story of *Deep Throat*.

A pretty, satisfying story. Controlled by the pleasure of the princess. Yet regarded as demeaning to Linda Lovelace. Why?

In her autobiography, Linda Lovelace argues that she was forced to perform acts of fellatio that were distasteful to her, not at all pleasurable. She says, in effect, that she was deceived, raped, and deprived of her fair share of revenue. So far as I know, these allegations have not been tested in a court of law. If they are true, then I think the criminals responsible deserve the penalties prescribed by law. But this issue does not bear on the question of erotic versus pornographic depiction. In the film, she convincingly projects pleasure.

The title of the film refers to a kind of fellatio in which the glans of the penis passes through the epiglottis. I find it difficult to believe that this could produce anything but nausea in the person performing the act. This physiological aspect is, I think, relevant to the debate, but not decisive. In the story, there is a symbolic transformation in which Linda Lovelace's throat becomes the archetypal hymen. Depending upon physiological circumstance, the rupturing of the hymen is more or less painful, but pain intermixed with pleasure, and optimally disappearing altogether. I am inclined to question the legitimacy of the symbolic equation on physiological grounds, but am confounded by the issue of masochistic pleasure. The premise of the depiction is that performing fellatio in the manner of deep throat is ecstatically pleasurable for Linda Lovelace. There is convincing evidence that some people take pleasure in acts I would find painful.

So far, the argument has focused on the depiction, leaving the viewer in the background. Even if one limits consideration to male viewers eighteen and over, diversities of all kinds compound with shifting attitudes and interests to produce a confusing array of possibilities. I will address the question of prurience, and bracket questions of arrested development, latent or overt aggression, and pathological forms of scoptophilia, transference neurosis, obsession, etc.

## OBJECTIFICATION AS A NEGATION OF DESIRE

In his discussion of obscenity, Sartre makes two points that are relevant here. The first is that "the obscene appears when the body adopts postures which entirely strip it of its acts and which reveal the inertia of its flesh." This is flesh stripped of intentionality, such as "certain involuntary waddlings of the rump." He describes this as a phenomenon in which flesh is isolated from its human meaning or purposiveness and reduced to "an unjustifiable facticity." In other words, the reification and objectification I have attributed to decontextualization. Sartre's term is "isolation." But this is on the side of the spectacle.

Sartre's second point has to do with the spectator.

> Revealed flesh is specifically obscene when it is revealed to someone who is not in a state of desire and without exciting his desire.[7]

If prurient interest is a form of desire, then Sartre's contention is that prurience negates obscenity rather than engenders it. This is a prima facie reversal of popular sentiment, hence worthy of consideration.

Sartre has already defined the object of desire as a body *"in situation."* The situated body is an "organic totality which is . . . desirable only insofar as it reveals not only life but also an appropriate consciousness."[8] In my terms, the object of desire is a person revealed in the rich context of human attributes, projects, values, beliefs, etc., including his or her own desires. Here is Sartre's definition:

> A living body as an organic totality in situation with consciousness at the horizon: Such is the object to which desire *is addressed.*

Sartre's account of desire culminates in a dreary cycle of sado–masochistic reversals because the very attempt to possess the desired object reduces it to an object deprived of consciousness and freedom. This is where I depart from Sartre: his pessimism stems from a dialectic of possession coupled with an ontological bifurcation of flesh into mutually exclusive elements of body and spirit.[9] But we agree that the object of desire is a person: a human body specified by context.

Following this line of reasoning, Linda Lovelace, as depicted in *Deep Throat,* is reified or "objectified," not so much by the prurient spectator who takes himself in hand because he can't touch her, as by the detached judge who witnesses her performance from the standpoint of neutralized or alien sexual motivation. Here the empirical evidence is overwhelming: charges of objectification and obscenity originate from the pulpit, the courtroom, and the outrage of feminists who see no beauty in X-rated films.

If, as Plato argued, beauty is the object of desire, then there is no beauty where there is no desire. Kant argued just the opposite: if there is interest, especially erotic interest, then there is pathology, but not beauty. I cannot settle this debate here, but I can point out the latent agreement between Plato and Kant: to objectify by decontextualization is to neutralize desire. They just have differing opinions about what to affirm with the honorific term "beauty," that is, whether it is good or bad to objectify.[10]

It is, perhaps, worthwhile to note in passing that women who make their living by taking their clothes off in front of male audiences are reported as unanimously and enthusiastically siding with Plato on this issue: they would rather strip in a bar than in a church, courtroom, or conference room.

There is a paradox in all this that may be illuminating. I argued first that the depictions of human sexuality generally taken as pornographic and demeaning because they objectify invite this criticism because they decontextualize. Fewer people are offended by *Basic Instinct* than by *Deep Throat,* and I would contend that this is in part due to the fact that the psychological structures of the sex object in one film were thematically questioned and scrutinized, whereas in the other they were largely ignored.

My second sequence of arguments tried to show that the disengagement of the spectator constitutes another kind of objectification or decontextualization that impoverishes the spectacle by neutralizing or alienating the desire that is its proper medium.

The paradox is that the depictions of sexuality at issue manifest an inner contradiction: in decontextualizing the sex object, they subvert their own purpose of trading on desire.

The paradox is that those who take offense at the objectification of sex make sex offensive by objectifying it.

What is illuminating about this paradox?

Contextualization humanizes. In traditional terms, to provide rich human context for sexual depictions is to present the sex object as a subject. Degrees of contextualization thus describe a spectrum from objectifying pornography to erotic depictions of sexual human subjects.[11]

The issue of contextualization is gender-neutral, at least on the side of the spectacle: crude pornography is egalitarian to the extent that it decontextualizes both men and women. On the side of the spectator, the empirical evidence seems to support a claim that male audiences will tolerate decontextualization more readily than female audiences. The main difference between standard X-rated fare and the films designed by women to engage female as well as male audiences is, for the most part, a difference of contextualization.[12]

I have heard it argued that male audiences not only tolerate but actually prefer decontextualized depictions. That may or may not be the case: it would be difficult to prove the point either way given the diversity of male perspectives and the paucity of erotic production to compare in popularity with the pornography that abounds. I do not know, but would surmise, that *Basic Instinct* attracted more male viewers than *Deep Throat*.

The point that can be established, however, is that the objectifying regard of those who judge all explicit sexual depiction, regardless of artistic merit and degree of contextualization, to be obscene and degrading has the character of self-fulfillment: to alienate one's own sexual response or prefigure it in a negative way is, ipso facto, to reduce erotic depiction to pornography.[13] Why would anyone claim that *any* explicit depiction of sexual activity is necessarily obscene and degrading?

The case can be made that depicting sexual acts is degrading, even when engaging in them is not, because the depiction violates the privacy of those engaged, or introduces a third perspective which corrupts the primal reproductive dyad. But that argument seldom appears.[14]

I can think of no other instance where the performance of an act is celebrated as potentially beautiful but its depiction is regarded in all instances as obscene and degrading. This leads me to wonder whether the animus expressed in the condemnation is not really an animus against sexual activity itself. I will take up the issue of the demonization of sex in a later phase of the argument. At this point I want to pursue the question of reduction by objectification and press the issue of the debasement held to result from decontextualization or the reduction of human spirit to flesh.

## REFLECTIVE DISTANTIATION

I have argued that it is an ontological mistake to bifurcate human existence into mutually exclusive realms of mind and body or spirit and flesh, and that this mistaken bifurcation is the result of uncritical acceptance of the Cartesian dualism that still functions as the latent framework of our thinking and valuing. The positive thesis I have put forward is that human flesh is permeated with human spirit, that the two are inseparable, hence, that to portray the body is to depict the mind or soul, as well.

At the level of prereflective engagement—which is the level congenial to the ecstasy sought both in interpersonal sexual relations and in solitary pleasure seeking—we live in our bodies without alienation or distantiation: our bodies fulfill the intentions they generate with a grace that can approach harmony. As the kite flies from the body of a martial artist who senses an imminent opening in his opponent's defenses, so does a caress reach out to adore the flesh intertwined with it. In the case of both gestures, the distinction between initiation and response is no longer sharp: there is an evocation that is not sequentially ordered in the manner of stimulus to deliberation to action; instead, there is an unfolding of corporeal intentionality that flows with the surges of the emergent situation in which it is enveloped. Merleau-Ponty describes this level of prereflective engagement as anonymous, as not inhabited by the discrete personal identity that arises with reflection and the alienating Cartesian cogito. We live the agon of combat or of sexlove in the midst of Dionysian transport, before or beyond the categories of the *principium individuationis.*

Just as the martial artist or athlete or dancer has to train deliberately in order to approach the level of harmonious fulfillment of corporeal intention, so do lovers have to learn to love spontaneously, to transcend the forms of alienation that inform mundane social praxis: one typically avoids expression of sexual interest in casual social encounters, and attempts to arouse sexual excitation are usually veiled.[15] Kierkegaard argued, against Hegel, that it is impossible for reflection to turn itself off, to achieve immediacy through the mediation of thought. And Western critics of Eastern thought often point to the paradoxes inherent in willing not to will or in the personal project of transcending ego involvement. Yet Heidegger has shown us that, in order to hit the nail squarely, we must learn to attend away from the hammer, incorporate it into our corporeal schemas, and let the hammer *be* in the mode of readiness-to-hand *(Zuhandenheit).* We can create automatic reflexes, although this description is lacking. Closer to the mark is the transition from deliberate and awkward attempts to teach one's body the movements of a dance sequence to the smooth and fluid movements through which that set of steps incorporates itself into bodily interpretations of a wide range of melodies and beats: one has to learn not to think reflectively about movement, but rather to let the forms sedimented into bodily acquisitions unfurl. As Merleau-Ponty puts it, we must place ourselves "in service to the sonata."

Another paradox: although I live the engaged moment in an anonymous mode, it is still I who perform the actions, still I who must take responsibility for the consequences of my behavior. One must distinguish between the anonymity of prereflective experience as it is lived, and the presence of an inchoate personal identity on the horizon of my experience. To use a Freudian analogue, the ego retreats during sleep, but the sleeping body is still mine, the incarnation of my self. For purely transcendental thought, there is no I unless there is conscious constitution of an ego. That is a mistake of pure transcendental thinking: the empirical fact of my bodily identity does not depend on transcendental constitution alone. If I am my body, my body is mine even in prereflective modes of existence, even when I live it in the mode of anonymity.

Furthermore, due acknowledgment must be made to the reality of the reflective or Cartesian cogito and its implications for human existence in general and sexlove in particular. Reflection does alienate my sense of myself, my amo,[16] in the act of thematizing it: I become an object for my own contemplative inquiry. Most traditional philosophy and psychology assign a double privilege to reflection. On the cognitive side, reflection is held to liberate me from biasing interests, to grant me access to a vantage capable of being taken up by others, to initiate a movement in the direction of objectivity and universality. On the practical side, this disengagement frees me from hot and hasty overreaction, and frees me for deliberation and rational choice; it allows me to array my options before my contemplative regard, weigh their probable consequences and associated values, and make a balanced judgment. Greek moderation depends on reflective distantiation; so does twentieth-century cool.

In our tradition, reflective distantiation has become more than an attitude privileged in moral evaluation and decision making; it has acquired positive moral value for itself. The condition for the possibility of moral behavior has become the content of moral behavior: to be ethical is to be rational, and to be rational is to operate at the level of reflective distantiation.[17] These are the underpinnings of the ethics of the universal, the generalizability criterion that informs the golden rule and the categorical imperative. This tradition is strong and noble. One must acknowledge its theoretical force and its historical merit. One must also acknowledge its internal incoherence: the attempt to provide rational grounds for privileging rationality is paradoxical and question-begging; at best one can offer a hermeneutics of rationality set forth within the context of a prior and undefended commitment to reason. This, in my view, is what Kant does in his *Critique of Practical Reason*.

The experiential foundation of the ethics of the universal is the recognition of the other as like unto myself, what Husserl called "pairing" or "analogizing apperception," and Merleau-Ponty called "transfer of corporeal schema." The founding experience is not predicated upon rationality if one defines rationality narrowly, as I have here, in terms of reflective distantiation.

The foundation is the experience of primordial communality or "syncretic sociability." Regarded from the standpoint of developmental or ontogenetic psychology, it takes place prior to the achievement of the Cartesian cogito and the emergence of the capacity for reflective distantiation. Reflection is founded upon the prereflective; the grounds for the rational are not rational. That does *not* mean, however, that the grounds of the rational are irrational: such an inference depends upon the dualism implicit in the law of the excluded middle term latterly designated as binary opposition.

To argue that reflection is grounded upon recognition and the demand of the other to accommodate her viewpoint within one's own—that is, the demand that motivates the self-alienation that reflection is—is not to deny the legitimacy of reflection or the values of rationality founded upon it; it is, rather, to incorporate those values within a wider perspective. The atrocities of reflective distantiation derive from the brutalization of consciousness, which denies humanity to the other by virtue of locating the human exclusively within the domain of reflective self-experience and regarding that domain as irredeemably private. To be human is to be a subject like unto me and the only such subject I can experience is myself: this is the origin of the brutalizing aspect of reflective distantiation, the reason that, in its cold calculations, does not include the recognition of the other. The egregious error here does not lie with reason or reflection; it lies in the severance of reason from its origin in primordial recognition at the prereflective level. It is pure reason that is capable of brutality.

The same error subtends the development of Western spirituality in its demonic form. Demonized spirit is spirit severed from its corporeal foundations, pure spirit: spirit that opposes itself to embodiment. The polarized thinking that posits human embodiment as antithetical to human spirituality is responsible for positing sexlove as lacking in spirituality. The depictions of sexlove currently labeled pornographic are vilified because the bodily representations, by virtue of being bodily, necessarily exclude the spiritual dimension. I have countered this thesis by maintaining that spirit is indissolubly intertwined with flesh, hence that the bodies portrayed in acts of sexlove manifest rather than exclude the spiritual dimension of human interaction. As will become apparent in the following section, the demonic capacity of human spirit, the capacity for ecstasy, can align itself with love as well as hate, can integrate itself with its fleshly dimension as well as posit itself in opposition to its flesh. Demonic experience is ecstatic experience, a form of transcending mundaneity, and can manifest itself in the figures of Eros as well as the figures of Thanatos: transcendence is a vertical vector that can point both up and down.

## ECSTATIC CARNAL UNION AND THE REVERSIBILITY OF FLESH

How are we to understand the spirituality of sexlove? Is spirituality essentially opposed to corporeality? Corporeal behavior is prereflective and anonymous. Spiritual behavior is reflective and personal. How, then, can spirituality manifest itself in expressions of bodily desire? The height of spiritual transcendence is an intense relation of the self to itself that, through the paradoxes of faith, puts one in relation with the godhead, the absolute within. The ipseity of my self, that which separates me from all others and constitutes the source of my unique value as an individual, defines my role in the overall scheme of things, hence puts me in relation to my creator. It also projects me into irredeemable solitude and silence. How can spirituality, so conceived, express itself through forms of bodily intertwining in which my self loses itself in a carnal relationship to another human being?[18]

Let me acknowledge the force of this challenge. The categories of spirit sedimented in our tradition—soul, mind, consciousness, subjectivity—are associated with principles of activity, volition, freedom, reason, and so forth. These categories are, in turn, linked with figures of the divine. Descartes identifies mind with "the natural light of reason" or *lumen naturale* that is the mark of the divine upon us, the bridge connecting us to godhead, and the part of us that can survive the death of the body to find immortality in the beatific vision or union with the divine. Opposed to the active subject or *res cogitans* is the passive object or material body. The appetites of the body object are the sources of the passions, which drag us back into the mundane causal order, subvert volition, freedom, reason, etc., and ensnare us in corruption, decay, and death. True love, in this model, is an active principle pointed in the direction of transcendence of the body toward the spirit, and sexlove or corporeal love involves a surrender to deathbound passion.

Even if one proceeds, as I have, by transcribing the metaphysics of this thesis into nontheological terms, that is, by reconceiving the figures of soul in the lexicon of reflection, one must acknowledge that it retains a measure of power and validity. Our capacity for reflective distantiation is intrinsically tied to our capacity to develop an awareness of context. Disengagement from the immediate claim of a given thematic concern frees us to become aware of the surrounding circumstances, including the possibilities for responding to them. It is this process of contextualization that allows us to distinguish the unidimensional enframing of pornographic depiction from the multidimensional enframing of erotic depiction. The difference between the hasty coupling of relative strangers and the intimate lovemaking of persons embarked on the project of knowing each other across a full spectrum of human experience is also illumined by the degrees of poverty and richness of the horizonal awareness informing the encounters.

The problem, then, is this: if reflective distantiation is required to develop the awareness of context that enriches and humanizes sexlove (and the depictions thereof), then does that not subvert my thesis that the proper sphere of erotic praxis is corporeal engagement at the prereflective level? If, at the level of prereflective engagement, we are caught up in fascination with the thematics of the other's bodily comportment, does that not obscure our horizonal attunement to the overarching complex of relations constituting the context of our encounter? Is corporeal intentionality not essentially lacking in spirituality, after all?

In *Women in Love,* Lawrence expresses distaste for Hermione's voyeuristic proclivities. He says, through Birkin, that Hermione prefers the remote vantage of spectator to the act of sexlove in which she is engaged.

> "Spontaneous!" he cried. "You and spontaneity! You, the most deliberate thing that ever walked or crawled! You'd be verily deliberately spontaneous—that's you. Because you want to have everything in your own volition, your deliberate voluntary consciousness. You want it all in that loathsome little skull of yours . . . . If one cracked your skull perhaps one might get a spontaneous, passionate woman out of you, with real sensuality. As it is, what you want is pornography—looking at yourself in mirrors, watching your naked animal actions in mirrors, so that you can have it all in your consciousness, make it all mental."

In response to a query by Ursula, Birkin expresses his own preference for dark sensuality, unmediated by reflection.

> "But do you really *want* sensuality?" . . .
> "Yes," he said, "that and nothing else . . . . It is a fulfillment—the great dark knowledge you can't have in your head—the dark involuntary being. It is death to one's self—but it is the coming into being of another."[19]

Here Lawrence is working through the polarized categories of the traditional mind-body bifurcation: either the light and deliberate volition of reflective consciousness or dark and involuntary submersion in the sensual body. Yet he speaks of "dark *knowledge,*" thereby confounding his categories.

In response to the problem just posed, I answer that it is a mistake to separate theme from horizon or to make reflective and prereflective modes of awareness mutually exclusive. The gestalt-theoretical principle of contextual relevancy states that theme and horizon inform each other: the gray figure appears dark against a white background and light against a black background; when the horse on which I bet heavily wins, the day brightens even though it may be cloudy. My prereflective engagement in sexlove is qualitatively influenced by the emotional context in which it takes place: if I am beset by guilt, my engagement is clouded by the desperation of willful ignorance of my circumstances and the possible consequences of my action; if we are coming together to purge ourselves of the lingering tendrils of animosity from a raging emotional conflict, there is, again, a semi-deliberate forgetting, but one tinged with joy and relief. Reflective awareness of past events and anticipations of future unfoldings frame the ecstatic present and impart a qualitative coloring. Temporal distinctions do not delineate the moment in a hard-edged way; the passage between theme and horizon is gradual and indistinct.

The martial artists, dancers, or lovers who train their bodies deliberately to incorporate formalized sequences into spontaneous responses demonstrate by their example the possibility of merging reflective awareness with prereflective action. These actions are deliberate and volitional, but they also have an automatic or unwilled aspect. The Zen of appropriate response can be described in the language of paradox—learned forgetfulness, involuntary spontaneity, etc.—but these paradoxes spring from awkward polarized categories rather than any mystery in the actions themselves. There is nothing mysterious about the learned ability to maintain balance on a bicycle in an unmindful way. These examples teach us that appropriate prereflective responses, responses attuned to the overall context, are acquired through practice, that they require preparation, and that they must be understood melodically, that is, from the standpoint of the interpenetrating flux of thick temporal moments: if time is conceived as composed of discrete atoms, there can be no melodic experience; past and future cannot inform the moment.

Spirituality has long been conceived as attunement to the whole, the all, the one, the encompassing. One does not name the Tetragrammaton because to do so would be idolatrous, that is, it would be tantamount to reducing the worldly horizon to a thematic object. Heidegger changed the course of Western thought by outlining the possibilities of attunement to the whole and granting to that *Stimmung* a nonthematic cognitive power that had been traditionally denied to mood. He can be criticized for failing to separate what he called Being from traditional metaphysical conceptions of the divine, but one can also take a more sympathetic view and congratulate him for seeing that the spiritual attunement to the whole celebrated in religious ritual can be understood as a more pervasive phenomenon than religious institutions typically acknowledge, and one that does not require extrarational theological commitments to be experienced. I maintain that the demonization of the flesh apparent in the preponderance of world religions, East and West, demonstrates a tendency within religion itself to reduce and reify human spirituality by opposing it to the corporeality that is its origin and sustaining force.

Returning to the question governing this phase of the debate—the question of the possibility of merging reflective categories of understanding with prereflective categories of engagement, or, in other words, the question of uncovering the spiritual attunement to the whole that can inform bodily engagement—I want to point to a phenomenon that strikes me as decisive. Loss of self in the ecstatic unification with the object of adoration has long dominated both the discourses of profane sexlove and the discourses of sacred divine love. Mystical union is mystical because it is irreducible to thematic categories, because attempts to express it in the categories of self and other or spirituality and corporeality lead always to the paradoxical need to obliterate the terms needed to start the discourse. Such discourses typically have recourse to an eccentric faculty of nondiscursive reason or intuition of the ineffable in its suchness.

The problem lies not with the incomprehensibility of the phenomenon, but with the inability to mediate binary oppositions: the negation that defines self as excluding other, and mind as excluding body, precludes the intertwining that is necessary to describe unification. The solution to the problem lies in recognizing the phenomenon that seeks to find expression in the opposing figures of sacred versus profane or spiritual versus corporeal union.

I cannot love a person I do not know—but I can engage in sexual intercourse with a person I know only superficially. Although intimate contact with another's body is, of itself, intimate contact with that person and inevitably brings with it some form of knowledge, that minimal knowledge amounts to an impoverished context and is commensurate with reduction of the other to an object upon which I project my fantasies. At the far end of the spectrum is ecstatic unification with an other whose ipseity is the focus of my desire. Here the quest is not projection of an immanent ideal, but rather recognition of the other in dimensions inaccessible to the discursive means of reflective thought. Touch is more intimate than vision; it affords a quality of reversibility that is not experienced from the distance of the gaze. It is true that to be seen by another is to feel the impact of her subjectivity in the look of love or hatred she directs toward me, but this may well be the synesthetic projection into vision of the exchange that takes place with the laying on of hands. A hug is different from a smile, and a hug is a relatively mild form of embrace.

The ecstasy of carnal union derives from the reversibility of touch, from the experience of feeling the touch of the other from an inside that is no longer inaccessible to me. The passionate touch of another takes me out of myself, beyond the superficies of my skin and into a sphere that encompasses the other's bodily experience. I do not coincide with her, I do not lose myself in her, but I am transported from the region of bodily ownness into that of the relation that transcends the individuals related: the I fades into the horizon, eclipsed by the we.[20] As the violinist merges with the music, placing her self in service to the sonata, so do lovers merge with the love that transforms them:[21] the carnal invocation of Eros is a participation in transcendence which opens a new vantage on the self that flows from its marginalization. Lovers who, in the ecstasy of carnal embrace, experience the touch of each other feel in their chiasmatic flesh the truth that we all know abstractly, that the whole is greater than the sum of its parts, that the love that eclipses the individuals marks them, wounds and humbles them with an ennobling scar. The affirmation of the caress that confirms my value in a manner I cannot achieve for myself opens me to the vulnerability of personal insufficiency: I am not fully myself in the absence of the love that has taken us beyond ourselves.

Plato described Eros as a daimon. So did Lawrence. In the sequel to the passage quoted earlier, Ursula asks Birkin about the "great dark knowledge" that comes with sensual ecstasy and transcends cerebration.

> "But how? How can you have knowledge not in your head?"
> "In the blood," he answered; "when the mind and the known world is drowned in darkness—everything must go—there must be the deluge. Then you find yourself in a palpable body of darkness, a demon—"[22]

Here is the truth of the personifications of love as Eros or some supervenient spirit manifesting godhead: their love eclipses the ipseity of the lovers upon which it is founded. The relationship of parts would not be what it is were the parts different, but the parts are no longer strictly individuated because they are parts of a transcending whole. The demonic is the transcendence. As the literature of love has acknowledged from the start, the demonic is awesome and sublime, both beautiful and frightful; it attracts and repels, and does so for the same reason: it eclipses the autonomy of the self; the dissolution of the relationship that grants dignity and nobility[23] casts the self back on itself and leaves it bereft. Love lost produces the demonic rage of rejection and the desperation for renewal evident in rebound romance. Since all love eventually does terminate in death (if not before), all love harbors anxiety and fear on its horizon and seeks to keep its essential relation to demonic hatred at bay. I depend on the beneficent demon of love for my well-being, but my lover can banish that friendly spirit as well as nurture it; in the negative potential of that power dwells the lingering specter of hatred.

Ecstatic invocations of Eros, the daimon of love, require incarnation. The spiritual dimension of love, deprived of corporeal expression in the ideal of Platonic love, degenerates into reflective isolation, narcissism, and solipsism. This is the truth that explains Socrates' despicable treatment of Alcibiades in the *Symposium*. One might rather pity Heloise and Abelard rather than emulate the substitute behavior to which they were reduced following his castration and banishment.

What is currently designated as spiritual and relegated to otherworldly and incorporeal forms of transcendence is more accurately understood through the human project of contextualization. To profane is to decontextualize, to objectify persons or actions by stripping from them the relations that endow them with meaning. It is not clothing that endows human bodies with dignity, but intentions gracefully fulfilled in action: not movement *simpliciter*, but movement that flows from antecedent to consequent, from motive to end, in a manner that betrays recognition of the humanity of the others engaged.

My desire seeks recognition in reciprocity on the part of your desire as your desire seeks its affirmation in mine. The stages through which this dialectic proceeds may be stages of intensification through the reversibility of reciprocation—although this growth may falter through phases of difficult communication or when obstacles intrude from the outside—or, at the other end of the spectrum, the progression may be brought to a halt when what I recognize in you is boredom or distaste. Sexlove is a dramatic and precarious unfolding, rife with potential for discovery, peripety,[24] suffering, and joy.

## CONCLUSION:
## SEXLOVE AND MIMESIS

Sexlove has always invited mimesis; it is a privileged subject matter for aesthetic representation. Critical assessments of these representations reflect the values—the desires, hopes, and fears—of the times and places in which they are delivered. Our time is one of ambivalence with regard to sexual mores, the kind of ambivalence that typically attends rapid transition. The one thing that media across the full spectrum of political persuasion seem to agree upon is that the market for pornography is lucrative and rapidly expanding.

> Last year [1996] Americans spent more on pornography and its satellite businesses (peep shows, strippers, computer porn, etc.) than they did on Hollywood movies, and vastly more than they did on rock and country music recordings combined.[25]

The subtitle of this article—"Is smut getting less sexy?"—expresses concern that increasing accessibility will make pornography banal.[26] The tacit assumption that I would challenge is that the appeal of pornography lies in its being forbidden, that the need for erotic depiction manifest in the art and literature of all cultures necessarily feeds upon the demonization of sex.

There is no doubt that much of what we label pornography is genuinely that, the depiction of whores. What makes a whore a whore is not simply the commercial aspect, the exchange of professional services for money (which in itself is unobjectionable), but the underlying reduction and displacement. Among the many motives for engaging in commercial sex—the loneliness of deprivation, the physical beauty of the commodity, the dislocation in social space attendant upon military service, business travel, and the like—the one that truly embodies contradiction is the desire to minimize engagement with the other's personal identity and involvement in the full range of the other's life. It is this decontextualization that makes a whore the kind of sex object that symbolizes the objectionable aspect of objectification. The wistfulness of commercial sex derives from the contradiction that desire fed by loneliness and attraction to beauty seeks to satisfy that need for love through means that thwart the ends of the erotic project.

Freud offers an insightful account of the love of harlots based on Oedipal motives: men choose the harlot to love because she does not invoke the purity of the pedestalled mother figure and the impotence generated by its attendant prohibition.[27] I would generalize this account and separate it from the hypothesis of the Oedipus complex. Men choose harlots because they free men from the burden of guilt that derives from the demonization of sex. When sex is demonized, every sexual incursion is an assumption of responsibility for depriving the object of her value. When men go to prostitutes, it is frequently because they would rather pay with money than with global responsibility.

The wistful quality of pornographic production derives from the same source: one seeks the pleasure of sexlove without the responsibility that would attach to a genuine encounter. The contradiction is also the same: one seeks love's affirmation in the absence of the context that love requires. Hence, the unsatisfying nature of the commercial consumption of sex. Given another Freudian hypothesis, that of aim-inhibited repetition, we can understand the proliferation of pornographic production: the quest never reaches its end and constantly renews itself.

Literature and dramatic production, in their highest instances, explore the possible modes of human existence. They demonstrate the connections between values and decisions, character and consequence. Only when they degenerate into kitsch, do they seek to provide the spurious pleasures of vicarious living. Erotic depiction that strives to represent the full range of structures, connections, and relationships constitutive of sexlove—that is, forms of mimesis that elaborate the horizons of erotic encounter, that seek to contextualize the intertwining of flesh rather than focus on mere slappings of meat—might well meet the most discerning standards of artistic production.

The proliferation of pornography is but another indicator of the prevalence of the structure of romantic love in our times, and an especially compelling indicator because the driving fantasy is exactly that, a phantasm, an image, an idealized abstraction from reality which is all the more abstract by virtue of the decontextualization it typically employs.

The movement beyond romance in the case of mimesis would mirror the movement toward carnal knowledge in real life, it would be a movement toward the recognition and exploration of character and setting that our highest forms of literary and dramatic representation have always sought to provide. The trend is already discernible, as American cinema follows European and Japanese leadership toward the goal of capturing the *eidos* of sexlove as it manifests itself across the spectrum of human emotion and understanding. We have long since departed from that tenet of the Aristotelian canon that requires violence to take place in a place removed from the spectator's perceptual field; I take it as a sign of health and vigor that we are beginning to have the courage to present the fleshly encounter essential to the development of carnal knowledge because we are coming to understand the crucial role it plays in the evolution (or devolution) of human character and love. If minds and bodies are inextricably intertwined, then, if we want to witness the emergence of character, we will have to steel ourselves to witnessing the bodily behavior that makes it apparent and compelling.

The next and final chapter attempts to consolidate the themes presented in the chapters leading up to it in order to articulate a theory of erotic love based on the thesis of the reversibility of flesh as it manifests itself in carnal knowledge. It is specifically directed toward the cognitive aspects of sexlove and the crucial role they play in distinguishing authentic love from romantic love, and in responding to erotic anxiety. The ancient Greek themes of mimesis and nobility (το καλου) are redefined to generate a theoretical understanding of the roles of perception and embodiment in the historical unfolding of the values associated with sexlove.

NINE

# THE FLESH OF LOVE

―――――――――――――――――

FLESH IS SENTIENT, historically situated, and in touch with itself through the chiasm of reversibility: what does this portend for the phenomenology of sexlove?

## COMMUNALITY AND ALTERITY IN MERLEAU-PONTY'S ACCOUNT OF INTERSUBJECTIVITY

Merleau-Ponty writes occasionally about love, but never addresses it thematically in a sustained way as, for example, he takes up the themes of space and time, motility and cognition, perception, language, history, politics, and so on. He does, however, write extensively on cognate themes that have a strong bearing on the question before us. Let me start by reviewing Merleau-Ponty's teachings on intersubjectivity, on primordial communality and alterity, as they bear on issues related to the perceptual and historical dimensions of carnal love or sexlove.

The traditional problem of other minds grows out of the mistaken assumption that we begin life in a solipsistic mode and learn somehow to recognize other human beings as such. The "somehow" remains inexplicable because the minds that define humans as human are conceived as hidden to all but first-person experience. Merleau-Ponty was, I think, the first philosopher in the Western tradition to break this paradigm by contesting the two axes around which it is constructed. He shows[1] that we begin life in a sphere of primordial communality characterized, not by solipsism, but by an indistinction of perspectives: the self-other distinction upon which the experience of privacy is predicated is absent from infantile experience; it is an acquisition that follows the development of reflexivity later in life. He also shows that mind or consciousness is incarnate, a modality of embodiment rather than a distinct entity different in kind from the flesh it permeates, and is revealed and concealed in the ways that living bodies open themselves to and close themselves from the queries of themselves and others. Merleau-Ponty's paradigm shift does not solve the traditional problem of other minds; it reconfigures the existential source of the problem—how far can I trust my understanding of myself and others?—in such a way as to allow answers to be ventured and tested in the interplay of experiential and theoretical inquiry.

Cognitive insecurity remains a problem in the sphere of human relations—as it persists as a problem for all kinds of knowing—just because what it is that we seek to know intrinsically transcends finite cognition. This is a matter of degree: how far I can trust my understanding of you, myself, a third party—or any other worldly being—is limited by the fission, dehiscence, or separation of beings Merleau-Ponty names as *écart*. In human relations, this obscuring alterity is inextricably bound up with the prime condition of revelation: that is, embodiment in space and time. Our skins separate us in space, and historical unfolding precludes the coincidence requisite to complete lucidity: we are adumbrated to ourselves and others; what allows us to know prevents us from knowing completely.

The distinction between space and time is abstract, as is the distinction between perception and history. It is true that I cannot now perceive what happened yesterday; it is also true that what I presently sense derives its sense from the context of its temporal unfolding. It is a mistake to separate perceptual presence from its historical horizon; it is also a mistake to conflate the two. We could never hear the melody if the notes did not *sound;* nor could we hear it if they didn't merge to portend other notes co-dependent upon differentiating silences. In the sensing of music, as in the sensing of other bodies, as in the sensing of all things, presentation presages withdrawal as retreat signifies a former presence.

Merleau-Ponty has been criticized for being a philosopher of sense who is guilty of demonizing non-sense. If there is a mistake here, it lies in the narrowing of sense, *sens*, to a model of cognition that is ultimately conceptual. This has the effect of classifying that which transcends conceptuality as nonsensical, meaningless, and ontologically vacuous. This is exactly the mistake that Merleau-Ponty corrected: by granting primacy to perception, to sensing, Merleau-Ponty assigned a primacy to carnal knowledge as the rich *fond* from which conceptuality draws in its process of clarification and refinement. For Merleau-Ponty, the nonsense lies in removing what we find difficult to conceptualize from the domain of sense. What it is that we find difficult to conceptualize is what we sense, be it wine, music, or love: that which transcends us, draws us to question, brings us together here, sets us apart here.

## CARNAL KNOWLEDGE AND COGNITIVE INSECURITY

Sexlove depends upon bodily sensing, hence upon carnal knowledge. The conceptualization undertaken here—in the text before you—is necessarily derivative upon the sensing that takes place when flesh intertwines. The hope is that this conceptualization will enrich the experience by articulating it, rather than obscure it by reducing it: my intent is to point to something we can sense, something we can know carnally, but only indicate with signifiers.

I have so far stressed the carnality of carnal knowledge, let me now turn to the knowledge, the cognitive aspect, of sexlove. I have argued that impersonal sex, pure sex, is an impossibility.[2] When bodies touch, persons come together and know each other. The knowledge may be unidimensional by design, but—impoverished though it may be and, I gather, often is—it is multidimensional by necessity, just because it is perceptual and synesthetic. The limiting case on the aloof end of the spectrum is not what concerns me here.[3] Here I want to address the project of pushing back the limits at the other end, where one seeks, not to separate the frisson from personal involvement, but rather to integrate them. What is at stake in this project is the affirmation of a kind of cognition, carnal knowledge.

Knowledge is the measure of sexlove. It is not the only measure: the categories of endurance, fidelity, and commitment, of intensity, ecstasy, and selflessness, of volition and compulsion, of vulnerability and defense, and so on are all relevant. There is, nonetheless, I now think, a privilege to the measure of knowledge: I submit that one cannot love a person one does not know. I submit that the less one knows a person, the less one loves *that person*. This is the principle that underlies my several critiques of romantic love.[4] Romantic love thrives on distance, obstacles, and the immanent ideal that is threatened by the knowledge of carnal knowledge. Cognition is the death of romantic love and the vital principle of authentic love, the love that seeks to intertwine with the ownmost being of another person, that seeks to sense the sense of another.

The sense of another: what might that be? For Merleau-Ponty, personal identity is corporeal and reveals itself through style, modality, movement, bodily behavior. The sense of another is that person's identity, that person's style; it is a sense that reveals itself through sensing, that is, through perception, the kind of sensing our bodies do. If I cannot recognize you, cannot distinguish you from others, I cannot love you. The recognition of other persons is primordially perceptual. Before we had the means to do otherwise, we reduced identity to signifiers on identifying documents: gray hair, green eyes, five feet ten inches in height, 165 pounds in weight. Now we demand photo ID on passports and drivers licenses. Photographs make it more difficult to falsify identity. Microchips may soon make it possible to incorporate movement and sound into identifying representations; that would make it even more difficult to pass oneself off as another. If we could identify others by signifiers, none of this would be necessary.[5]

The distance of signifiers from what they signify increases the possibility of deceit: representation facilitates misrepresentation. It is possible to dissemble oneself across a table, but more difficult than it is in a chat room we enter through computers. That may account for the growing popularity of computer dating: it fosters the distance upon which the illusions of romantic love thrive; it allows us to have a semblance of the experience of love without intimate carnal knowledge intruding to shatter the ideal and dispel the immanent fantasy; above all, it reduces the vulnerability intrinsic to the fleshly contact of sensing another who is carnally present. People who meet in disembodied cyberspace, who begin to love there, and subsequently marry, invariably report the various phases of corporeal or perceptual contact—by telephone and then in person—as involving a dramatic change of aspect, a displacement of a conceptual ideality by a perceptual gestalt. They approach such encounters gingerly and with apprehension, knowing that their history together will be transformed by a process neither can control. They are shy in the face of transcendence.

The possibility of deceit compounds cognitive insecurity in the erotic domain. The vulnerability intrinsic to loving may be the prime source of the dissemblance that historically has attended the rites of courtship and mating: one cannot reveal one's love without fearing the other's betrayal and rejection; therefore, one protects oneself with a mask that one can laugh off if it is betrayed and scorned. Posturing and imposture seem to be constant attendants to sexlove across history and sexually reproducing species. It may be, as Nietzsche suggests, that we are all actors and cannot do without our masks even if we would. It may also be, as Levinas suggests, that the transcendence of the human is manifested in the portentous inscrutability of its face. I offer the humbler truth that we cannot remove our faces as easily as we can doff a mask, and even the transformations of time never quite succeed in complete transfiguration: something recognizable always shines through.

Time also reveals the sense behind the sequence of masks we choose to wear. Historical unfolding is betrayal, revealing identity as its melody emerges through the notes of imposture. The felicitous truth is that, given time and fortunate happenstance, romance betrays love. Because we are embodied, and those who learn to identify our bodies and sense them eventually come to know more and more of who we are. The good fortune required is that self-betrayal result in acceptance and affirmation rather than rejection. Some of that good fortune may, indeed, depend on happenstance, but it is also true that some may not.

Deceit revealed as such is the prime source of erotic disenchantment, rejection, and the transformation of love into other emotions. This is doubtless true in the case of romantic love where any revelation is a threat to fantasy, and sustaining the deceitful illusion is a necessary condition for the conceit of romance. Yet romance is resilient—as Stendahl notes, the collapse of the first crystallization is typically but a phase in the construction of the second— those who dwell in and for illusion eventually learn to tolerate the vicissitudes of its dialectic, even to celebrate them for the sake of intensity and the frisson which is the telos of romance.

Deceit revealed is far more of a threat to authentic love because it betokens the loss of its object. If I learn that you are not the person I love, then I have lost my love and it is displaced by mourning and melancholia rather more than hate. The romantic fears the loss of the experience of love, the ecstatic frisson; the authentic lover dreads the loss of the person loved. Love based on knowledge of the other cannot survive the revelation that betrays the falsity of the cognition because the person known and loved no longer exists: this new you is but an unsettling simulacrum of the person I love. This death means that I can no longer perceive the person I love. That person still exists, just as a biologically dead loved one still exists, but exists as an absence in the interstices of my lifeworld where, despite my reflective knowledge of her nonexistence, my habitual anticipations of her appearance are betrayed by a continuous succession of disappointments. If I learn through the betrayal of deceit that you are not the person I love, then when I see you, what I sense is loss, what I experience is mournful nostalgia and longing for a past that once was present, but present in the mode of dissemblance, a mirage.

Hate is an emotion based on threat. Actualization of the fear of rejection may inspire hatred and the project of revenge, but that is more likely to occur in romantic love, where bubbles can burst in an instant, rather than in authentic love, where cognitive paradigms shift more slowly: dream figures change abruptly; perceptual themes evolve. It is also the case that we are complicit in the deceit practiced upon us, that we demand it; especially in romantic love, I demand that you fulfill an antecedent ideal and dissemble all departures from it. In authentic love, your departures from my expectations are a source of wonder and inquiry; a new adumbration sensed forces me to adjust my cognitions. In one case, disclosure portends dissolution; in the other, it demands accommodation.[6]

Romantic love is bound to attenuate and die—or transform itself into other erotic modes—just because the encroachment of knowledge must erode the formation of new crystallizations. It is the nature of perception to displace fantasy when the two collide.

Authentic love must also contend with death. Biological death, the death consequent upon deceit, or the death of another transfiguration consequent upon change. Persons are historical, they come into being and pass away, they become. I may change and you may not affirm the person I have become: if youth and the physical beauty associated with it are what one loves in others, the love will fade over the years. If I stop sensing you, stop questioning, you will become someone else I no longer know. If I stop growing and start decaying, and you are paying attention, you will cease to affirm me erotically, although you may remain loyal to me for other reasons. But if you mature, become a fuller realization of the values I originally affirmed in you, my love will grow and displace its immature incarnations. The little deaths here are happy ones.[7]

Sexlove is a quest for carnal knowledge. As such, it is intrinsically limited by the very transcendence of the other presupposed in the quest: the distance or separation (écart) that poses the question of the other's own identity also opens the possibility of continuing wonder, discovery, and mutual growth.

## MIMESIS AND το καλου

The state of primordial communality in which we begin life is based, as noted earlier, on syncretic sociability or indistinction of perspectives. Merleau-Ponty

characterizes this state in positive terms as founded upon the "transfer of corporeal schema," a process of recognition or bonding or identification-with-
out-identity, and in negative terms as founded upon the absence in the infant
of a body image or visual representation of itself.

> To the extent that [the infant under six months of age] lacks this visual con-
> sciousness of his body, he cannot separate what he lives from what others
> live as well as what he sees them living. Thence comes the phenomenon of
> "transitivism," i.e., the absence of a division between myself and others that
> is the foundation of syncretic sociability.[8]

Transitivism can be analyzed into moments of projection and introjection or
conceived under the general heading of mimesis, as long as one is careful not
to model these activities on their adult or reflective and deliberate forms: the
infant does not set out to mime, it just picks up behaviors as we sometimes
find ourselves unthinkingly reproducing locutions that permeate our sociolinguistic environments.

   Later in life, following the recognition of its body as separate from others
and the development of reflective awareness, the adolescent experiences a
phase of intense alienation accompanied by hyper-reflexive concern about its
own identity. It is not mere coincidence that this is the stage of the body's
sexual maturation, the stage at which the changeling is thrust into the excit-
ing and threatening arena of sexlove. The passage from infancy to adolescence
is marked by a qualitative and quantitative intensification of cognitive insecurity whose source is the recognition of alterity: the birth of selfhood is at the
same time estrangement from self and others. It is accompanied by a nostalgia
for lost innocence and unity with self and others. This nostalgia is a key element in the historical dimension of sexlove, and constitutes a moment in
which history and perception merge to provide direction for the erotic quest.
It is the anamnesis that guides our recognition of love.[9]

   The unification models that have dominated the literature of love from
Plato through Hegel to the present—where the currently prevalent cynicism
is parasitic upon the notion of unity it delights in proclaiming to be impossible—are founded on nostalgia. This is evident in Aristophanes' myth in the
*Symposium;* it is also evident in Freud's account of the Oedipal structure and
Ferenczi's account of the Thalassa complex: what is sought is a backward
movement to the unity from which we have fallen. For Hegel, the dialectical
movement forward to unity is governed by the paradigm of the *return* of Absolute *Geist* unto itself, a retrieval of the unity lost in the fall into history. The
unity conceived in these various ways might better be conceived as the unity

experienced in the mode of primordial communality or syncretic sociability. That is, I think, the experiential ground for the nostalgia that has traditionally guided sexlove.

This ground is unstable. It is based on an infantile quality of experience which is structured by ignorance or unawareness. The infant's perspective does not recognize itself as a perspective, but it is nonetheless a perspective. What is experienced as communality frequently is, indeed, communality, but occasionally is not. How many instances of infanticide and child abuse need be cited here? How many instances of children, young and old, cleaving in desperation to parents who continually abuse their infantile love? How many instances of otherwise decent persons recapitulating with their own children the historically structured atrocities of their own childhoods? Nostalgia can guide us back to a unity that never was; it may obscure, under the infantile and illusory category of unity as coincidence of perspectives, the genuine telos of communality that is dynamic harmony based on reversibility—something very different from a totalizing fusion that negates individuality.

Infantile mimesis is unreflective and automatic. When recapitulated in adult life, we attribute it to dark forces dwelling in the unconscious and regard the repetition as a fixation, as a failure to develop, as compulsive and destructive. The unconscious, as conceived here, is the vehicle of history operating recursively to produce cyclical variants of itself. Its unconsciousness, its lack of lucidity, is what makes it tragic, what permits the gratuitous return of the same—when lucidity would open alternatives. "I'll teach you some respect." Is that what Ouranos said to Kronos, what Kronos said to Zeus?

The culprit is not mimesis. The culprit is nostalgia for an infantile quality of experience.

Mimesis is the driving force of eros. Listen to what Phaedrus says in the *Symposium*.

> The principle which ought to guide the whole life of those who intend to live nobly cannot be implanted . . . by anything so effectively as by love. . . . I mean the principle which inspires shame at what is disgraceful and ambition for what is noble. . . . Suppose a lover to be detected in the performance of some dishonorable action . . . ; I assert that there is no one . . . whose observation would cause him so much pain in such circumstances as his beloved's. (*Symposium*, 178c–e)

This is a bit more subtle than Phaedrus might have realized. The lover seeks to behave nobly in the presence of the beloved. According to what measure of nobility? That of the beloved? No: the lover's measure of nobility is one that is projected upon the beloved as much as recognized within her, a measure that the lover then introjects in his own ideal identity. She would want me to do this, therefore I will do it. But why should I not do it on my own? Why do I need her? Because I am defining myself in her eyes. Why her eyes, why not the eyes of somebody else? Because I attribute two things to my beloved: first, nobility on her own part and its correlate, the ability to discern it in others—this very nobility was the reason I chose to love just her—and, second, I attribute to her the project of knowing me—that sensing of me being the condition for her choice of me as her beloved.

The Greek word translated here as nobility is το καλου. The Greek term is rich and overdetermined; it means aesthetically attractive or beautiful, it also means morally good or virtuous; indeed, it means both of these things at once, the intersection of goodness and beauty, as though one could not be either good or beautiful without being both. το καλου is that which one seeks in one's beloved; to see someone as an instance of το καλου is already to feel the tug of Eros.

What is needed to complete Phaedrus's thought in the passage quoted is the structure of reversibility. I sense my love as embodying το καλου. That is part of what it is to love her. Another part of loving her is my desire to be loved by her, also to be sensed as embodying το καλου. Only to the extent that one embodies το καλου can one recognize it in another. The recognition is akin to that which takes place when two persons sharing the same affinity or set of attitudes or tastes begin to discover their common ground: if you are not a sailor, it is difficult to pass yourself off as such with someone who is really a sailor. The difference is that το καλου names a global posture or disposition, a style of being, the recognition of which in another takes some time and testing.

Were it not so, the process of mate selection would be far less complex. The posturing, the defenses employed to protect one's self-esteem in the face of the vulnerability attendant upon self-disclosure, and the idealizations at work in the early phases of loving all conspire to compound the difficulty of discerning the style of the other's being-in-the world. The notes that constitute the melody are stretched out in time and circumstance, and one must listen carefully to hear how they fit together. Listening, attuning oneself to the nuances and portents of another person's behavior, is difficult enough under ordinary conditions, but during the phases of crystallization when the norm is overestimation and projection of ideality, when the gestures of courtship are ambiguous by design and all declarations are veiled and deniable, the project of coming to know another human being is anything but instantaneous. The thunderbolt of instant recognition is my prime contender for the paradigm of *méconnaissance:* the thralldom into which one falls when struck by Cupid's arrow is sheer romance; it means that one's immanent ideal has found a vehicle that accepts the construction, that there is a resonance between my projections and hers. How, then, can one discern between mystification and recognition?

The short answer is that one cannot. There is no set of criteria that can be applied in a short period of time to determine whether this new relationship has the potential to grow. The long answer is that the idealizations and constructions will inevitably be displaced by the reality of the other as the contact between the principals extends over time and variation in situation. Relationships transcend the relata: the gestalt that formulates itself against the background of the lifeworld is not under the control of either party, but it does eventually make itself manifest to both, although never in a final way. Sooner, of course, is better than later: better before moving in together or marrying or having a baby. And this is where the modicum of power we can have in regulating our own erotic destinies comes into play.

## REVERSIBILITY AND CARNAL KNOWLEDGE

How to facilitate or even accelerate the process of genuine recognition? This is one of the main questions this book set out to answer. One has to have a sense of what one is looking for in order to be able to find it, or to identify it if one stumbles upon it. My hope is to have awakened the project of looking, to have described carnal knowledge as the knowing that takes us beyond romance to a more fulfilling kind of love, and to have provided some indication of what one is looking for and where it might be found. In this domain of human existence, as in all others, there is no way to circumvent the necessity for judgment: ambiguity permeates all of experience, every theme can be seen in multiple contexts, but it is especially pervasive in the erotic sphere, hence the difficulty of judgment is compounded here. How does one subsume this datum, this piece of behavior, this string of events, etc. under the appropriate category? That is the form of the concrete question, and the answer, of course, is that there is no meta-rule that can be applied to ensure success. Finite existence is precarious, and nowhere more precarious than in loving.

This much, however, can be said and said with confidence. If one is looking for true romance, one will not find it—because truth and romance are incompatible. To search for the sustainable illusion is to seek in vain. To know that is already to have improved one's chances for erotic fulfillment. To know that knowing another is a prime condition for loving the other is to open oneself to the possibility of knowing more about a prospective partner than one would were one to search for a measure in feeling, in quality of emotional response, alone. It is a notorious truth that good sex does not necessarily betoken genuine love, and it is also true that genuine love does not ensure good sex—genuine love frequently survives illness, aging, and accidents of all sorts that affect the physical capacity to make love—but it certainly facilitates it. After all, the carnal knowing I have attempted to describe does entail paying attention, listening, attuning oneself to the nuances of the other's gestural life.

Beyond that, carnal knowledge as described here is predicated on the notion of the reversibility of flesh, the ability we have to sense the other's sensing of ourselves. One has to be aware of this capacity in order to undertake the project of developing it deliberately. Sensate focus has been a dominant technique in sex therapy for the past three decades, and there is little doubt that it enhances the sexlove of most of the couples who undertake the training. In my perusal of the literature, however, there is little evidence to indicate awareness of why it works, what underlying structures of human embodiment are called into play. Sensate focus, under different rubrics, has been advocated in practice of Tantric yoga for centuries, but also without explicit awareness of the structure of reversibility that explains why these practices are as effective as they are.

There is nothing at all mystical about the phenomenon of reversibility. If you shake hands with yourself, there is an indistinction of subject and object: which hand is doing the feeling and which hand is being felt? It is not clear, the two roles merge, although the two hands retain their separate identities. Clasp an inanimate object, a doorknob, for example, and the quality of experience is markedly different. One feels the doorknob, by virtue of feeling oneself; the feel of the doorknob resides in the sensations we have in our hands, but we do not feel the doorknob feeling us. When we shake hands with another person, however, that experience differs qualitatively from both grasping the doorknob and shaking hands with oneself: we are aware, at the perceptual level, of being sensed by another. In the case of erotic touching, this difference is even more pronounced. The difference between a genital caress that is self-administered and one received from a lover cannot be explained away by the difference in mood and context: the touch of another is qualitatively different from one's own touch—massage parlors of all kinds would lose revenue were this not the case.

Sartre argued that I discover the subjectivity of another human being when I feel the impact of the other's look. This is one of those genuine discoveries that we have always known to be true. When I feel your eyes upon me, especially when they meet and reverberate with mine, I am acutely aware of being seen by another sentient being because I experience your sentience. That is why the experience can be acutely uncomfortable—or profoundly moving. The same thing is true in the case of the other's touch: to be touched is necessarily to touch, it is also necessarily to feel the touch of the other person, to come in touch with that person's own experience. Sartre also argued—mistakenly, I think—that the look of the other was necessarily objectifying, that it has to reduce the one looked at to object status, and through that objectification pose a threat to the freedom of the one objectified.[10] We have seen that the premise of Sartre's argument, the premise that consciousness and body are distinct and disjunct, is wrong: to look at my body is also to look at me because my consciousness permeates my flesh. There are, indeed, looks that are demeaning and diminishing, but there are also looks that are approving and encouraging. The same is true of touch. Battery is not a gesture of love (or rather is a manifestation of negative emotional intensity which may or may not be an expression of love turned demonic), but caresses—which on Sartre's own account depend upon consciousness "swooning" into the flesh—are or can be modes of expressing affection, desire, and affirmation.

Caresses are not unidirectional. To touch is to be touched, and the feeling of being touched includes awareness of the other's sensing. The roles of the toucher and the touched are reversible: I do not merely infer your arousal from such measurable things as engorgement of erectile tissue or retraction of the clitoris, I feel your excitement in the kind of synesthetic perception that allows animals to sense the moods of their handlers. This is the carnal knowledge, the direct contact with another, that takes lovers beyond romance into genuine intimacy. It is not fusion—the unification model just does not fit this phenomenon—because I retain my separate identity, but it does produce an indistinction of perspectives. The indistinction produced differs from infantile modes just because separate identities, exactly what the infant has not yet learned about, are retained. But what the two modes have in common is a blurring of boundaries. Neophyte lovers, like neophyte dancers or athletes, may have to concentrate on technique and pay deliberate attention to the results they fail or succeed in producing; but once the partners are attuned to one another, once they have incorporated the Zen of resonating with the whole of the experience, deliberation gives way to harmonious expression, and the relata give themselves over to the relation that transcends them. They are in service to the love they invoke. They do not make love so much as they summon Eros, as we invoke Morpheus by miming sleep.

The knowing of carnal knowledge is not the only kind of knowing that love depends on, but it is basic to sexlove. Feeling your affirmation of me at the carnal level builds my confidence in your love and allows me to risk further disclosure. But the risk remains a risk—what you learn may be off-putting. I may, for example, risk disclosing an affinity for a form of sexual expression that strikes you as disgusting. Initiation of any new practice burdens the initiator with fear of rejection. But, if the couple has built a relationship of trust and respect over a period of time, the inertia of the relationship and their historical solidarity may well sustain them through the crisis. Carnal knowledge resonates with the other kinds of knowing—the sense I have of your multifaceted identity, your moods and tastes, the style that informs all of your actions—to generate a rich sense of your being.[11] It is this encompassing sense of who you are and what you want to be that informs my growing recognition and affirmation of your nobility, your embodiment of το καλον.

It is the invariable hope of sexlove that loving another will awaken the other's love, and this hope is based on the reversibility of carnal knowledge. You should return my love because what I love in you is the goodness and beauty I value and have sought to embody in myself: my recognition deserves recognition. But recognition is a phased process, not a switch that gets turned on all at once. My demand for recognition may be premature and leave you with the sense that we do not yet know each other well enough; you may fear that I am more in search of recapitulating the intensely pleasurable frisson I have experienced with other persons than I am motivated by the desire to establish intimate contact with you. If one person is impetuous and the other prudent, if we live in differing tempos, the process of recognition is more difficult.[12]

## RECOGNITION AND ANAMNESIS

Sartre was right in arguing that the project of loving is the project of being loved, but, I think, mistaken in interpreting this as driven by the vain attempt at possessing a freedom as a freedom. What my love awakens in me can—but need not—be the infantile quest to achieve unity and peace by domination and engulfment of the other's perspective, the cannibalistic quest to consume the otherness of the other and assimilate it; this is truly self-defeating, a project in which success necessarily betokens failure. The anamnesis at work in authentic love is guided by the project of finding myself in my beloved, and finding myself affirmed by her reciprocation of my love, but the finding, the discovery, intrinsic to that project presupposes the alterity or *écart* that separates me from what I am and keeps the two of us from coinciding.[13]

The history that guides the recollective aspect of love, its anamnesis, is a history obscured by infantile amnesia which continues to work its way through us. It is often said that, to love another, one must first love oneself. Lacking self-esteem, I cannot believe in your esteem for me and must seek to manipulate it through the Sartrean dialectics of fascination and seduction. Lacking self-esteem, I cannot believe in reciprocity. If I do not embody the values of το καλου, I cannot recognize them as embodied in you. What is it to embody such values? What recognition is at work in this embodiment?

One emerges from infancy and early childhood with a legacy of values and a mixed sense of one's own worth, both of which have been assimilated more or less uncritically. The transformations of adolescence, however, call these values and self-assessments into question. Psychoanalysis is right in turning to the structures of early experience to find the sources of adult neurosis, and right again in the project of seeking lucidity as the means of transcending them. But it is mistaken in reading history only backward, in reducing present attitudes to their antecedents. History is also prospective and creative. Nowhere is this more apparent than in the vicissitudes of sexlove. We all recapitulate the violence of mate selection writ large in the drama of Romeo and Juliet: we must all leave the home clan and violate the turf of another clan in the process of finding a partner in sexlove.

Every potential partner is always already spoken for in some way or other. Even if you are not in an erotic relation when we come together, I am still a threat to those who are close to you. Time spent alone with me is time taken from your friends and maybe even your work. To enter an amorous relationship with you may—and usually does—generate consternation in my family: is it too early in life for this diversion from the rigors of preparing for adulthood; am I ready for the risks of a sexual encounter; are you an appropriate partner, one who will foster the values my family has tried to inculcate in me? Freud and Bataille may be right in arguing that the primal prohibition is sexual in nature, that civilization consists in the repression or diversion or sublimation of sexual aims, but they failed to see the implications of that thought. We all do become sexual in one mode or another.[14] Most of us violate the injunction to keep our sexual aims and behavior in line with established civil structures: we sense that we know better, and that sensing, that corporeal knowledge, necessarily leads to transgression and transformation, the genesis of new forms, destruction and creation. We eat the apple.

One must look forward as well as backward to understand the historical process of anamnesis. I sense in my beloved an instantiation of το καλου that differs from the models imbued in me, for better or for worse, in the prehistory of my early years. She is not a facsimile of Mother; she is roughly my own size. He is not Father under a different name enforcing another prohibition; he demands yes rather than no. The crux is this, exactly this: the values imparted in my prehistory prohibited the carnal knowledge of sexlove and called obedience to that prohibition virtue; the values I affirm in myself and my beloved in the pact of sexlove celebrate the beauty of that experience and designate it as bound up with the good. The question is whether sexlove fosters civilization, as Phaedrus argues, or undermines it, as at least one reading of Freud and Bataille would have it—not to mention Plato and Aristotle, Augustine and Aquinas, and the host of those who advocate suppressing or sublimating the carnal for the sake of the spiritual.

How much does the qualitative unfolding of history depend on recognizing and embodying το καλου in the celebration of sexlove? And how much does the qualitative dimension of that celebration depend on our ability to transcend our own prehistories? Responses to these questions foreshadow new conceptions of civilization with moral and political infrastructures differing significantly from those now in place. I have argued that we live in a time of erotic malaise, that our culture espouses and enforces unhealthy and counterproductive values in the domain of sexlove, that we all suffer from the demonization of sex that stems from our Platonic-Christian heritage.[15] This has the pernicious consequence of generating a dilemma that all of us must face.

If we attempt to liberate ourselves from the norms and values that amount to a demonization of sex, we will encounter social resistance and evoke condemnation from those committed to the existing institutions. Adolescents typically do defy the existing norms, and they are punished for it in insidious ways. There is no way not to internalize negative self-assessment when negativity exudes from the woodwork of one's days. One may, and most adolescents do, continue to be defiant, but the price of that defiance is paid on both sides of the generation gap. We care about our youth and lament their recalcitrance, unaware through our own structures of denial that the intrusive strictures through which we express our care are exacerbating the problem rather than pointing the way toward solution. When it comes to sex, we want them to learn to swim before they get in the water; we somehow manage to avoid acknowledging that they are already in over their heads. Over their heads because their heads have been filled with leaden superstition and their bodies are surging with sexual incentives. They may chant the mantras of permissiveness—if it feels good, do it—but the need to chant betrays the bad conscience we have poked into their skulls.

There is hope here, but it is distant. We are distributing condoms with the message not to use them. And they are not using them. Because that would acknowledge before the match ignites that they intend to play with fire. Beyond that, however, we are establishing with our sexual hypocrisy an attitude among adolescents that adult values are generally hypocritical, thereby creating a spillover effect that undermines our more legitimate values and the attempt to instill them in the youth. The hope resides in the fact that mimesis plays as strong a role in the formation of character as reinforcement by reward and punishment: as we grow toward sanity, that will transmit itself to the youth.[16]

It is as true for adults as it is for children that to go against the prevailing norms of sexual behavior is to suffer at the hands of those who take it upon themselves to enforce those norms. The other horn of the dilemma is that we suffer if we do not depart from the sick norms of demonized sex. Either way, we suffer. Given the choice, I think it is wiser and nobler to suffer in the quest for higher and healthier ends. Prudence dictates propriety, and *phronesis* or practical wisdom names a task rather than a solution: it is a matter of sorting out the acts for which we might take pride from those that are truly shameful. I do not think that Augustine got it right when he argued that it is appropriate to feel shame for our sexual nature, that this is divine punishment for our quest for carnal knowledge. I wonder if he would have altered his doctrine if he had foreseen that exactly that doctrine has generated the multimillion dollar industry that now caters to prurience, or if he had understood that the surest way to dispel prurient curiosity is to foster knowledge.

Mimesis is how the forms are instantiated. But what I mime is not το καλον in the celestial sphere of pure ideality, it is το καλου where I find/project it as emergent in myself and embodied in another. If what is truly virtuous is the quest to find out what is truly virtuous—if the friendship of the good is a mutual quest to embody and sense το καλου—then its highest

forms are not Platonic. The anamnesis that makes history rather than recapitulating sedimented forms looks backward critically: harmony, as we all know,
is not pre-established—that is an illusory past grounded in a nostalgic prescience that can only be fulfilled in the future.

————————

Dedicated to the memory of Maurice Natanson

# CONCLUSION

## PRACTICAL IMPLICATIONS

### PREMISES

THIS IS A BOOK about sexlove. Sexlove permeates human existence, hence it ramifies across the full spectrum of human affairs. The segment of that spectrum I intend to take up here is defined by a principle of relevance to the personal lives of individuals. Global conclusions regarding the implications of the viewpoint set forth in the body of this text will have to be placed in abeyance: utopian visions, fascinating as they are, will remain on the horizon; I want to focus on the concrete bearing the ideas in this book might have on the decisions we can actually make for ourselves and make now—without waiting for the millennium.

In the process of writing this book I was frequently daunted by the heterogeneity of individual humans and the diversity of their cultural heritages. How could I hope to generate hypotheses or address the cacophony of competing values in a way that would be relevant to persons other than myself? The contemporary critique of universalist writing, the attempt on the part of one situated individual to speak to or about all persons in all places and times, quite properly induces humility. But that caveat, itself, speaks in the voice of universality. And the sun comes up in the east for all of us, although your winter may be my summer. My point here is that there are general structures of human existence—death and the opposed thumb, for example—and although they may apply in different ways for differently situated persons, they still apply: some people bury their dead, some incinerate them, a few shoot them off into space, but nobody just casually throws the bodies away. The final judgment about the bearing of my offerings on your life—whether and how these ideas might apply to you—is necessarily yours to make.

I have argued that sexlove should not be tied as closely as it is to the processes of procreation. I have also argued that the two cannot be completely divorced: biological causality has psychological and sociological consequences. The values that currently govern sexual morality were generated in times when human life was less abundant, shorter, and riskier than it now is. Species survival then depended on fostering human propagation, as now it depends on managing population growth. As a species, we are permanently in heat. If it is a reasonable goal to limit our direct progeny to small numbers, then the percentage of sex acts we perform pointed toward the telos of reproduction will be minuscule. Some couples at some times work hard to make babies, but many many more diligently contrive to avoid that consequence. It is myopic, I think, to continue to focus our sex values on one of the functions of sex that, for the most part, we seek to circumvent.

If sexlove is not driven exclusively—or even primarily—by the telos of reproduction, then the values that govern our practices might well be adjusted to fit the goals that, in fact, do constitute our primary motivations: pleasure, intimacy, communication, love. These goals do not exclude reproduction, but they govern it: we reproduce for a host of motives, including love, but reproduction is not an end in itself for us, and most of us who make babies are not at all motivated by concerns for species survival. What follows from this?

As already argued in chapter 3, the most obvious consequence is to lift the sanctions against nonreproductive sex acts, that is, the ones traditionally labeled as perverse: masturbation, fellatio, cunnilingus, anal sex, and so forth. Although they are still on the law books and are still being used to prosecute individuals, these sanctions are slowly attenuating, and there is little need for further comment here. Except, perhaps, to reinforce the further consequence that the core animus against homosexuality—that aspect of natural law theory that ties sex to potentially reproductive acts—loses its ground, thus opening the way for homosexual love to express itself with dignity and without fear of legal prosecution.

The most important consequence of freeing sexlove from the reproductive dyad is to acknowledge explicitly what has long been the case, that the values informing erotic praxis are the same values that govern the other domains of human action. The argument against generating a canon of specifically sexual values has also been set forth in chapter 3, but further commentary is warranted in this case. If we refuse to demonize sex, if we refuse to assign special stigmata to sex offenses, then the calculus that attempts to balance punishment against damage inflicted begins to change character. At best, this calculus is imprecise and admits of wide variance in judgment from place to place, court to court, jury to jury, but it is evident to me, at least, that there is a long-standing practice of treating offenses associated with sexuality as especially heinous. If, for example, one compares the stigma attached to persons accused of sexual harassment with that accruing to the perpetrators of legal harassment, such as those employed by the Internal Revenue Service, one sees gross disproportionality between damage suffered and consequences to those responsible for inflicting the damage. The results are not yet in, but I am confident in predicting that the dollar amounts awarded to individual plaintiffs in the recent sexual harassment class action suit against Mitsubishi will be incommensurate with the amounts awarded to plaintiffs suing the IRS, given the relative gravity of damage inflicted.

The demonization of sexuality, the assignment of negative value to sexual acts as such—a negativity redeemed only by their reproductive function—is a threat to all persons who are sexual, hence a threat to us all. In chapter 9, I claimed that the sexual values being foisted upon the youth reflect both our concern for our young and our hypocrisy. Our Judao-Christian heritage formally recognizes the passage into adult status with a coming of age ritual, bas mitzvah or bar mitzvah or confirmation, at a time that roughly coincides with the development of secondary sexual characteristics and achievement of the capacity for reflection.[1] These rituals date back to agrarian cultures in which couples married in their mid-teens. They mark a social recognition of the changeling's passage into adult status and sexual activity. They also mark a desire on the part of the social entity to regulate the unruly process of mate selection.

As the statistics come in on matters such as teenage pregnancy, abortion, and the proliferation of unwanted children, spread of sexually transmitted diseases among the youth, and so on, it is clear that there is need for guidance, even control. It is also clear that the measures taken so far are ineffective. We are distributing condoms and introducing courses in sex education in our public schools, but the trend of the statistics continues upward. Why?

The hypothesis I would offer is that the intent of these well-conceived measures is undermined by the moral horizon in which they are placed. We purport, for political reasons, to present knowledge and the means to act on it in a value-neutral way. We refuse to acknowledge that this area of human experience is sacred in the sense of being laden with taboo and prohibition. Advocates on all sides of the debate surrounding these highly controversial measures manifest the fervor that has always surrounded the domain of the sacred. Absolute commitments collide, the debate stalls, the contest moves into the streets, and eventually into courts of law. I doubt that this process can be streamlined to minimize the violence and suffering attendant upon it, but I would like to try anyway.

My thought is a simple one. If the figures of the sacred and the rites engendered to enforce prohibition are themselves just means adopted to enforce norms dictated by prudence, then the solution lies in assessing the norms in accordance with the guidelines of practical reason. This thought is not new. It can be reduced by a simple ad hominem argument to a commitment on my part—which I happily acknowledge—to side against the fear-inducing techniques of mystification in favor of an ethics of cooption based on appeal to long term self-interest. What may be new is my claim that the youth will respond more favorably to demonstrations of their own self-interest than they will to thinly veiled threats they perceive as grounded in hypocrisy. We cannot persuade them to do as we say when that conflicts with what they see us do. We *can* model behavior that manifests sanity, compassion, and emotional satisfaction. We can show them that it is possible to be successfully sexual. And we can teach them how to do it, once we have developed our own knowledge.

Compare our success in teaching the youth how to drive. The incidence of drunken driving is down in general, and the statistics for teens are following—with an understandable lag behind the general trend. Driving is hazardous. So is drinking. But they are both fun things to do, adult things to do. Just a matter of developing good judgment, recognizing the values and practices that balance risk of pain against good times to be had. We did this by letting the truth be manifest.

The truth about sexlove is not so different. Good times are to be had, but risk management is essential. It is a bit more complicated, to be sure, but the stakes are actually lower. Much better to have a pregnant child or a diseased child or a psychologically disturbed child, a child that can be helped, than to have a child hopelessly dead or maimed.

The problem is not technique. Condoms help. So does education. The problem lies in acknowledging that children begin to be sexual when they reach puberty. There is no way for them just to say no to what is happening to themselves. They know that. And they identify those who tell them otherwise as the more or less well-intentioned fools we truly are when we deny a manifest truth. It is scary to turn over the keys of the car to your kid. So we do everything we can to prepare the kid to manage the risk. But we prefer not to know about the sex thing. Too threatening. Why? Well, we don't feel guilty about driving.

We are passing down a legacy of guilt, mystification, and incompetence. At best, we are failing to transmit what we do know, and, at worst, we are tempting them with Adam's apple when we should be serving it at table. The apple signifies knowledge, carnal knowledge, knowledge of our bodies and their capacities to generate pleasure and pain, love and hate.

Sex isn't dirty; it's just dangerous. As it is with all dangers, so it is with sex: the more you know about it, the better able you will be able to handle it. The knowledge of which I speak includes, but is not limited to, the physiological facts of reproduction and transmission of diseases. Beyond that, it includes the critical assessment of prevalent norms and understanding of the psychological and sociological structures informing sexual behavior that this book has attempted to address. How might we hope to live a life of sexual sanity in a culture afflicted with sexual malaise? The first step in working out one's own answer—and in guiding those looking for solutions—is to pose the question in a thematic way.

### THEMATICS

#### PROMISCUITY

I am advocating affirmation of our sexual being. Does this amount to a covert advocacy of promiscuity? That depends, of course, on how one defines the term. A person is promiscuous, in my judgment, if that person has too many sexual partners for his or her own good, or for the good of the partners involved. Given that definition, I am not an advocate of promiscuity. But, how many is too many?

Under the model currently informing the sexual morality to which many pay lip service but few observe—the model of virgin marriage and lifelong exclusive fidelity—one should have one sole partner, and promiscuity starts with the second. Few adhere to this model, and that is well, even at the price of hypocrisy, because it turns mate selection into a game of chance uninformed by experience and comparison.

Two is okay, then. Maybe even preferable to one. What about three or four or ten or a hundred or five hundred or five thousand? Where does one draw the line? How could one draw the line? How would I prove that a range from twelve to twenty-four is better than a range of forty-eight to sixty? Or vice versa? Why would anyone attempt to do that?

Many parents view it as a disaster if their child starts going steady—and keeps going steady—in high school. They tell their children to play the field. Many parents are upset if their child has not entered a permanent relationship by age thirty. Children are upset if their parents split up and take new lovers or spouses. Older children think it is cute if their parents begin to date again in their later years after the untimely death of a spouse. I neither espouse nor repudiate these sentiments. I cite them to show that the number of partners that is appropriate for a given individual depends on structural variables such as time of life, antecedent commitments, and cultural milieu. In Hollywood, if you are seen with the same person several times, tongues begin to wag. In Grand Rapids, it works another way.

The number also depends on individual goals, tastes, and proclivities. Long term exclusive relationships offer benefits that short term multiple relationships do not. And vice versa. For a marriage minded person, a succession of partners is an indicator of an empty and unfulfilled life. For such persons, trust, loyalty, steadfastness, and a quality of intimacy that can only be nurtured in an abiding relationship are essential to personal happiness. For a gay caballero (in either or both senses of the term), such a relationship would be confining and oppressive, as it would for a merry widow or sex goddess. For some people, action, variety, intrigue, and a degree of intensity that cannot be sustained for long are necessary for the quality of life they want. Nor is it the case that one is committed to a given pattern throughout the course of a lifetime. The same person may adopt a pattern of serial monogamy in adolescence, take up exclusive monogamy during child-rearing years, pass into a period of recreational sex with multiple partners after the marriage terminates in death or divorce or debilitating illness, and then lose interest in sexual relationships altogether.

There is no number. Promiscuity is a term of opprobrium we apply to people we think are behaving badly. Sometimes, it is apt. If your son is a philanderer, you are not going to be a contented grandparent, nor will you be if he is a recluse headed in the direction of self-willed autism. If you have unprotected sex with large numbers of partners, your chances of catching a sexually transmitted disease are excellent. Even if you insist on condoms, your likelihood of getting sick increases as the number of contacts goes up. Apparently one in five American adults has herpes, and condoms are less than perfect in protecting against transmitting it. Chlamydia is also frightening: carriers are frequently unaware that they have the disease.

One is a bad number. So is fifty-two times fifty (averaging one partner a week for fifty years). But, if you are a devout Roman Catholic priest, one is too many; and if you are a prostitute by profession, one a week is too many for a sugar daddy and too few for a woman with a book. In between these extremes there is a range of options, and one cannot say a priori which is best. A posteriori, however, it is relatively easy to tell. The prime measure is satisfaction.

Satisfaction of what? One's own sense of το καλου.

## PHYSICAL BEAUTY

> *Diotima:* "The object of love, Socrates, is not, as you think, beauty."
> *Socrates:* "What is it then?"
> *Diotima:* "Its object is to engender and bring forth in beauty."[2]

Traditional interpretations of the *Symposium* regard the ugly Socrates as the genuine lover and the physically attractive Alcibiades as an example of love that does not understand its proper end. Socrates is the quintessential teacher; through his midwifery he gives birth to the genuine eros that resides within us all and nurtures it into *philia*. I contest this. Alcibiades was aware enough to choose Socrates as his beloved, and Socrates failed to nurture this auspicious seed into flower. Perhaps this is another instance of Plato's frequently deployed strategy of pointing toward the path of success by concretely portraying a failure. If so, it is the only time I can think of when the role of illustrating failure is assigned to the mature Socrates.[3]

The issue here is beauty. The Greek word translated as beauty in the passage above is το καλου. And whatever one makes of the aporetic love nonaffair between Alcibiades and Socrates, the issue of reality versus appearance in the case of beauty is thematic throughout the dialogue. Easy, then, to say that mere physical beauty is, at best, a distraction and, at worst, a deficit in the search for genuine love. Easy to attribute this to Plato, who typically argues that the perceptual world and what we see in it is constantly changing, hence not as trustworthy and real as the unchanging forms that are the true objects of philosophical contemplation.

I have argued against regarding the worlds of perception and thought as mutually exclusive. I have argued in favor of acknowledging that the *eidos* as perceptual physiognomy has a greater claim to reality than the *eidos* as idea, that the latter is parasitic upon the former.[4] I have appealed to an older understanding of το καλου which regards physical and spiritual beauty as inseparable. Does that mean that I am committed to saying that it is impossible for ugly people to love and be loved? I think it does. This acknowledgment has generated hostility to my ideas on more than one occasion. I welcome the philosophical agon, but want to avoid summary rejection.

Inner and outer beauty coincide in behavioral style. Style is adverbial, it describes the how rather more than the what of appearance, and it is temporally extended. There is little of style in a still photograph; style, like melody, manifests itself in unfolding. Individual notes, isolated and decontextualized, may be clean and pure, but they are neither harmonious nor cacophonous. So it is with behavioral style, which is why it takes a while to begin to see the beauty or ugliness of a person. We can identify physical beauty from a photograph; we cannot identify το καλου that way.

It is impossible to love someone whose behavioral style becomes recognizable as ugly. It is impossible because what makes the style ugly is a lack of human pathos, a failure to affirm in others, through the structures of reversibility, the value one assumes for oneself. Indeed, it may be a failure of self-affirmation that is responsible for that kind of ugliness, that lack of pathos. Ugly is unlovable because ugly can't love.

Is this sophistry? Have I ducked the issue by defining beauty in covertly spiritual terms? I have certainly refused to reduce beauty to meat, to merely physical attributes, but have I failed to do justice to the central role I have accorded to flesh and physiognomy?

Sometimes we find older persons unloving and unlovable because they have become irascible and cranky, incapable of a word of affirmation or approval. Cranky people have bad dispositions, they manifest unpleasantness over time; interpersonal negativity has become integral to their styles of behavior. The English colloquial term *cranky* is derived from the German *krank,* which means ill, sick, or diseased. It is difficult to be affirmative when one has suffered chronic pain over a long period of time and there is only darkness ahead. One may love a cranky parent or grandparent when their bodies have become painful burdens, but this love might better be described in terms of loyalty and commitment, sustained by memory and nostalgia for better times. If during a period of respite, the person you knew becomes recognizable again, a more robust sense of loving returns, one that is discernibly different in quality from the endurance of the bad times.

This example is rather far removed from the domain of sexlove, but it may help as a transitional thought. The point it seeks to illustrate is that a certain minimal level of physical health is required as a condition for the ability to affirm self and others, that is, to love. One may be steadfast and loyal to a spouse in advanced stages of Alzheimer's disease, but one cannot love someone one no longer knows, someone in whom one can awaken no sense of recognition. The emotional attachment evident in such cases may be strong and admirable, it may resemble love in several ways, but it is not the love I have attempted to describe in this book simply because the cognitive aspects of reversibility have eroded.

Health, physical fitness, the appearance associated with reproductive competence, and other such sheerly physical attributes have recently been studied as objective measures of sexual attractiveness or beauty. A typical experiment design is to ask subjects to look at a series of photographs and rank order them from very attractive to repellent. The photographs selected as attractive are then found to depict persons who share such objective characteristics as symmetry of features, a given proportionality in the dimensions of chest, waist, and hips, a certain height to weight ratio, etc. Other studies attempt to show that the sense of physical beauty is variable over cultures and times. The emaciated American flapper girl or Parisian gamin of the 1920s gave way to the voluptuous pin-ups of the World War II era, it was argued, because the insecurities of the war which led to baby boom reproduction, demanded a figure that symbolically represented security and abundance.

Such studies are reductive by intent: they try to isolate one set of mensurable variables and demonstrate that it has an important function in qualitative determinations. If we take such variables as these as indicative of what is meant by physical beauty, then it is evident that they cannot do justice to the conception of beauty named by το καλου, just because they intentionally disregard behavioral style and other components of appearance that do not lend themselves to objective measurement. If one goes beyond this impoverished domain to include behavioral style, as I have, one has, indeed, departed from the merely physical, but one has not, ipso facto, leapt into the domain of the purely spiritual. There is no appeal to inner qualities, the presence or absence of which is crucial to personal value but which cannot be detected in manifest action as, for example, the behavior Kierkegaard's Knight of Faith is indistinguishable from persons lacking his faith. Nor is my appeal to an outward glow radiating from an ineffable and invisible inner core posited as the occult cause for an individual's beauty. This claim is more difficult to substantiate, but perhaps I can establish it obliquely by considering the case of merely physical beauty coupled with behavioral ugliness, the case of cruel beauty.

## CRUEL BEAUTY

> Come away, come away, death,
> And in sad cypress let me be laid;
> Fly away, fly away, breath:
> I am slain by a fair cruel maid.
> (Shakespeare, *Twelfth Night*, II, iv, 51.)

Secondary narcissism, the narcissism of the mirror, has long been associated with cruel and unfeeling behavior. The psychological structure here is easy to understand. The child who is fair of face sometimes fails to develop the social awareness and concern for others that the rest of us have to acquire in order to elicit positive responses from those around us: approval is taken as a birthright. The romantic idealizations of mate selection come to rest on fair faces, and sometimes stop there for too long. One internalizes the affirmation radiating from the beatifying desire of the host of aspirant lovers without having to do anything but smile at the mirrors they hold up. Here is the dark side of reversibility. If beauty is the object of desire and I am automatically beautiful, my love for myself translates into love for the other as automatic affirmation, a thing that reflects my beauty without choosing to do so—a thing I use as I use all things, with tacit contempt, without asking the chair whether it would like to be sat upon.

Perhaps there is room here for a compelling sociobiological explanation for the phenomenon of the ugly duckling. The notorious beauty of the ephebe that emerges on the far side of puberty, all self-absorbed and self-sufficient, is a cruel and unusual beauty. Unusual because the process of adolescence typically involves an extended period of monstrous disproportionality and awkwardness. There are many reasons why adolescents are shy; some of them we have already seen, but this one is new: the hyper-reflexivity of the changeling is a mirroring phenomenon, but what is mirrored is an ungainly body that has lost the competence of childhood and stumbles like a colt into its emergent flesh. Perhaps this period of awkward sociality, this period of public defiance manifesting a private desperation for the approval it seeks among its peers, is a necessary phase in the development of an organism capable of the nurturing love necessary for successful reproduction and contribution to the gene pool.

There is such a thing as mere physical beauty or ugliness—the *eidos* we see in momentary snapshots or in one scene of a tragedy in four acts—and it plays a part in the evolution of the individual. Sunday's child may have a leg up on the rest of us, may learn to mirror back the sunny disposition people take to be reflected in its face. But Sunday's child may also, like the witch in *Snow White,* fall into the mirror of pathological narcissism. The unfavored child may learn to court approval by projecting it, or may learn to reflect the disdain he or she experiences as a lifelong strategy of wistful denial. Parental role models are crucial. Our parents teach us how to wear our faces; they have lived for a while in faces that usually resemble ours, and they can transmit vanity or humility (or their reaction formations).

Cruel beauty is an oxymoron in my lexicon. Cruelty cannot be beautiful. Those who are fair of face and form but behave destructively soon begin to appear ugly. The limiting case is the masochist, the person who seeks to be dominated and cruelly mistreated. Sacher Masoch would pay women or inveigle them through his own techniques of seduction and manipulation to beat and humiliate him. Doubtless, for him, his dominatrix would be beautiful, an object of desire. The categories of dominance and submission, of cruelty and acquiescence, begin to interpenetrate here, and threaten to confuse. But the matter resolves if we ask ourselves how Masoch would have reacted to genuine torture, humiliation, and real danger of maiming or death. Had he been a prisoner of war and subjected by a physically attractive woman to such terrors as the White Angel visited upon his victims, he would not have been sexually aroused or gratified, would not have seen his tormentor as beautiful. Masoch depended on the compassion and benevolence of his dominatrices, and on the control he exerted over them through money or affection. Had he recognized genuine sadistic intent in the behavior of one of them while he was bound and helpless to resist, I think his reaction would have been one of fear and loathing. Genuine sadistic intent: are we back, once again, to purely spiritual categories?

We can learn to love whole persons or fixate on partial objects. Whole persons are manifest in the style of their behavior. A snapshot is a partial object, a fetish. As it is with works of art, so it is with persons, the beauty that is immediately apparent may or may not wear well, may or may not evolve into το καλου. Only by stretching our simile can we attribute an inner spiritual beauty to da Vinci's painting of Mona Lisa: beneath the painted surface, there is only stretched canvas. What we see and call spiritual is a smile resonating between lips and eyes, a human gesture, a piece of behavior. If Mona Lisa, herself, managed to step out of the frame, we might eventually recognize her as a lovely person. Or we might find ourselves in the company of "a cold and lonely, lovely work of art," as Nat King Cole feared. In this case, as well as in the case of Masoch's dominatrix, it would depend upon a harmonious synthesis of the adumbrations of her behavior as her truth unfolded over time.

This temporal emergence of *ethos* or personal character may be the source of what we mean by inner or spiritual beauty, but it cannot be divorced from its flesh. Gestural grace requires a body. Bodies have to train themselves to be graceful; an inner representation, even if coupled with the will to enact it, is insufficient. And so I rest my case on this point. I have argued against bifurcating human existence into mutually exclusive realms of body and spirit. In the case of beauty and ugliness, then, it cannot be a matter of two separate lines of causality, one visible and one invisible, coming into some unthinkable coincidence. It must rather be corporeal intentionality revealing itself along a spectrum of modalities we find more or less attractive or repulsive. I have defined beauty in categories that include the spiritual, to be sure, but I have done so because it would be a mistake, the mistake of bifurcation, to have done anything else. What we call spirit or soul is a manner of being of flesh.

## The Beauty of Romance and το καλου

One of the tensions embodied in romantic love is the coupling of two disparate needs: one is the need to remain ignorant of the flesh and blood reality of the other, to avoid carnal knowledge in order to be able to sustain the immanent fantasy; the other is the need to have a flesh and blood presence upon which to project the idealization. Now we have a clearer understanding of how that is possible. I can fit snapshots into my fantasy album. If my moments of contact are of brief duration, if I protect my ideal from the obtrusion of your behavioral style by limiting exposure to selected shorts, I can fit those parts into a gestalt of my own fabrication, and avoid having to accommodate your being as an emergent whole. If we are complicit in the strategies of romance, if we carefully arrange to meet under conditions that foster romance—idyllic settings, candlelight and wine—if we carefully groom and clothe our bodies to project a photogenic image, if we orchestrate the encounter to avoid discord (or to heighten the sweet joy of reunion after an emotional collision), we can fill each other's albums with the illusions we cherish.

The positive side of this, as we have seen, is the transformative aspect, the attempt to become the ideal I project, the attempt to make myself worthy of the affirmation I seek. The negative side is the fragility of the fantasy, its tendency to dissipate into the ordinary with overexposure and the encroachment of carnal knowledge. The challenge posed throughout this book is that of sustaining the growth and self-transcendence of striving to actualize an ideal through the intimacy of prolonged contact in quotidian reality rather than avoiding that carnal knowledge by means of the strategies of the typical romantic *pas de deux* which are designed to sustain the illusions.

The question we confront now is how concretely this might be done.

One of the strategies that comes to the rescue of romantic love when its intensity is threatened by the boredom of encroaching familiarity is the lovers' quarrel. It is a characteristic of lovers' quarrels that they endow a trivial issue with emotional weight disproportionate to the significance of the precipitating event. This disproportionality is not adventitious, but essential, as we shall shortly see. One person is fifteen minutes late for a rendezvous, and the other is livid. Words, often rather unpleasant words, are exchanged, and the relationship is suddenly in question. What was to have been a joyful occasion is now filled with tears, pain, and recriminations. The lovers separate, cool off, reconsider, rise above ego investment and pride, and come together again, passion rekindled, in a blissful reunion. Each apology seeks to be more abject than the last, acknowledgment is made on both sides that the matter was truly of no consequence, and the event is forgotten. This sequence recapitulates itself at regular intervals. The inflammatory event remains trivial, but the heat of the quarrels escalates, and hasty words turn into hasty actions: the lovers rush off into the arms of others, property is damaged, physical violence occurs, outside intervention may become necessary. The real crisis comes when the lovers have to face the fact that they have become dysfunctional as a couple. They have to find better ways of settling their disputes, or they have to part company. When they part company, they find new partners and reenact the same drama. This is an old, dreary story, well known to family court justices and marriage counselors.

The precipitating event is trivial. It is the occasion, however, for a nontrivial confrontation. The trivial event is the means by which deeper and darker forces, genuine fears and antagonisms too awesome to be named or brought into the light of day, can express themselves and seek release or catharsis. In Freudian terms, they are the emissaries of the unconscious. In the example at hand, the failure to be on time for a meeting, it may be jealousy or fear of betrayal that is at work, or it may be some other insecurity, some sense that one is overcommitted, that one's emotional investment is not matched on the other side, a deep anxiety that one is not loved. Or it may be a genuine hatred of the other, the truly unspeakable.

As we have seen, love is never pure; love is always love-hate. It is always love-hate because hatred is a response to threat and we are threatened by our vulnerability, our emotional dependence on the other for our own welfare. The greater the love, the greater the vulnerability, hence the larger the threat of the hatred on the horizon of the relationship. The child screaming its hate of its mother in the supermarket is expressing in infantile and demonic form the anxiety attendant upon all profound love. So is the wickedly vituperative or abusive spouse.

The difference between romantic love and authentic love is carnal knowledge, knowledge of oneself as well as the other. The knowledge that the romantic lover tries to avoid is knowledge that the authentic lover seeks out. When authentic lovers find themselves in heated antagonism over a trivial affair, they seek to uncover, name, and confront the demon they know is there.

I am really angry that you were late because it makes me feel that you don't care enough about me to be on time. People are seldom late for an occasion of pleasure. My anger is rooted in the fear that you don't love me in the way I need to be loved.

Okay. I am angry that you are angry. I don't think you are handling your insecurity in a responsible way. You know that I am seldom late. It is not a recurring pattern. You also have plenty of evidence for my abiding love for you. But you insist on more. Your insecurity—which we both have—is manifesting itself as a project of control. You use unwarranted anger to manipulate my behavior and demand unreasonable proofs of my affection. That is unfair and counterproductive. It makes me feel like an object you want to own rather than a person you are strong enough to love. It makes me create my own defenses and withdraw from you emotionally.

There may be some truth in what you say. I'll think about it.

Well, we both know that I am not as demonstrative as I might be. Maybe if I offered reassurances instead of waiting for your demands, I could short-circuit the problem.

At the end of such an exchange, the air would not be clear and pure again. The problem has been recognized as real, as grounded in frailties on both sides. There is difficult internal housecleaning to be done by both parties. They would not fall into bed for a jolly romp that would make everything better again. The confrontation would generate reflective distantiation. They would brood and try to succeed at the monumental task of being honest with themselves, trying to avoid both self-serving blaming of the other, on one side, and facile apologies to get beyond the negativity, on the other. They might even seek counsel from a third party. And chances are that, if the frailties at stake are tightly woven into the dispositions of the persons involved, similar confrontations await them in the future.

In the meantime, however, all the other aspects of the relationship will continue to reinforce it. He may be deeply committed to his career, occasionally inattentive, and not as overtly affectionate as she would have him be. But he is strong and protective, unfailingly loyal, and funny. He is also unpredictable, shows up with masses of flowers and reservations for a weekend alone together in a retreat for lovers. She may be a bit possessive and overly sensitive to slight. But she is also smart and honest and understanding, quick to see, and generous in response. Each sees qualities in the other to emulate. If they cycle through the inattentive/manipulative debate again, it will be on a different level, building on earlier insights, renewing the project of growth and self-transcendence.

The beauty that is nobility, το καλου, is the beauty that engenders beauty in one's lovers and in oneself. Just as Diotima said.

It may be that the negativities uncovered in the process of mutual discovery are devastating to the relationship. One may be forced to realize that the other is weak and incapable of rising above self-indulgence. Or that this apparently noble person is full of deceit, that irresponsibility and inability to face unpleasant truth permeate his or her character. If this happens, the relationship is at an end: the person one had loved, may, indeed, still love, no longer exists. The person standing there before me is not the person I love, but a stranger dwelling in a familiar body. Or this person is someone I have known for quite some time; this flaw that is tragic to our relationship is one that I have known in the mode of denial. After my coming to awareness, I may choose to continue in a relationship, but this will be a different relationship: we have both changed, she is no longer the person I thought she was, and I am no longer the person who thought of her that way.

There is a ticklish point here that needs to be mentioned but cannot be resolved in a book. Is love compatible with the project of changing one's partner? The trait I wish to change is something about the individual, part of his character I cannot affirm: how can I then be said to love this person? No person, myself included, is a complete instantiation of all the values I cherish, everybody has room for growth: how could I love a person and not want her to grow? If my lover is a recovering alcoholic or substance abuser, or if my lover habitually abreacts the scars of parental abuse, or if my lover earns his or her living in a trade I cannot respect . . . does that nullify my love? You smoke cigarettes and show no real sign of wanting to kick the addiction, therefore I will stop seeing you. If you want to see me anymore, stop smoking. Pitfalls on both sides. The fact is that serious flaws are just that; they pose serious threats to the individual and all who are intimate with the individual.

All relationships are conditional: this is a necessary correlate of human finitude. All relationships come to an end with death. Literally. Heloise and Abelard live on in literature, but they are dead and so are the Brownings. There are conditions that are tolerable, others that are not, and a host of imponderables in between. Great love has been known to overcome great obstacles. This is the core of the romantic tradition. The lovers surmount the insurmountable, and then the book ends. Worldly obstacles—towering mountains, raging seas, bitter family feuds—are not at stake here. What is at stake in love are persons, their bodies, and the histories sedimented in their flesh. Whether love will be ennobling or disabling is contingent upon the persons involved, the nature of the relationship that develops when they come together, and the vicissitudes of fate. We have but a modicum of influence over these three variables.

What one can change within oneself, other persons, and the world at large is a matter of judgment. Judgment is informed by knowledge. The more one knows, the better judgments one makes. One's erotic fate can be profoundly affected by the judgments one makes. Carnal knowledge is not the only knowledge that is relevant to loving, but it is indispensable.

To love is to put oneself at risk. Not to love is to turn the risk of catastrophe into a certainty. Meaning, as I understand that abstract term, refers to relatedness: the meaning of a thing is how it is related to other things, its place within an overarching whole. The relationship that confers meaning, the relationship that, more than any other, defines our relationship to the transcendent whole of human existence . . . is, I believe, love.

# BIBLIOGRAPHY

Aquinas, Thomas. *On the Truth of the Catholic Faith*. Trans. Vernon J. Bourke. Quoted in *Sexual Love and Western Morality*. Ed. D. P. Verene. New York: Harper and Row, 1972.

Aristotle. *Poetics*. Trans. Richard McKeon. New York: Random House, 1941.

Aristotle. *Nichomachean Ethics*. Trans. Ross. London: Oxford University Press, 1963.

Bataille, Georges. *Erotism: Death and Sensuality*. Trans. Mary Dalwood. San Francisco: City Lights Books, 1986.

————. *The Story of the Eye*. Trans. Joachim Neugroschel. San Francisco: City Lights Books, 1987.

de Rougemont, Denis. *Love in the Western World*. Trans. Montgomery Belgion. New York: Harper and Row, 1974.

Dillon, M. C. "Sartre on the Phenomenal Body and Merleau-Ponty's Critique," *The Journal of the British Society for Phenomenology* 5, No. 2 (1974).

————. "Merleau-Ponty and the Psychogenesis of the Self," *Journal of Phenomenological Psychology* 11, No. 1 (1978).

————. "Toward a Phenomenology of Love and Sexuality," *Soundings* LXIII, No. 4 (1980).

————. "Merleau-Ponty on Existential Sexuality: A Critique," *Journal of Phenomenological Psychology* 11, No. 1 (1980).

————. "Love, Death, and Creation," *Research in Phenomenology* XI (1981).

————. "The Phenomenon of Obscenity in Literature," *Journal of Value Inquiry* 16 (1982).

————. "Romantic Love, Enduring Love, and Authentic Love," *Soundings* LXVI, No. 2 (1983).

————. "Merleau-Ponty and the Reversibility Thesis," *Man and World* 16 (1983).

————. "Erotic Desire," *Research in Phenomenology* XV (1985).

————. "Desire: Language and Body," *In Post-Modernism and Continental Philosophy*, ed. Silverman and Welton. Albany: State University of New York Press, 1988.

————. "Desire for All/Love of One: Tomas's Tale in *The Unbearable Lightness of Being*," *Philosophy Today* 33, No. 4 (1989).

———. "Sexual Norms and the Burden of Sexual Literacy," *Journal of Phenomenological Psychology* 23, No. 2 (1992).

———. *Merleau-Ponty's Ontology*. Bloomington: Indiana University Press, 1988. Second edition with supplement on "Truth in Art." Evanston: Northwestern University Press, 1997.

———. "Sex, Time, and Love: Erotic Temporality," *Journal of Phenomenological Psychology* 18, No. 1 (1987). Reprinted in *Sex, Love, and Friendship*, ed. Soble and Kirshner. Atlanta: Rodopi, 1997.

———. *Semiological Reductionism: A Critique of the Deconstructionist Movement in Postmodern Thought*. Albany: State University of New York Press, 1995.

———. "Am I a Grammatical Fiction?—The Debate over Ego Psychology." *Merleau-Pouty's Later Works and Their Practical Implications: The Dehiscence of Responsibility*, ed. Duane H. Davis. Amherst, N.Y.: Humanity Books, 2001.

———. "Decrypting Desire: Beyond the Postmodern Blues." In *Imagination and its Pathologies*, ed. James Morley. Cambridge, Mass.: MIT Press, forthcoming.

Foucault, Michel. *The History of Sexuality, Volume I: An Introduction*. Trans. Robert Hurley. New York: Random House, 1980.

———. *The Use of Pleasure: Volume 2 of The History of Sexuality*. Trans. Robert Hurley. New York: Pantheon Books, 1985.

Freud, Sigmund. "Instincts and Their Vicissitudes." Trans. Cecil M. Baines. In *General Psychological Theory*, ed. Philip Rieff. New York: Macmillan, 1963. First published in *Zeitschrift*, Band III, 1915. Reprinted in *Sammlung, Vierte Folge*.

———. "A Special Type of Object Choice Made by Men." Trans. Joan Riviera. In *Sexuality and the Psychology of Love*, ed. P. Rieff. New York: Macmillan, 1963. First published in *Jahrbuch*, Band II. Reprinted in *Sammlung, Vierte Folge*, 1918.

———. "The Taboo of Virginity." Trans. Joan Riviera. In *Sexuality and the Psychology of Love*, ed. P. Rieff. New York: Macmillan, 1963. First published in *Sammlung, Vierte Folge*, 1918.

———. *The Ego and the Id*. Trans. Joan Riviere. New York: W.W. Norton, 1962. First published in 1923 by Internationaler Psychoanalytische Verlag, Leipzig, Vienna, and Zurich. Reprinted in *Gesammelte Schriften*, Band VI, 1925.

Graves, Robert. *The Greek Myths*. London: Penguin Books, 1960.

Heidegger, Martin. "On the Essence of Truth." Trans. John Sallis. In *Martin Heidegger: Basic Writings*, ed. David Farrell Krell. New York: Harper and Row, 1977.

Kierkegaard, Soren. *Either/Or*. Vol. 1. Trans. David F. Swenson and Lillian Marvin Swenson. Garden City, N.Y.: Doubleday. 1959.

Lacan, Jacques. *Feminine Sexuality: Jacques Lacan and the école freudienne*. Ed. Juliet Mitchell and Jacqueline Rose. Trans. Jacqueline Rose. New York: W.W. Norton, 1982.

Lawrence, D.H. *Women in Love*. New York: Viking Press, 1960.

Locke, John. *An Essay Concerning Human Understanding*. Ed. Fraser. New York: Dover, 1959.

Malraux, André. *La Monnaie de l'absolu*. Quoted in Merleau-Ponty. "Indirect Language and the Voices of Silence." In *Signs*, trans. Richard C. McCleary. Evanston: Northwestern University Press, 1964.

Merleau-Ponty, Maurice. "The Child's Relations with Others." Trans. William Cobb. In *The Primacy of Perception and Other Essays on Phenomenological Psychology, the Philosophy of Art, History and Politics*, ed. James M. Edie. Evanston: Northwestern University Press, 1964. "Les Relations avec autrui chez l'enfant." In *Les Cours de Sorbonne*. Paris: Centre de Documentation Universitaire, 1960.

————. "The Experience of Others." Trans. Fred Evans and Hugh J. Silverman. In *Review of Existential Psychology and Psychiatry* 18 (1982–83). "L'expérience d'autrui." In *Bulletin du Groupe d'études de psychologie de l'Université de Paris (1951–1952)*. Paris: Centre de Documentation Universitaire.

Miller, Fred D., Jr. "Aristotle on Natural Law and Justice." In *A Companion to Aristotle's Politics*, ed. David Keyt and Fred D. Miller, Jr. Cambridge, Mass.: Basil Blackwell, 1961.

Norton, David L., and Mary F. Kille (Eds.). *Philosophies of Love*. Totowa, N.J.: Rowman & Littlefield, 1971.

Ovid. *The Metamorphoses*. Trans. Horace Gregory. New York: Viking Press, 1958.

Partridge, Eric. *Origins: A Short Etymological Dictionary of Modern English*. New York: Greenwich House, 1983.

Person, E. S. *Dreams of Love and Fateful Encounters: The Power of Romantic Passion*. New York: Penguin Books, 1989.

Plato, *Symposium*. Trans. W. R. M. Lamb. London: Heinemann, 1961.

Ricoeur, Paul. *Freud and Philosophy: An Essay on Interpretation*. Trans. Denis Savage. New Haven: Yale University Press, 1970.

Sappho. *The Poems of Sappho*. Trans. Suzy Q. Groden. Indianapolis: Bobbs-Merrill, 1966.

Sartre, Jean-Paul. *Being and Nothingness*. Trans. Hazel Barnes. New York: Washington Square Press, 1966.

Solomon and Higgins (Eds.). *The Philosophy of (Erotic) Love*. Lawrence: University of Kansas Press, 1991.

Stendahl. *Love*. Trans. Gilbert and Suzanne Sale. Harmondsworth, England: Penguin Books, 1975.

Verene, D. P. (Ed.). *Sexual Love and Western Morality: A Philosophical Anthology*. Second edition. Boston: Jones and Bartlett, 1995.

# NOTES

## CHAPTER ONE
### NAMES OF LOVE

1. Thus, love and hate are not mutually exclusive opposites, but limiting points of a continuum in which positive and negative aspects intertwine. One seeks to find ways to maximize the positive—that is one of the aims of this book—but, as I shall try to show, that requires acknowledging the inevitability of the darker aspects of love. The more one loves, for example, the more one is vulnerable to the vicissitudes of the beloved's freedom and fate.

2. Plato's *Meno* inquires about the essence of excellence or virtue *(arete)* and Plato raises the paradox in reference to that subject matter, but it can invoked with regard to any subject of inquiry, as I invoke it here on the issue of love.

3. See chapter 9.

4. Actually, as will become apparent in chapter 5, she was true to one precept (the principle that romantic love takes precedence over the conventions of marriage), but broke with another (the principle that consummation is to be deferred indefinitely because it preordains the death of love). Romantic love yearns for the unattainable. If Guinevere had loved Lancelot, but remained chaste, she would have been a truer romantic.

5. See M. C. Dillon, "Romantic Love, Enduring Love, and Authentic Love," *Soundings* LXVI, No. 2 (1983).

6. Soren Kierkegaard, *Either/Or,* Vol. 1, trans. David F. and Lillian Marvin Swenson (Garden City, N.Y.: Doubleday & Company, 1959), 37.

7. I am referring here to such thinkers as Sigmund Freud, Georges Bataille, and Jacques Lacan. Simply put, the argument runs as follows. The primal law, the law that generates the very idea of law (hence institutes culture as such), is the law of exogamy, the law that prohibits incest. The birth of civilization is the point at which the incest that is apparent in nature among animals is explicitly prohibited among clans of protohumans. This is the point that marks the difference between the unconscious animal instinct to reproduce and the human consciousness of desire. Human desire is, thus, the product of the institution of a symbolic ordering, a law prohibiting certain forms of sexual activity. The linguistic act that names a prohibition in articulating this first law thereby

transforms natural inclination into something new, human desire—animals may behave prudently in recognizing a danger as such, but they cannot speak, hence cannot behave in a consciously lawful way.

8. Bataille's novel, *The Story of the Eye,* trans. Joachim Neugroschel (San Francisco: City Lights Books, 1987) is a *tour de force* in which we are presented with a sequence of erotic episodes that escalate in violence from an idyllic opening scene in which beautiful youth loses its innocence by making love in defiance of the prohibition against underage sexual expression to a final act of sexual outrage in which a cleric is seduced, subdued, raped, and murdered. The point at stake is Bataille's claim that what makes human desire what it is and separates it from innocent animal desire is its telos of transgression. Human desire is a cultural phenomenon that feeds itself on violating the sacred, according to Bataille, and could not exist if it did not provide itself with laws to break.

I think Bataille's analysis of the piquance of forbidden fruit is acute and on target, but reductive and ultimately misleading insofar as it purports to account for the full range of human desire. I contend that the prohibitions constitutive of the sacred are grounded in prudential considerations—sex is dangerous of itself—and then become institutionalized in religious symbolism with a false guise of autonomy derived from forgetfulness of its pragmatic origins. We create our gods for our own purposes, but they tend to run amok.

The point at stake here is that, if desire is driven *exclusively* by the motive of transgression, it is tragic, futile, and bound to death. The very idea of fulfillment or satisfaction is ruled out from the start. If I violate the prohibition, then desire dies. If I do not violate the prohibition, I am not satisfied. Once I have broken a given law, the desire to transgress it disappears: I have laid waste to its transcendence, emptied it of pleasure and enticement. I must go on to the next prohibition in search of a new frisson. Each success spells the death of desire. And I awaken from my ecstasy surrounded by the blood and excrement of the dead priest. This is the logic of romantic love at work. It is the dark side of romance, but it is genuinely romance: I want what I want *because* it is out of reach, forbidden.

If, on the other hand, the goal of my desire is carnal knowledge of another human being, each success opens further mystery, beckoning me on toward the enticement of deeper revelation. I want what I want because it gives me pleasure and fulfillment. I awaken to the prospect of further vistas, further challenges to my acuity. Death awaits us all, to be sure, but the piquance of life does not lie in hastening the event.

9. 'Semiological reductionism' is my term for the thesis that meaning (significance, relation in general) in human experience is necessarily the product of mediation by signs [Greek, *semata*], symbols, signifiers, or language. See M.C. Dillon, *Semiological Reductionism: A Critique of the Deconstructionist Movement in Postmodern Thought* (Albany, N.Y.: State University of New York Press, 1995).

CHAPTER TWO
ALETHEIA, POIESIS, AND EROS

1. Plato, *Symposium,* trans. W. R. M. Lamb (London: Heinemann, 1961), 111.

2. Michel Foucault, *The Use of Pleasure: Volume 2 of The History of Sexuality,* trans. Robert Hurley (New York: Pantheon Books, 1985), 225.

3. Stendahl, *Love,* trans. Gilbert and Suzanne Sale (Harmondsworth, England: Penguin Books, 1975), 275–278.

NOTES TO CHAPTER TWO 163

4. *The Poems of Sappho,* trans. Suzy Q. Groden (Indianapolis: Bobbs-Merrill, 1966), 20.

5. Ovid, *The Metamorphoses,* trans. Horace Gregory (New York: Viking Press, 1958), Book XV, 421.

6. Denis de Rougemont, *Love in the Western World,* trans. Montgomery Belgion (New York: Harper and Row, 1974), page references in the text.

7. See M. C. Dillon, "Romantic Love, Enduring Love, and Authentic Love," *Soundings* LXVI, No. 2 (1983).

8. "Just as the simple taboo created eroticism in the first place in the organized violence of transgression, Christianity in its turn deepened the degree of sensual disturbance by forbidding organized transgression." Georges Bataille, *Erotism: Death and Sensuality,* trans. Mary Dalwood (San Francisco: City Lights Books, 1986), 127.

9. "In the psychiatrization of perversions, sex was related to biological functions and to an anatomo-physiological machinery that gave it its 'meaning,' that is, its finality [i.e., reproduction]; but it was also referred to an instinct which, through its peculiar development and according to the objects to which it could become attached, made it possible for perverse behavior patterns to arise and made their genesis intelligible." Michel Foucault, *The History of Sexuality, Volume I: An Introduction,* trans. Robert Hurley (New York: Random House, 1980), 153.

10. "It is evident . . . that every emission of semen, in such a way that generation cannot follow, is contrary to the good for man. And if this be done deliberately, it must be a sin. Now, I am speaking of a way from which, in itself, generation could not result: such would be any emission of semen apart from the *natural* union of male and female. For which reason, sins of this type are called contrary to nature." Thomas Aquinas, *On the Truth of the Catholic Faith,* III, i, trans. Vernon J. Bourke, quoted in *Sexual Love and Western Morality,* ed. D. P. Verene (New York: Harper and Row, 1972), 121, emphasis added.

11. "A law being that which is *laid* down, *law* not too surprisingly comes, through Middle English *lawe,* earlier *laghe,* from Old English *lagu,* law, akin to and probably from Old Norse *lög,* law, originally the plural of *lag,* a layer or stratum, a due place, synonym Old Saxon *lag,* Old Frisian *laga.*" Eric Partridge, *Origins: A Short Etymological Dictionary of Modern English* (New York: Greenwich House, 1966), 353. Pokorny (the *American Heritage Electronic Dictionary*) and the *Shorter Oxford English Dictionary* give similar accounts.

12. See chapter 3 below, "Natural Law and Sexual Morality."

13. For an account of the psychogenesis of desire, see M. C. Dillon, "Merleau-Ponty and the Psychogenesis of the Self," *Journal of Phenomenological Psychology* 11, No. 1 (1978).

14. The lived body provides an ambiguous, but non-arbitrary measure for modes of erotic regulation. Castration of preadolescent males preserves the soprano range in their voices. Clitorectomy may or may not dampen the development of erotic interest among preadolescent females. Circumcision may have salubrious effects, but perhaps at the expense of pleasure. The list goes on: some cultures tattoo the bodies of the youth; others pierce earlobes, nipples, penises, noses, tongues; some bind feet, and others elongate necks or flatten heads. No culture leaves the body intact, unaltered, unadorned, unpainted, unstyled. Call it mutilation or enhancement, we modify the bodies of our youth in order to adapt them to our purposes, and usually without soliciting the consent of the individual. I take bodily motility or functionality as a paradigm of freedom, and freedom as a measure of civilization. The point here is tenuous and might be defended better than I have,

but it is worthy of consideration: the lived body provides a measure of the deployment of power lurking behind social construction.

15. See M. C. Dillon, *Semiological Reductionism,* chapter 6, for a critical exegesis of Derrida's account of desire.

16. André Malraux, *La Monnaie de l'absolu,* 125. Quoted in Merleau-Ponty, "Indirect Language and the Voices of Silence," in *Signs,* trans. Richard C. McCleary (Evanston: Northwestern University Press, 1964), 57.

17. "Of Don Juan we must use the word *seducer* with great caution . . . . This is not because Don Juan is too good, but because he simply does not fall under ethical categories. . . . [Don Juan] does not seduce. He desires, and this desire acts seductively. . . . I suppose he is a deceiver, but yet not so that he plans his deceptions in advance; it is the inherent power of sensuousness which deceives the seduced, and it is rather a kind of Nemesis." Soren Kierkegaard, *Either/Or,* Vol. 1, trans. David F. Swenson and Lillian Marvin Swenson (Garden City, N.Y.: Doubleday, 1959), 97. Tell that to Donna Anna, Soren, or to her father, the Commandatore, who sends Don Giovanni off to hell in a triumph of moral outrage.

18. "As letting beings be, freedom is intrinsically the resolutely open bearing that does not close up in itself." Martin Heidegger, "On the Essence of Truth," trans. John Sallis, in *Martin Heidegger: Basic Writings,* ed. David Farrell Krell (New York: Harper and Row, 1977), 133.

19. "The inordinate forgetfulness of humanity persists in securing itself by means of what is readily available and always accessible. This persistence has its unwitting support in that bearing by which Dasein not only ek-sists but also at the same time in-sists . . . ." Ibid., 135.

## CHAPTER THREE
## NATURAL LAW AND SEXUAL MORALITY

1. Precepts of specifically sexual morality and precepts of general morality may be distinguished by the criterion of extension: general moral precepts range over all dimensions of human behavior; specifically sexual moral precepts apply exclusively to sexual conduct. As will be evident in the argument that follows, these two areas overlap, and this overlapping generates confusion.

2. *Roth v. United States,* 354 U.S. 476 (1957). A similar position was taken in the recent rejection of the "Communications Decency Act" regarding the regulation of sexual content on the Internet.

3. The obvious exception is the law of exogamy, the prohibition against incest. My response to this will be brief, as little rests on the point. Like sanctions regarding property, sanctions regarding consanguinity are pervasive but highly variable from culture to culture. Property, blood, food, sexual behavior, etc. are generally sanctioned, how they are sanctioned is specific. The law of exogamy operates at a level different from the appeal to universality.

One might also acknowledge the force of the argument that contends that the law of exogamy does not originate as a specifically sexual precept, but rather as a precept designed to reduce strife generated by competition for mates within the clan. This argument also accounts for the animus against incest in cultures where the dangers of homozygosity are unknown and the biology of reproduction little understood.

4. I am arguing here against the demonization of sex as such: the idea that sex is inherently evil and can be redeemed only by appeal to supervening principles. "It is reasonable . . . that we should feel very much ashamed of [sexual] lust, and reasonable too that those members which it moves or does not move by its own right, so to speak, and not in full subjection to our will, should be called pudenda or shameful parts . . . . Surely any friend of wisdom and holy joys, who lives in wedlock but knows, as the Apostle admonished, 'how to possess his bodily vessel in holiness and honor, not in the disease of lust like the gentiles who do not know God,' would prefer, if he could, to beget children without this kind of lust." St. Augustine, *City of God,* trans. Philip Levine (Cambridge, Mass.: Harvard University Press, 1966), 4:345–401.

5. See Fred D. Miller Jr., "Aristotle on Natural Law and Justice," in *A Companion to Aristotle's Politics,* ed. David Keyt and Fred D. Miller Jr. (Cambridge, Mass.: Basil Blackwell, Inc., 1961), 279–306. The interpretation set forth here takes its departure from this excellent article and guidance provided by my colleague at Binghamton University, Anthony Preus, although neither should be held accountable for it.

6. "Aristotle finds it necessary to adopt [a] biological perspective [on natural law and justice] because he has repudiated the metaphysical foundations of Plato's theory of natural law and justice. Plato's *Laws* represents justice and law as 'natural' in the sense of having a divine origin (see IV.715e7–716a3, 716c4–6; X.888d7–890d8). Nature in Plato's *Republic* is a transcendent, eternal and immutable principle involving the theory of Forms. Aristotle has replaced this with a notion of nature as a principle of change which is inherent in substances and which, in the sublunary realm at least, holds always or for the most part." Ibid., 289.

7. "Biology is not a value-free science for Aristotle. On the contrary, it explains the presence, structures, and interrelationships of organs in terms of their value for living, teleological systems." Ibid., 292.

8. "Human beings have their left limbs detached most of all the animals because they are according to nature *(kata phusin)* most of all the animals; now the right is by nature *(phusei)* better than the left, being separate from it, and so in human beings the right is most right [among all the animals]." *De Incessu Animalum,* a18–22. The translations of Aristotle's works in this section are Miller's.

9. "Nature does nothing in vain, but always the best possible concerning each kind of animal with respect to its substance. Therefore, if one way is better *(beltion)* than another, that is also according to nature *(kata phusin)*" (2.704b12–18).

10. Miller, op. cit., 291.

11. At stake is the issue of attributing intent to nature at large. Under the Aristotelian account, right-handedness does not emerge from the intentions of natural entities, it is a supervenient principle which informs nature. Animals and humans do not choose to be right-handed in order to survive; nature designs us to be right-handed to ensure our survival. If nature makes nothing in vain, that means that nature is driven by an intent whose origin lies beyond the intentions of natural entities, an intent or purpose transcendent to the organisms comprising nature.

12. The terms are taken from Merleau-Ponty. See M. C. Dillon, *Merleau-Ponty's Ontology* (Bloomington: Indiana University Press, 1988), 67.

13. As Miller puts it, the ideal system is one in which "the lawgiver uses his practical rationality to frame a constitution and to fashion laws which bring the polis into a just or natural condition: that is, which will promote the common advantage of the citizens in the sense of enabling them to realize their natural ends and attain the good life. Although nature constrains the lawgiver in that he must cooperate with the nature of the citizens, he nevertheless has considerable room for inventiveness and discretion in crafting the conventional component of political justice." Op. cit., 305.

14. "Nature makes nothing in vain, and human beings are the only animals endowed by nature with logos or speech. Human speech serves to reveal the advantageous and the harmful, and hence also the just . . . and the unjust. . . . Nature [also] endows humans with the desire to live together because life in political communities is necessary for their common advantage." Ibid., 293–294. Here Miller cites *Politics* III.6.1278b17–30.

15. "Aristotle is seeking in his different discussions to accommodate . . . common beliefs *[endoxa]* as far as possible, but he is not merely taking these beliefs to be given and putting them, as far as possible, into a coherent system. He is also seeking a deeper normative theory which tries to draw upon 'things that seem to be the case' in order to justify common ethical beliefs and correct them if necessary. As part of this method, he argues that the principles of ethics depend upon principles of his natural and metaphysical works which are themselves defended by reference to nonethical *endoxa* and *phainomena*." Ibid., 282.

16. This distinction between the empirical and the trans-empirical depends upon a narrow conception of the empirical, which I shall abandon eventually. Narrowly defined, the empirical domain is value-free, hence any prescription or norm would have to be justified by appeal to a trans-empirical domain. One of the key theses being presented here is that this narrow definition is reductive and cannot ultimately be sustained.

17. The dogmatic tone of these remarks stems from the need for brevity and, I trust, will be vindicated by the use subsequently made of them. The polemical aspect is sheer self-indulgence for which I offer apologies to those who want them.

18. I leave it to scholars better versed in ancient Greek thought than I to determine whether the use of the craftsmanship analogy about to be criticized is properly ascribed to Plato or to Socrates.

19. "We call that which is in itself worthy of pursuit more final than that which is worthy of pursuit for the sake of something else, and that which is never desirable for the sake of something else more final than the things that are desirable both in themselves and for the sake of that other thing, and therefore we call final without qualification that which is always desirable in itself and never for the sake of something else.

"Now such a thing happiness, above all else, is held to be; for this we choose always for itself and never for the sake of something else. . . ." *Nicomachean Ethics,* 1.1097a30–b1, trans. W. D. Ross.

20. Note that I understand intent as qualified by deliberation, some degree of thematic awareness or choice. I remain silent on the issue of such ascriptions of intent to nature as are latent in the family of concepts grouped under such headings as instinct, drive, conatus and associated with "unconscious" tele such as survival of the organism, the species or perpetuation of nature at large.

21. Miller's essay, "Aristotle on Natural Law and Justice," interprets Aristotle as arguing on the basis of an analogy between natural justice and right-handedness. In this context, Miller raises the following questions.

> In what sense could Aristotle claim that natural justice is "superior" or "stronger," by analogy to right-handedness? And even if an analogy could be found, why suppose that it would support normative conclusions? Does the fact that the right hand is generally stronger than the left imply that it is better? (Op. cit., 288)

Miller tacitly acknowledges that Aristotle does infer the value of its superiority from the fact that the right hand is generally stronger.

The standpoint I am developing contends not so much that it is valid to infer values from facts, but that it is a mistake to separate the two in the first place. I do not think Aristotle made that mistake. I do think Aristotle made the mistake of conceiving natural entities as entelechies in a way that attributes to nonhuman aspects of nature the kind of deliberate intentions evident in human teleology. What I have been calling "the onto-theological fallacy" is a species of anthropomorphism.

22. A hypothetical imperative takes the form of an "if-then" assertion known in traditional formal logic as a hypothetical statement: *if* you want this, *then* you must do that. The antecedent, or "if" clause is a matter of contingent fact: one may or may not want this. Hence, the force of the *must* in the consequent, or "then" clause, is dependent upon the contingent desire expressed in the antecedent. Kant's categorical imperative—so act that the maxim of your act can be willed as a universal law—is not dependent upon contingent desire, but is held to govern all human action: it tells us what we must do under all circumstances.

23. Traditional natural law morality as applied to the sexual domain has based itself on such norms as the male-female reproductive dyad and male superiority as supernatural intentions discernible in nature. I have already repudiated the notion of supernatural intent, but the prudence I advocate prompts me to state explicitly that I regard perversity in sex just as I do perversity in other domains as practice contrary to human intent. I do not recognize any specifically sexual morality, but seek to subsume sexual behavior under the same precepts that govern other domains of human interaction. It is my intent to promote an environment in which consenting adults are free to do whatever they please with themselves and each other, subject only to self-imposed constraint based on knowledge of risk. Nor do I think that either gender—or any gender—enjoys general superiority over any other, although I do think that we are all constrained by genetic coding and bodily attributes.

## CHAPTER FOUR
## SEXLOVE: MARGINALITY AND RECTITUDE

1. I should note here that we are not in general agreement as to what constitutes rape, what degree of consanguinity is acceptable, or what age is appropriate to establish as the age of consent.

2. There are even advocates for bestiality. Their arguments may be found in the Internet newsgroup devoted to that subject: alt.sex.bestiality.

CHAPTER FIVE
ROMANTIC LOVE

1. "Some argue that Eros, hatched from the world-egg, was the first of the gods since, without him, none of the rest could have been born; they make him coeval with Mother Earth and Tartarus, and deny that he had any father or mother, unless it were Eileithyia, Goddess of Childbirth." Hesiod, *Theogony*, 120.

"Others hold that he was Aphrodite's son by Hermes, or by Ares, or by her own father, Zeus; or the son of Iris by the West Wind (Alcaeus, quoted by Plutarch: *Amatorius*, 20)." Robert Graves, *The Greek Myths*, Vol. 1 (London: Penguin Books, 1960), 58.

Plato offers a similar account in the *Symposium* where Pausanius argues that there are two goddesses of love, heavenly Aphrodite (the primordial figure, a symbol of spiritual love), and earthly Aphrodite (younger and lesser, symbolizing physical love). *Symposium*, 180c–181d.

2. "This difference it is that distinguishes Tragedy and Comedy also; the one would make its personages worse, and the other better, than the men of the present day." Aristotle, *Poetics*, 1448a10–20.

3. Gays and lesbians are doubly oppressed—they are vilified not only for being sexual, but for being sexual in a manner contrary to nature—but they have no exclusive claim on the closet. The closet is where we are all supposed to conduct our sexual affairs. Sexual liberation is a task for us all, and gratitude is due to all who take the risk to carry the banner.

4. The greatest living Plato scholar I know, Harrison J. Pemberton, contends that Socrates "knew" the third truth as well, demonstrated that knowledge by conducting himself in accordance with it. To which I reply: maybe. But if he did, he failed to pass it along to his primary pupil and doxographer. Or so I am about to argue. (The failure of teachers to teach what *they* think is most important to their students is endemic to the profession. As this very essay may demonstrate, the students always take away what *they* think is most important.)

5. *Symposium*, trans. Walter Hamilton (London: Penguin Books, 1951), 95 (212a).

6. This point is controversial and heavily contested. Jacques Lacan, for example, has argued that personal identity is a sociolinguistic construct, a *méconnaissance* or mystification driven by the structures of desire and the symbolic forms through which these structures work themselves out. The issue of personal identity will be taken up in the next chapter. I have also addressed it at length in other work. See "Desire: Language and Body," in *Postmodernism and Continental Philosophy*, ed. Silverman and Welton (Albany: State University of New York Press, 1988), 34–48, and "Am I a Grammatical Fiction?—The Debate over Ego Psychology," in *Merleau-Pouty's Later Works and Their Practical Implications: The Dehiscence of Responsibility*, ed. Duane H. Davis (Amherst, N.Y.: Humanity Books, 2001), 309–324.

7. Nobility is the English term typically chosen to translate the Greek noun το καλον. I shall have much more to say about this word and the various ideas attached to it in the closing chapters of this book. For the moment, suffice it to say that I learned the term from Plato but will follow it along a different path.

8. Theosebeia. This is my transliteration of the Greek θεοσεβεια, the service or fear of god, religiousness.

9. "If the Other loves me then I become the unsurpassable, which means that I must be the absolute end. . . . The object which the Other must make me be is an object-transcendence, an absolute center of reference around which all the instrumental-things of the world are ordered as pure *means*. . . . The beloved can not will to love. Therefore the lover must seduce the beloved, and his love can in no way be distinguished from the enterprise of seduction. . . . To seduce . . . is to risk the danger of *being-seen* in order to . . . appropriate the Other in and by means of my object-ness . . . by means of making myself a *fascinating object*." Jean-Paul Sartre, *Being and Nothingness,* trans. Hazel Barnes (New York: Washington Square Press, 1966), 481, 484.

10. The gender assignment in this paragraph is deliberate. Historically, the role of the lover is active and, therefore, masculine, whereas the role of the beloved is to be passive, the object of pursuit, and, therefore, feminine. Assignment of specific roles in human relations based on gender comes close to being a definition of sexism. What follows from this is the truth that romantic love has been defined historically in sexist terms. That may be yet another reason for repudiating it. It should, however, be noted that the literature of the romantic tradition is rife with role reversals, that these role reversals are endemic to romance, hence that the characterizations of masculine and feminine roles do not necessarily coincide with the actual genders of the personae involved. Cleopatra is portrayed by Shakespeare as the active partner in her relationship with Marc Anthony.

11. "Toward a Phenomenology of Love and Sexuality," *Soundings* LXIII, No. 4 (1980); "Romantic Love, Enduring Love, and Authentic Love," *Soundings* LXVI, No. 2 (1983); "Desire for All/Love of One: Tomas's Tale in *The Unbearable Lightness of Being,*" *Philosophy Today* 33, No. 4 (1989): 347–357.

12. Quoted in an appendix to Stendahl, *Love,* trans. Jean Stewart and B. C. J. G. Knight (Harmondsworth: Penguin Books, 1975), 281.

13. "Tristan and Iseult do not love one another. They say they don't, and everything goes to prove it. *What they love is love and being in love*. . . . Tristan loves the awareness that he is loving far more than he loves Iseult the Fair. And Iseult does nothing to hold Tristan. All she needs is her passionate dream. Their need of one another is in order to be aflame, and they do not need one another as they are. What they need is not one another's presence, but one another's absence." Denis de Rougemont, *Love in the Western World,* trans. Montgomery Belgion (New York: Harper & Row, 1974), 41–42.

14. Or no justice or no friendship or no truth, etc.

15. Socrates' opening argument in the *Symposium* (200a–204c) characterizes love in the categories of desire as lacking the goodness and beauty it seeks in its object: "Love is in love with what he lacks and does not possess" (201b). But the argument concludes with the lover coming "in contact . . . with the truth . . . and becoming . . . immortal himself" (212a).

16. The relationship between Derridian desire and Hegelian desire is developed in detail in chapter 6 of *Semiological Reductionism,* "Ungodly Desire, Unnatural Desire."

## CHAPTER SIX
## VIRTUAL BODIES / BODIES OF FLESH

1. If you were convincingly cross-dressed, however—and I were unmindful of that possibility—I might miss you. Paradigms, especially gender paradigms, are constitutive of

anticipation, and anticipations have a strong bearing on identification: if my sister were artfully disguised as a man, I might well pass her by without recognizing her.

2. Derrida argues that there is no way to account for the origin of signifiers. He claims that signifiers signify by virtue of their ideality, that is, by remaining the same over time and being recognized as a repetition or iteration. The first, or original, signifier would thus have to be an original repetition. The notion of first or original repetition is a deliberate oxymoron. As I interpret it, his intent here is to assert that we are always *already* caught up in language, that the very idea of a first linguistic event is inconceivable from within the standpoint of the signifying species.

3. That is, by combining the transcendentalist thesis that language structures the human world with the empiricist thesis that language is a response to the world we perceive. These arguments, presented in truncated form here, are articulated in the first two chapters of *Semiological Reductionism*.

4. See my essay, "Am I a Grammatical Fiction?—The Debate over Ego Psychology."

5. You may manifest this in what Heidegger called the "deficient mode," but I would assert that denial of this form of care is, in classical Freudian terminology, denial, and either pathological or inauthentic. "I don't care," in this instance, means what it usually means, that is, I care too much to admit it to myself or others, I do not want to—or cannot—acknowledge my vulnerability.

6. "The identity of the same *man* consists . . . in nothing but a participation of the same continued life, by constantly fleeting particles of matter, in succession vitally united to the same organized body." John Locke, *An Essay Concerning Human Understanding,* ed. Fraser (New York: Dover, 1959), Vol. I, Book II, chap. 27, para. 7, 444. Subsequent references to Locke's *Essay* refer to page numbers in this chapter.

7. Principle of individuation: the basis for establishing a unique personal identity.

8. "Since consciousness always accompanies thinking, and it is that which makes every one to be what he calls self, and thereby distinguishes himself from all other thinking things, in this alone consists personal identity, i.e., the sameness of a rational being: and as far as this consciousness can be extended backwards to any past action or thought, so far reaches the identity of that person; it is the same self now it was then; and it is by the same self with this present one that now reflects on it, that that action was done" (*Essay,* 449).

9. The form of love that culminates in *Liebestod* is a pathology of romance.

10. Søren Kierkegaard, "Rotation Method," in *Either/Or,* Vol. I, trans. D. F. and L. M. Swenson (Princeton: Princeton University Press, 1971), 294.

# CHAPTER SEVEN
## MOTHERLOVE AND SEXLOVE

1. To be fair to Freud, it should be noted that the Oedipal attachment does not become thematic until the phallic stage (at four or five years of age). At that time the child has begun the process of self-other differentiation, although the bonds of symbiosis remain strong and residues of transitivism and mimesis are apparent. Nevertheless, the critical point retains its validity. Whether the primal attachment to mother is regarded as grounded in prenatal experience or in the oral phase during breast feeding, this founding moment takes place during a period of syncretism and indistinction between self and

other. As will become evident as the argument unfolds, Freud's mistake is to attribute to the awakening child a quality of sexual experience that does not begin to emerge until puberty. Freud anticipates this criticism and responds with resolute defiance.

"I am today no longer satisfied with the statement that the primacy of the genitals is not effected in the early period of childhood, or only very imperfectly. *The approximation of childhood sexuality to that of the adult goes much farther and is not limited solely to the establishment of an object-attachment.*" Freud, "The Infantile Genital Organization of the Libido," trans. Joan Riviere, in *Sexuality and the Psychology of Love,* ed. Philip Rieff (New York: Macmillan, 1963), p. 172, emphasis added. First published in *Zeitschrift,* Bd. IX, 1923.

2. This attempt is originally oblivious of pain caused to the other, hence not motivated by the attempt to cause it.

3. Sigmund Freud, "Instincts and Their Vicissitudes," trans. Cecil M. Baines, in *General Psychological Theory* (GPT), ed. Philip Rieff (New York: Macmillan, 1963), 99.

4. "Instincts . . . ," GPT, 102.

5. Paul Ricoeur, *Freud and Philosophy: An Essay on Interpretation,* trans. Denis Savage (New Haven: Yale University Press, 1970), III, 3, 483–93, "The Implicit Teleology of Freudianism: The Question of Sublimation." "All the procedures or mechanisms that are set into operation by the constitution of the higher agency, whether they be called idealization, identification, or sublimation, remain unintelligible in the framework of an economics. . . . Freudianism lacks a suitable theoretical instrument to render intelligible the absolutely primal dialectic between desire and the other than desire." *Freud and Philosophy,* 489–490).

6. "At the very beginning, in the individual's primitive oral phase, object-cathexis and identification are no doubt indistinguishable from each other." Freud, *The Ego and the Id,* trans. Joan Riviere (New York: W. W. Norton, 1962), 19.

7. "As a substitute for a longing for the father, [the ego ideal] contains the germ from which all religions have evolved. The self-judgment which declares that the ego falls short of its ideal produces the religious sense of humility to which the believer appeals in his longing. As a child grows up, the role of father is carried on by teachers and others in authority; their injunctions and prohibitions remain powerful in the ego ideal and continue, in the form of conscience, to exercise the moral censorship. The tension between the demands of conscience and the actual performances of the ego is experienced as a sense of guilt. *Social feelings rest on identifications with other people, on the basis of having the same ego ideal.*" *The Ego and the Id,* 27, emphasis added.

8. This argument is elaborated in my essay, "Merleau-Ponty and the Psychogenesis of the Self," *Journal of Phenomenological Psychology* 9, No. 1–2 (1978).

9. Amscan: the term is one I have adopted to refer to an individuated perspective, the global standpoint of a unique and discrete person. See my essay "Am I a Grammatical Fiction?—The Debate over Ego Psychology."

10. *The Mourning Bride,* III, viii.

11. Nor, for that matter, is the self-other relation a binary opposition in the first two pairs of opposites, but that is a separate issue which requires its own separate treatment.

12. With all due respect (and much respect is due) to Mitchell and Rose in *Feminine Sexuality,* Mother's desire is not definitive of the infant's emergent sense of self—as every flesh and blood mother knows. Mother is a powerful influence, but the infant's body has a

mind of its own. Jacques Lacan, *Feminine Sexuality: Jacques Lacan and the école freudienne,* ed. Juliet Mitchell and Jacqueline Rose, trans. Jacqueline Rose (New York: W.W. Norton, 1982).

13. Perhaps it is necessary to say that it is possible for a seductive mother to take her child as a lover if that is an essential demand in her pathology. This structure has its own etiology. It may also be necessary to acknowledge that my account is unabashedly value laden, but to deny that these values are grounded in anything resembling the natural law theory analyzed and criticized in chapter 3. Biology—and psychology, sociology, economics, etc.—certainly plays a role in the premises of my arguments, but there is no appeal to cosmic design or divine intent. Indeed, any such appeal is explicitly repudiated. Nature imposes limits, human reason contrives to work within and upon them.

## CHAPTER EIGHT
## SEX OBJECTS AND SEXUAL OBJECTIFICATION

1. This French term can be translated as "misunderstanding," but that rendering is misleading. The usual practice among translators is to leave the term in French.

2. I think most parties to the debate would agree that some version of the principle of otherness applies in self-self or narcissistic relations, as well.

3. It may be worth noting that Buber himself stresses that the principle of otherness is retained in I-Thou relations.

4. *Merleau-Ponty's Ontology* (Bloomington: Indiana University Press, 1988). Second edition with supplement on "Truth in Art" (Evanston: Northwestern University Press, 1997).

5. Kore is Greek for maiden, damsel, bride. Like the Latin *puella,* it designates the transitional phase of a female's life when she awakens sexually and makes the passage from maidenhood to womanhood. On the surface, this would not seem to apply to Linda Lovelace, who is already sexually active; in symbolic terms, however, her hymen remains intact until the mystery of her sexual desire is plumbed.

6. "Primitive custom appears to accord some recognition to the existence of the early sexual wish [which fixates the maiden's libido upon the father figure] by assigning the duty of defloration to an elder, a priest, or a holy man, that is, to a father-substitute" (81). "The act of defloration ... liberates an archaic reaction of enmity towards the man, which may assume pathological forms, and leads to the primitive fear of virgins and the strategy of delegating the act to some powerful figure other than the bridegroom." Freud, "The Taboo of Virginity," trans. Joan Riviera, in P. Rieff (ed.), *Sexuality and the Psychology of Love* (New York: Macmillan, 1963), 85. First published in *Sammlung,* Vierte Folge, 1918.

7. Jean-Paul Sartre, *Being and Nothingness* (BN), trans. Hazel Barnes (New York: Washington Square Press, 1966), 520–521.

8. BN, 502.

9. See M. C. Dillon, "Sartre on the Phenomenal Body and Merleau-Ponty's Critique," *The Journal of the British Society for Phenomenology* 5, No. 2 (1974).

10. I would hope to forestall the obvious objection by acknowledging that Plato discriminates between higher and lower forms of desire, that the higher forms are higher by virtue of being spiritual/intellectual as opposed to physical, and that it is

possible to interpret his standpoint as a prelude to the Christian demonization of the flesh. Nonetheless, the higher forms of desire remain forms of Eros for Plato. Plato was content to sublimate desire; Kant sought to suppress it altogether in aesthetic judgment.

11. Contextualization is the key variable, but not the only one. Pornographic depiction is also rendered pornographic by the relative absence of artistry. The actors and actresses are frequently beautiful in physique, but almost always artless in performance. The scripts defeat their own ends by their poverty of craft and production. It is a tribute to the beauty of the human form and the intense significance of acts of love and pleasure that these depictions manage to capture such a wide and avid audience.

If one asks why there is a poverty of art and beauty in contemporary depictions of sexuality—when the subject of sexuality has forever been a privileged subject of artistic depiction—one raises another host of questions, which I place under the heading of the demonization of sexuality. As Bataille contends, there is evidence that social and religious prohibitions have contributed to the constitution of desire. In maintaining a social posture of prohibition, we may be assigning the roles of sex object and its portrayer to bad actors and hasty producers.

It could also be that beauty of physique and acting ability relate to youth in contrary ways.

There is another irony in prohibition: if Bataille is right, then those who would drive the depiction of sexuality farther underground would have to blame themselves for intensifying the desire for profane depiction.

12. This, of course, remains to be supported by evidence, but I cite the work of Candida Royale, who produces and markets X-rated films under the label of Femme Productions.

13. Here I would cite Catherine MacKinnon's argument that there is no difference in kind between the act of rape and the act of depicting human sexuality.

14. See M. C. Dillon, "The Phenomenon of Obscenity in Literature," *Journal of Value Inquiry* 16 (1982) for an extended treatment of the privacy argument. As I understand it, the privacy argument is grounded in natural law theory and its assertion that any departure from the male-female reproductive dyad is contrary to the intent of nature and its creator.

15. In the current environment of political rectitude enforced by legislation against sexual harassment, overt expression of sexual interest may, under varying circumstances, lead to official censure, fines, or imprisonment.

16. "Amo" is a neologism. It refers to the full range of experience and history that designates a unique perspective or sociopersonal identity. The term is designed to undercut the distinction between the ego of American schools of ego psychology and the transpersonal transcendental consciousness that is the focus of European attention. In my view (Dillon, "Am I a Grammatical Fiction?—The Debate over Ego Psychology"), the polarization of the two schools around this distinction undermines the theoretical cogency of both.

17. This is especially evident in the domain of the mores currently governing the initiation of erotic interaction: manifestations of sexual interest in another person must be oblique and deniable; courtship rituals, especially in the opening phases, are routinely expected to incorporate dissemblance and deceit. One must maintain the posture of reflective distantiation in the process of declaring emotional engagement.

18. As will be apparent to those who know him, my touchstone here is Kierkegaard and the problems he confronts in *Fear and Trembling* when he juxtaposes his erotic relationship to Regine Olsen with the passionate inwardness and solitude of his relationship to the Christian God. As I read Kierkegaard, it is apparent that (1) his categories, the categories of Cartesian dualism as they inform Hegelian metaphysics, entail recognizing that these two relationships are mutually exclusive, and (2) Kierkegaard wanted to identify the two relationships by means of the logic of paradox in which finite and infinite, immanent and transcendent, can be brought together. The categories he inherited drove Kierkegaard from Regine. The categories I am attempting to develop would allow him to love her, but would confound his Christian faith. I think he is exactly right in construing the choice between God and Regine as an either/or that only the logic of contradiction can supervene. I also think he made bad choices—both in the case of love object and in the case of categories.

19. D. H. Lawrence, *Women in Love* (New York: Viking Press, 1960), 36.

20. It would be well, I think, to underline the difference between what I am describing as the ecstasy of carnal union and the mystical union described variously by such diverse thinkers as Meister Eckhart and Hegel. In Hegel's words, such union "excludes all oppositions, [and] ... is not finite at all. . . . In love, life is present as a duplicate of itself and as a single and unified self." G. W. F. Hegel, unpublished manuscript quoted in Solomon and Higgins (eds.), *The Philosophy of (Erotic) Love* (Lawrence: University of Kansas Press, 1991), 117.

In mystical union, the self is lost. All individuation is obliterated in the formation of a unitary whole. In the ecstasy of carnal union, the self is experienced as a part of a transcending relationship whose meaning for itself is transformed by the relationship. Mystical union precludes otherness; carnal union feeds on the transcendence of the other and the relationship that envelops self and other.

21. I am indebted to Ethel Person for inviting my attention to the transformative aspect of sexlove. "Love changes more than the scope of the lover's experience; it changes the lover as well." E. S. Person, *Dreams of Love and Fateful Encounters: The Power of Romantic Passion* (New York: Penguin Books, 1989), 66.

22. *Women in Love,* 36.

23. The idea here expressed with the term *nobility* is better expressed with the Greek term, το καλου, which will be explicated in chapter 9.

24. "A peripety is the change ... from one state of things within the play to its opposite. . . . A discovery is . . . a change from ignorance to knowledge, and thus to either love or hate . . . ." Aristotle, *Poetics,* trans. Richard McKeon (New York: Random House, 1941), 1452a22–32.

25. "Porno for Mom and Pop," *Civilization: The Magazine of the Library of Congress* 4, No. 3 (1997), 35.

26. Along these lines, the author quotes Heinrich Blücher's response to a lecture defending pornography given by Norman Podhoretz at Bard College in the 1950s: "'You are taking all the fun out of sex! ... Don't you know that pornography soon becomes boring?'" Later in the article, Larry Flynt is reported to believe that "after an initial glut, it would take a mere decade of legalization for the sex industry to wither away for lack of titillation." "Porno for Mom and Pop," 35.

27. Freud, "A Special Type of Object Choice Made by Men," trans. Joan Riviera, in *Sexuality and the Psychology of Love.*

CHAPTER NINE
THE FLESH OF LOVE

1. See chapter 7.

2. "Sacred Love, Profane Love, and Love." Written in 1979, unpublished.

3. This theme was developed in chapter 8.

4. See chapter 5.

5. I acknowledge the prerogative here granted to vision, to that kind of sensing, but I appeal to the doctrine of synesthesia to temper this privilege: we see texture, we see gesture in the expression frozen in a photograph; the person's style is revealed in an impoverished fashion, but a partial revelation is still a revelation. The thoughts summarized here are explored in chapter 6.

6. The question of the viability of a heuristic of full disclosure which obtrudes here will have to be postponed. My sense is that there is a positive dimension of privacy that is grounded in the inevitability of *écart*: every imperative I have encountered, including the commandment to disclose the full truth, demands judgment in its execution.

7. I cannot see any room for happiness in the biological death of a person one loves.

8. Merleau-Ponty, "The Child's Relations with Others," trans. William Cobb, in *The Primacy of Perception and Other Essays on Phenomenological Psychology, the Philosophy of Art, History and Politics,* ed. James M. Edie (Evanston: Northwestern University Press, 1964), 135. "Les Relations avec autrui chez l'enfant," in *Les Cours de Sorbonne* (Paris: Centre de Documentation Universitaire, 1960).

9. "The perception of other people . . . depends heavily upon our pre-established relations with others prior to this particular perception. It has roots in our whole psychological past. Each perception of another person is never simply a momentary event. Such a perception is not therefore a pure reception of a certain content which is given as such. It is always a deeper relationship, a relation of coexistence with that aspect of the other person which is presented." Merleau-Ponty, "The Experience of Others," trans. Fred Evans and Hugh J. Silverman, in *Review of Existential Psychology and Psychiatry* 18 (1982–1983): 40–41. "L'expérience d'autrui," in *Bulletin du Groupe d'études de psychologie de l'Université de Paris (1951–1952)* (Paris: Centre de Documentation Universitaire).

10. See chapter 8.

11. See chapter 6.

12. See M. C. Dillon, "Sex, Time, and Love: Erotic Temporality" *Journal of Phenomenological Psychology* 18, No. 1 (1987). Reprinted in *Sex, Love, and Friendship,* ed. Soble and Kirshner (Atlanta: Rodopi, 1997).

13. Were I to coincide with myself and at the same time with goodness and beauty, I would be divine perfection, not my embodied and becoming finite self. The thought of a loving god is a thought I cannot think, and even those who believe in it acknowledge that god's love for humanity is a mystery that defies comprehension.

14. In positive modes of assertion and expression, and privative modes of denial and chaste withdrawal. The point here is that chastity is a form of explicitly sexual behavior which lives the sexual motives it finds in itself or others in the mode of negation and denial.

15. See chapter 4.

16. It might be well to note here that I am not advocating promiscuity or unfettered recreational sex among either youth or adults, nor do I think children could or should be left to generate their own solutions. I do think the youth will react to the patterns they discern in adult behavior, that they are subject to our influence, and that we would do well to examine our values and modify our practices with this in mind. In the conclusion I will sketch what I take to be the practical implications of the theories set forth in the main text of this book.

## CONCLUSION

1. See chapter 2.

2. *Symposium* 206e. I am indebted to Karsten Harries for inviting my attention to this passage and opening my eyes to its implications.

3. The young Socrates, however, is a bit of an ingenue and depicted as such in the *Parmenides*.

4. See chapter 5.

# INDEX